Coronado National Memorial

AMERICA'S NATIONAL PARKS SERIES

Char Miller, Pomona College, *Series Editor*

America's National Parks promotes the close investigation of the complex and often contentious history of the nation's many national parks, sites, and monuments. Their creation and management raises a number of critical questions from such fields as archaeology, geology and history, biology, political science, and sociology, as well as geography, literature, and aesthetics. Books in this series aim to spark public conversation about these landscapes' enduring value by probing such diverse topics as ecological restoration, environmental justice, tourism and recreation, tribal relations, the production and consumption of nature, and the implications of wildland fire and wilderness protection. Even as these engaging texts cross interdisciplinary boundaries, they will also dig deeply into the local meanings embedded in individual parks, monuments, or landmarks and locate these special places within the larger context of American environmental culture.

Death Valley National Park: A History
by Hal K. Rothman and Char Miller

Grand Canyon: A History of a Natural Wonder and National Park
by Don Lago

Lake Mead National Recreation Area:
A History of America's First National Playground
by Jonathan Foster

Coronado National Memorial: A History of Montezuma
Canyon and the Southern Huachucas
by Joseph P. Sánchez

Coronado National Memorial

A History of Montezuma Canyon and the Southern Huachucas

JOSEPH P. SÁNCHEZ

UNIVERSITY OF NEVADA PRESS *Reno & Las Vegas*

America's National Parks
Char Miller, *Series Editor*

University of Nevada Press | Reno, Nevada 89557 USA
www.unpress.nevada.edu

Cover photograph by George H. H. Huey / Alamy
Cover design by Erin Kirk New

Library of Congress Cataloging-in-Publication Data
Names: Sánchez, Joseph P., author.
Title: Coronado National Memorial : a history of Montezuma Canyon and the southern Huachucas / by Joseph P. Sánchez.
Description: Reno : University of Nevada Press, [2016] | Series: America's national parks | Includes bibliographical references and index. |
Identifiers: LCCN 2016043636 (print) | LCCN 2017014336 (e-book) | ISBN 978-0-87417-473-1 (e-book) | ISBN 978-1-943859-31-3 (paperback : alkaline paper)
Subjects: LCSH: Coronado National Memorial (Ariz.)—History. | Montezuma Canyon (Ariz.)—History. | Huachuca Mountains (Ariz.)—History, Local. | Land grants—Arizona—Huachuca Mountains—History. | Land settlement—Arizona—Huachuca Mountains—History. | Mines and mineral resources—Arizona—Huachuca Mountains—History.
Classification: LCC F817.C5 (e-book) | LCC F817.C5 S35 2016 (print) | DDC 979.1/53—dc23
LC record available at https://lccn.loc.gov/2016043636

The paper used in this book meets the requirements of American National Standard for Information Sciences—Permanence of Paper for Printed Library Materials, ANSI/NISO Z39.48-1992 (R2002).

First Printing

Manufactured in the United States of America

For

Alphonse and Helen Brodeur

Contents

Preface

The southeastern corner of Arizona has always been a region of historical importance to the state of Arizona as well as to the neighboring states of New Mexico and northeastern Sonora, Mexico. The international ambiance of the region sets the stage for a historical drama of epic proportions. Yet the history of the area is little known, save for individual histories of towns and settlements that dot the area. Long before the coming of Europeans, Native Americans migrated into the area and settled along the Sonora and Arizona rivers. They lived their lives in an uncertain world and were constantly poised to defend their lands against all comers. The expedition led by Francisco Vázquez de Coronado passed through the area in 1540–42 and made note of the people, the flora and fauna, and the land. By the 1680s Spanish colonial settlements sprang up just to the south of the Huachucas around Cananea and Bacanuchi. The settlers, seeking a new beginning, came to farm and ranch. Some came as miners. It is from these settlements that Spanish colonial settlers began to prospect in the Huachuca Mountains and Montezuma Canyon. Following Mexican independence from Spain, such interests persisted into the Mexican territorial period between 1821 and 1853. After the Gadsden Purchase Treaty of 1853, in which Mexico sold a large tract of land known presently as southern Arizona to the United States, a growing number of Anglo-Americans ventured into the Huachucas seeking mineral wealth. Nearby places established in the nineteenth century, such as Bisbee, Tombstone, and Fort Huachuca, are best known for events that have attracted the popular mind in lore, history, and literature. Despite the Spanish/Mexican period settlements in the area, the history of that small corner of southeastern Arizona and northeastern Sonora has been largely ignored because it was perceived to be a pass-through area mentioned in historic documents that have long since been tucked away in archives. Yet as an area of settlement mining and ranching, its history is rich in genealogies, events, and economies that contributed to the development of the area. In the long run, the historical process of empire, nation building, and world economies briefly cast the region of southeastern Arizona and northeastern Sonora into a world forum.

On the other hand, much has been written about the larger region of southeastern Arizona and northeastern Sonora. In many ways, this study complements those efforts, for the region's past as seen and interpreted through history's window bridges both countries for nearly four centuries. The present volume, *Coronado National Memorial: A History of Montezuma Canyon and the Southern Huachucas,* is about a place that is tied to the history, heritage, and patrimony of Spain, Mexico, and the United States, as well as to regional Native American tribes. The history of Montezuma Canyon is not about its local perspectives, but about the global aspects of its ties with the wider world. As such, the history of Montezuma Canyon is part of the historical evolutionary pattern that shaped the region and two countries.

In the context of a fast-changing world, early Hispanic settlers and Native American tribes in the area of northeastern Sonora and southeastern Arizona adapted to a dynamic historical process that evolved quickly before them.[1] Under Spain, Hispanic settlers quickly established forms of governance, such as the required *cabildo* (town hall), along with minor town officials including an *alcalde* (mayor), as well as legal processes. History had taught the settlers well, for under Spain they had worked mining projects and protected their lands under the contractual laws governed by the Laws of the Indies, Las Siete Leyes (The Seven Laws), and other compilations of Spanish laws. Litigation for mining rights, the use of water, common lands, sales, and transfers of land was carried out publically before the world and documented. Under Mexico laws, regulating land grants changed but little between 1821 and 1853 in terms of legal practices and interpretation of the law governing those earlier concessions. For example, land grants originally held under Spain were left alone and acknowledged as legal entities. Meanwhile, the Mexican government did issue new land grant ordinances that followed revised provisions. The War of 1846 between Mexico and the United States raised new questions about land grants and their disposition. Under governance by the United States, however, Spanish and Mexican land grants in the greater Southwest would be adjudicated differently. Following the Gadsden Purchase Treaty (1853), the area of southern Arizona underwent a profound change. A synopsis of the history of some of those grants narrated in this study presents a snapshot historical perspective in regard to how the grants were created and their final disposition as they are generally perceived by the descendants of those who pioneered the settlement of the Sonora–Arizona frontier. With the United States' laws, adherence to the old Spanish and Mexican property and mining laws would also be tested.

The history of mining in Montezuma Canyon serves as a microcosm in which to view the larger picture of mining, which served as both a magnet for settlement and the desire for wealth. Montezuma Canyon, with its potential mining, is what drew some settlers to the area. Through good times and bad, they stayed, risking their lives, and farmed and ranched the area to survive. All the while Montezuma Canyon beckoned but never delivered on its promises of mineral wealth. Today, the inventory of abandoned mines at Montezuma Canyon within Coronado National Monument indicates sixty-two mine shafts, adits (a horizontal or nearly horizontal entrance to a mine), and test pits. No one knows how many other efforts were made historically to find mineral wealth there. Indeed, the early history of Montezuma Canyon is about people on both sides of the border who learned to work the legal systems of Spain, Mexico, and the United States in order to keep their lands and their values alive. It is about a people who learned to adapt, for they are still there. In many ways, their story revolves around the same historical processes that shaped the greater Southwest.

Montezuma Canyon itself holds many secrets—some might never be revealed. Gradually Montezuma Canyon became a corridor for illegal entry into the United States from Mexico. Often little is known about such activities. The summer of 2007, however, exposed one of many such events that might never be known. Although many issues plague the United States–Mexico border, the human dimension is often overlooked in the enforcement of policies.

On Friday, June 29, 2007, a life-and-death drama unfolded in Montezuma Canyon at Coronado National Memorial. Not far from safety, two sisters, among others, had illegally crossed from Mexico into the United States where their hopes and aspirations could be realized. One of them, 34-year-old Marta Yolanda González-Pineda from Jalapa, Guatemala, complained of stomach and knee pains. That evening, as sunlight faded, her sister, Angela González-Pineda, concerned about her sister's dire situation and who, by then, had fallen unconscious, left her to summon help. While she was gone, Marta Yolanda died from dehydration, a common cause of death among undocumented immigrants who cross the deserts of Sonora and southern Arizona as temperatures hover in excess of 100 degrees. Meanwhile, Angela was taken into custody by the Border Patrol.[2]

Coronado National Memorial, at the time, reported that Border Patrol agents discovered the woman's body in "Montezuma Canyon a mile west of the park visitor center on the afternoon of June 30th." Later that day, the officers from the Cochise County Sheriff's Department transported the body to the medical examiner's office. An investigation by the Border Patrol was undertaken.[3]

The death of the young undocumented immigrant woman that occurred in Montezuma Canyon is neither an isolated case nor an accident of time and place. The memorial is known to be a pass-through area for undocumented immigrants entering the United States. Evidence such as "empty . . . bottles, food cans, etc."—especially near the old mine sites—appears to be signs that undocumented immigrants use Montezuma Canyon as a stopping place before moving on.[4] Such an occurrence is not solely incidental to Coronado National Memorial but to other national parks along the border as well. Ironically, once the borderline was drawn on a map, traditional access to the land and the historical rite of passage changed with policies on both sides of the border. Thus, in summer of 2007, Montezuma revealed another theme in its history—one that was not necessarily new to the area—but one that remains to be written.

Today, Montezuma Canyon, once a topographic marker to early Indian and Spanish colonial settlers and travelers, sits as a gateway to history and a reminder of the common history shared by the United States and Mexico. In the late nineteenth and early twentieth centuries, the historical secrets housed by Montezuma Canyon had all but disappeared from mind and sight. By the 1960s, many of those stories slowly began to re-emerge as the National Park Service (NPS) rediscovered them and put them on display at Coronado National Memorial.

Each episode has left its mark on the history of southeastern Arizona and northeastern Sonora. What is the history of the region? Why is it worth knowing? In regard to those questions, this book examines the history of the region as a part of our national experience, but also adds a relatively new dimension to that history. In the late 1930s the U.S. Congress, seeking a way to commemorate the four hundredth anniversary of the Coronado Expedition, ultimately established Coronado National Memorial. Today, the succeeding staffs at Coronado National Memorial interpret the legacy of the expedition and its historical significance to our national story. The histories that evolved at Montezuma Canyon, furthermore, mirror events that occurred within the region of southeastern Arizona and northeastern Sonora. Apache and other tribes, for example, once occupied Montezuma Canyon, as did Spanish, Mexican, and Anglo-American miners and settlers. By now, however, the NPS is one of the longest-known occupants of Montezuma Canyon. As the keeper of its history, the NPS strives to preserve and protect Montezuma Canyon's resources and heritage for future generations to appreciate and learn about a part of our national past and experiences within the context of that little corner of earth shared by two countries.

The author is indebted to Robert Spude, historian, NPS, Santa Fe, New Mexico. Dr. Spude, now retired, not only inspired the creation of this history, but he also read through the entire manuscript and made invaluable suggestions to strengthen its presentation. Coronado National Memorial's superintendent and staff, particularly Denise Shulz, chief of interpretation, deserves a note of appreciation in not only aiding and abetting this study to go forward, but for making Coronado National Memorial accessible for my site visits to Montezuma Canyon. Similarly, the staffs at the Archivo Histórico Diplomático in the Secretaria de Relaciones Exteriores and the Archivo General de la Nación, both in Mexico City; the NPS's Western Archeological and Conservation Center (WACC), Tucson; the Arizona Historical Society, Tucson; the Special Collections Library at Arizona State University, Tempe; the Arizona State Department of Mines and Minerals, Phoenix; the Arizona State Library, Archives and Public Library, Phoenix; the Bisbee Mining and Historical Museum, Bisbee; and the Bancroft Library, University of California, Berkeley, deserve special thanks and acknowledgement for their professional assistance to the author. I would be remiss without a note of appreciation to the late Larry Miller for his supportive contributions to this effort. I especially thank my wife, Loretta Sánchez, for her assistance in combing through research depositories in Arizona and her accompaniment in my field surveys of Montezuma Canyon.

Portions of this manuscript are revised and expanded from *Between Two Countries: A History of Coronado National Memorial 1939–1990* (2014, Rio Grande Books), by Joseph P. Sánchez, Bruce A. Ericsson, and Jerry L. Gurule; and an earlier study commissioned by the National Parks Service, "Forgotten Pathways through Montezuma Canyon: Coronado National Memorial Historic Resources Study," by Joseph P. Sánchez.

NOTES

1. I define the historical process as an occurrence, a state of, or a phenomenon that has to do with the evolution of an idea or concept that ties to an event or a series of events. The historical process is a function of the interactions of the affairs of humankind with time, events, the sequence and continuities of events, causes, and effects; and the change or changes that develop as a consequence. The historical process can provide directionality. In summary, the historical process is evident in these questions: Who are we?, Where do we come from?, and Where are we going? In the historical dialectic, the historical process is best defined as an unanswerable paradox that can never be completed because it is something that is in a perpetual state of becoming.

2. "Officials Recover Three Bodies from Desert," Brady McCombs, *Arizona Daily Star,* July 2, 2007.

3. Andy Brinkley, "Death of Illegal Immigrant," *Inside NPS,* July 11, 2007.

4. Robert Spude to Joseph P. Sánchez, e-mail correspondence, July 12, 2007.

Coronado National Memorial

Introduction

The Many Faces of Montezuma Canyon

Because the Memorial lacks visible remains and is not the site of any dramatic occurrence, its historical value lies in the fact that it is able to set a reflective mood suitable for contemplation of the Coronado Entrada.

—Hugo H. Huntzinger, Superintendent,
Coronado National Memorial, 1970[1]

Montezuma Canyon sits nestled within the Huachuca Mountains at Coronado National Memorial in southeastern Arizona. Facing the San Pedro River Valley, the location of Coronado National Memorial was predicated on a route determined by historians to be near the place where explorers of the Coronado expedition (1540–42) entered the present-day United States from Mexico.[2] Still, much of the story about Montezuma Canyon is tied to many facets of the history of Mexico, Spain, and the United States. Indeed, Montezuma Canyon's association with the Coronado expedition gave it added significance. In the sixteenth century, a mere forty-eight years after Columbus's first voyage, the Coronado expedition had thrust North America onto the stage of the Age of Discovery, a world history milestone in the annals of European expansionism. By the early 1540s Mexico City, forged from the ruins of Tenochtitlan, had become one of the great centers of the Spanish Empire. Significantly, the historical events tied to Montezuma Canyon have often been played out on an international stage. In that way, Montezuma Canyon's past is part of a binational story that brings together broader themes found in the histories of the United States and Mexico.

Geographically and metaphorically, Montezuma Canyon itself became the focal point where Spanish and Mexican period miners and ranchers, Native Americans, early Anglo-American mining entrepreneurs, and homesteaders crossed paths. Indeed, Montezuma Canyon and Montezuma Peak, both within Coronado National Memorial, form pivotal points offering panoramic vistas of places where a pageantry of

Native Americans, settlers, and miners converged at different times. That pageantry could also include present-day National Park Service (NPS) personnel, because by now they represent the long-term continual settlement and development of Montezuma Canyon. Ultimately, the United States NPS became the sole owner of the land with its wide panoramic view that, seen from Montezuma Peak, overlooked and hosted historical events associated with present-day Coronado National Memorial. Aside from serving as host to many such events, Coronado National Memorial has, indeed, acquired a history of its own. Many events associated with Montezuma Canyon would have been long forgotten had not the NPS rescued them from certain oblivion.

To that end, this study addresses and identifies historical themes tied to Montezuma Canyon that shaped the history and society throughout that region. It also explores the historical land-use patterns on both sides of the adjoining border, and, in particular, Montezuma Canyon with its many ravines, throughout the Spanish colonial period and the Mexican period, as well as the early Anglo-American period in the late nineteenth century following the Gadsden Purchase Treaty of 1853. The history of settlement, mining, and ranching binds those periods together thematically and leads into the late twentieth century, when they came together as part of a heritage and patrimony commemorated at Coronado National Memorial. Finally, the role of the NPS in the development of Montezuma Canyon lends yet another dimension to the identity of Coronado National Memorial. In order to understand the purpose of Coronado National Memorial and its historical resources, one must know its past.

A presidential proclamation in 1952 established Coronado National Memorial and set aside the designated property to be protected and preserved for future generations.[3] Shortly afterward, in 1954, funding was appropriated for the memorial, and the first superintendent of Coronado National Memorial, Carroll Burroughs, was hired.[4] For its first five years, Coronado National Memorial operated out of rented quarters at a mine that Grace Sparkes called "the State of Texas Mines" in Montezuma Canyon, which then constituted an inholding—that is, private property within a national park. Sparkes, who later sold the State of Texas Mines to the NPS, had been a longtime booster for the establishment of Coronado National Memorial.

The story behind Montezuma Canyon and the creation of Coronado National Memorial is intertwined with the prehistory and history of southeastern Arizona and Sonora. Its early history runs from the Spanish contact period in the sixteenth century to the Spanish and Mexican settlement and mining periods between 1680 and 1853. Too, its history includes the early Anglo-American homesteading and mining ventures following the Gadsden Purchase Treaty as well as vignettes that occurred during the Civil War. The modern history surrounding Montezuma Canyon dates from the middle 1930s when the Coronado Cuarto Centennial Commission, aimed at celebrating the Coronado expedition of 1540–42, conceived the idea of a national park along the United States–Mexico border.

Associated with the creation of Coronado National Memorial were issues that sprang from historical U.S.–Mexican relationships during the nineteenth century. The United States–Mexico War of 1846 had tarnished relations between the two countries. In 1853 both countries again crossed paths when Mexican dictator Antonio López de Santa Anna, in need of funds, sold a part of northern Sonora, Mexico, to the United States. In time, a part of the purchased territory became known as southern Arizona. Another piece of the Mexican concession included New Mexico. Although Mexican citizens were outraged by the sale of a portion of their country, the signing of the Gadsden Purchase Treaty ushered in a new era for southern Arizona, which had once been part of Pimería Alta on the northern Sonoran frontier. Pimería Alta, or the northern extent of the Tohono O'odham and other tribes, included a large territory from northern Sonora to the Gila River that ran from its headwaters in New Mexico to the Colorado River. For his part in the transfer of sovereign land, Santa Anna was exiled to Venezuela in 1855. Between Mexico and the United States, Indian lands were included in such negotiations.

Although this volume does not deal with technical aspects of European sovereignty over Native American tribes, it does assess the conflicts between tribes who inhabited the region surrounding the Huachuca Mountains and settlers during the Spanish colonial, Mexican, and Anglo-American periods. The question of European sovereignty in the Americas is at odds with its antithesis: contested homelands. Territoriality is a theme in the history of humankind, and is often decided by the victor. In many ways the Huachuca Mountains exemplify this concept because they set the stage in which the conflict between Spanish, Mexican, and Anglo settlers and their Apache counterparts fought for control of the area.

Throughout the nineteenth century, following the Gadsden Purchase Treaty, punitive expeditions from the United States and Mexico crisscrossed the area in search of Apache who both countries viewed as the problem. Both employed Native American scouts and allies, an old practice among them, to track Apache raiders who attacked their settlements. Indeed, during the Spanish colonial period Spanish settlers at Bacanuchi depended on the support of their Indian allies, among them Opata warriors, to defend their towns and ranches against their common enemy, the Apache.[5] The use of Indian allies by Spanish and Mexican settlers against Apache raiders was not isolated to Sonora. In other areas, such as New Mexico, Spanish settlers depended on Pueblo Indian allies to support them against Apache, Navajo, Ute, and Comanche attacks.[6]

Then, too, varied opinions about the causes of Apache attacks persisted. Some Spanish militarists expressed sympathetic views about the Apache. Of the more enlightened attitudes about the Apache, some Spanish officials explained that the aggressive behavior of the Apache was a response to intruders onto their lands rather than a response to the innate character of Apaches. They agreed that the Apaches waged war against settlers and miners because they had trespassed on their lands and had exploited the people and the resources. They robbed, some explained, because hunting alone did not support their needs. Bernardo de Galvez, a military commander, wrote, "If the Indian is no friend, it is because he owes us no kindness, and. . .if he avenges himself it is for just satisfaction of his grievances."[7] In 1799 Viceroy Antonio de Bucareli confided to José de Galvez, the intendant general of New Spain, that "an impartial judge could. . .see [that] every charge we might make against them would be offset by as many crimes committed by our side."[8] Thus, Spanish officials and settlers did not fail to understand their own role in provoking war with the Apache or other tribes, but in the wake of a devastating raid, the reasons for the provocations did not matter. Each side, on the other hand, justified its reasons for war against the other. Such reactions were not exclusive to Spanish settlers, but were also found in Anglo-American settlers and miners who came into the area in the middle nineteenth century.[9] Ambivalent views of the Apache persisted well into the twentieth century. Perhaps Geronimo said it best in 1905, when he met President Theodore Roosevelt. In explaining why he fought to protect his homeland, Geronimo began with a traditional greeting and then said these words: "Great Father. . .Did I fear the Great White Chief? No. He was my enemy and the enemy of my people. His people desired the country of my people. My heart was strong against him. I said he should never have my country."[10] Anthropologist Keith Basso, writing about the Western Apache, echoed Geronimo's historical perceptions about the ambiance of their homeland, its attendant heritage, and the importance of the land to the well-being of its people. In many ways, his statement reflected a universal sentiment shared by many Native Americans. Basso wrote, "For Indian men and women, the past lies embedded in features of the earth—in canyons and lakes, mountains and arroyos, rocks and vacant fields—which together endow their land with multiple forms of significance that reach into their lives and shape the way they think. Knowledge of places is therefore closely linked to knowledge of the self, to grasping one's position in the larger scheme of things, including one's own community, and to securing a confident sense of who one is as a person."[11] In that regard, the contest over control of Montezuma Canyon serves to remind us of the many powerful actors and forces who participated in the numerous historical experiences that occurred there, both positive and negative. Such experiences were shaped and shared by Spain, Mexico, the United States, and regional Native American tribes.

Historically, the question of sovereignty has raised other issues beyond those related to Apache defense of their homeland on both sides of the international boundary. The resulting border between Mexico and the United States had significant ramifications in regard to immigration, trade, and land tenure, especially as they affected Mexican land grants and mining interests. Just as quickly, discrepancies regarding the exact location of the boundary in certain areas developed, as did other problems related to smuggling, and a host of law enforcement dilemmas that sprang up in the first fifty years following the 1853 treaty.[12] By the middle of the twentieth century, a small segment of the United States–Mexico boundary would include a new landowner, the NPS, with the southern boundary of Coronado National Memorial that abuts the international boundary between Mexico and the United States.

Establishing the international boundary would be the first order of business following the Gadsden Purchase Treaty. Soon thereafter, the United States and Mexico formed a boundary commission to survey the present boundary line from the western bank of the Rio Grande below El Paso to the California coast. On January 31, 1855, U.S. and Mexican boundary commissioners, Lt. William H. Emory and José Salazar y Lárregui, respectively, met and agreed on the first boundary marker at El Paso. Moving westward from there, they surveyed the line between Sonora and Arizona. The line ended on the California coast south of San Diego.

Still, although monuments marked the boundary, for the most part during the remainder of the nineteenth century the boundary in the immediate environs of the memorial was virtually invisible.[13] Border problems followed as settlers moved into the San Pedro River Valley on the United States side of the international boundary. Towns sprang up, as did numerous mining camps. Especially after the Tombstone boom, the Arizona–Sonora border became a corridor for illegal activities inclusive of smuggling and cattle rustling on both sides of the line. The vagueness of the physical location of the boundary obscured enforcement jurisdictions. One customs agent, Jeff Milton, recalled an incident that occurred in the late 1880s when he apprehended a smuggler on the San Pedro River, who was convicted and sentenced to the Yuma Territorial Prison. Later, Milton learned he had captured the Mexican south of the border.[14] There were other instances such as when, in 1892, Mexican customs officials actually crossed the border, surrounded the station in Bisbee, Arizona, and arrested a Mexican national wanted by the law in Mexico.[15]

Some issues such as the boundary discrepancies were readily remedied. The unclear location of the international boundary caused much confusion in regard to jurisdictions. Given the overlap of land and mineral claims along the border, mine operators demanded a thorough and clearer marking of the boundary line. In 1882 a binational tribunal agreed to the erection of immovable and recognizable monuments, and subsequent treaties confirming the Gadsden Purchase Treaty boundary. Between February 1892 and May 1895, the boundary commission marked the border with 258 six-foot-high concrete and cast iron obelisks. The segment of the boundary that abuts Coronado National Memorial is marked by boundary markers numbers 100, 101, and 102.[16] Thus, the border and its markers are a part of the historical scene that can be viewed from Montezuma Canyon and its adjoining peak at Coronado National Monument.

Coronado National Memorial abounds with historical themes and resources that are interpreted by NPS personnel at the memorial's visitor center. Interpretation topics range from flora and fauna to historic land-use patterns for ranching, grazing, mining, dude ranching, and homesteading. They also include the road that passes through the heart of Montezuma Canyon, which was constructed in 1933–35 by the Civilian Conservation Corps when the land still belonged to the U.S. Forest Service.[17] Prior to the construction of the road, vehicular travel was not possible through Montezuma Pass. The anonymous author of a brief report entitled "History of Coronado Activity" summed up the early history of the road:

> Prior to the 1930's travel around the south end of the Huachuca Mountains was accomplished by traveling into Mexico then crossing back into the United States. In 1930, the U.S. Immigration Service closed this route. In December 1933 the Civilian Conservation Corps set up a 250 man camp in Ash Canyon and a second 250 man camp in Sunnyside Canyon to construct a road over Montezuma Pass. By May 1933 the Sunnyside crew completed the road to the top of Montezuma Pass from the west. The Ash Canyon crew completed the east side up to the second horseshoe bend. The crews were transferred to the Grand Canyon in the summer. The Sunnyside crew returned in the fall of 1934 and completed the road. The Montezuma Pass road was opened to the public in May 1935. The road cut the distance from the Brown ranch on the southeast side of the Huachuca Mountains to the D'albini ranch on the west side from 103 miles to eleven miles.[18]

The road through Montezuma Canyon is part of the significant pattern of developments at Coronado National Memorial and its environs.

The road also leads to other well-known historical attractions in the area. Nearby, Tombstone and Bisbee, in their own ways, had become centers for tourism. Tombstone was a boomtown that quickly declined along with its silver lodes. Famous for the "Gunfight at the OK Corral," Tombstone lived on, and continues to exist as a tourist attraction. Across the San Pedro Valley, Bisbee and its associated mines in the Mule Mountains grew as the market for copper and tourism ebbed and flowed. The establishment of Fort Huachuca and Sierra Vista introduced a new era for the area as a large urban population center grew in the midst of surrounding communities such as Wilcox and Benson.

Coronado National Memorial became an attraction with its festival, hiking trail, and overlook, from which the San Pedro Valley can be viewed. In the 1960s a visitor center and wayside exhibits were developed to enhance the telling of the history of the region. The park also acquired the mining property within its boundaries for, among other reasons, possible historical interpretation. In late 1986 the NPS acquired the State of Texas Mines (see chapter 5). Soon afterward, old buildings at the site were removed and trash was cleaned up, and a mine safing team came from Death Valley National Park to install safety netting across most of the openings, shafts, and adits. In late 1988 Superintendent Joe

Sewell reported that ten mines within the memorial's boundary had been sealed.[19] At that point, the property was considered "an excellent interpretive area and a detailed prospectus" was drafted.[20] A State of Texas Mine trail was considered to provide new scenic vistas and highlight the historical role of mining in the region.[21]

Although the history of mining is a dominant theme in the later history of Montezuma Canyon, its earlier history is significant for understanding the development of the area over time. Early migrations into the area date to prehistoric times. The forefathers of many regional tribes inhabited the area for hundreds of years before the coming of Europeans. Thus, the prehistoric period set the stage for humankind's presence in Montezuma Canyon as it related to other sites in the region. Although there are few remnants there in comparison to other areas of richer finds in southeastern Arizona and northern Sonora, early Native American tribes in the surrounding area did use the canyon for hunting and as a place of refuge.

The possibility of finding evidence of prehistoric occupation of Montezuma Canyon attracted George A. Teague, an archeologist with the Western Archeological and Conservation Center (WACC) in Tucson, and his crew, including Krista Deal and Lynne D'Ascenzo. Following the acquisition of the State of Texas Mines in 1986, Teague's survey began on September 23, 1987, when Deal and D'Ascenzo traveled to the site. In their survey, they concentrated on forty acres surrounding the State of Texas Mines. For the next two days, they mapped the area and, on September 25, at day's end, they had completed their task. They wrote, "Approximately forty acres of the Old Sparks [*sic*] property (which encompasses the State of Texas Mine) was archeologically surveyed with several outlying mining features recorded."[22] No prehistoric sites in the immediate survey area were found. Their initial report in that immediate area of the mines showed no artifacts and the area was cleared of any prehistoric archeological sites.[23]

Although Montezuma Canyon, similar to the Huachuca Mountains, contains evidence of prehistoric activity, the region, nonetheless, is filled with evidence of centuries of human occupation and land-use. Long before the Spanish imagined golden cities to the north of Mexico, hunter-gatherer groups had developed agricultural communities along the river basins of southern Arizona. The San Pedro River Valley, within sight of Montezuma Peak, served as home to certain tribes who were, for a short while during the Spanish Colonial period, the objects of missionary efforts for conversion to Christianity.

In the early 1950s, as the idea of a Coronado National Memorial was becoming a reality, archeologists unearthed intermingled bones from humans and mammoths in the nearby San Pedro and Sulphur Springs valleys. When tested, those artifacts proved to be some 11,000 years old.[24] The prehistoric culture that developed in the area was given the name Cochise by archaeologists for the county in which they found many of the sites that defined it. Stages within the Cochise culture, which lasted from about 10,000 to 2,500 years ago, were taken from local geography as well. The ultimate stage of Cochise culture is named San Pedro in honor of archeological finds in the valley adjacent to the Coronado National Memorial.[25] Several Cochise culture sites, primarily from the Chiricahua stage (8000 to 3000 BC), have been found in Montezuma Canyon.[26]

Over time, through the movement of people and ideas, various regional cultures developed, among them the Mogollon, Hohokam, and Salado. The San Pedro River lay at the margins of these cultures. Ruins within the valley and its tributaries exhibit mixtures of characteristics and influences, and scholars disagree as to the exact relationship between the groups in the area or cultural affiliations of each site.[27] The exact relationship between the prehistoric cultures studied by archeologists and the groups that first met the Spanish in the fifteenth and sixteenth centuries is also less than certain.

It appears that several sites in the San Pedro Valley were settled during the few centuries preceding the arrival of the Spanish. Evidence of human occupation during that period has been found within the boundaries of Coronado National Memorial.[28] According to archaeologist Harold Sterling Gladwin, the San Pedro Valley was one of only a few centers of the great sedentary cultures to survive in the Southwest as late as 1400.[29] At that time, ancient Indian peoples built pueblos on the San Pedro River and Babocomari Creek and at the mouths of the major canyons along the eastern edge of the Huachuca Mountains.[30] Despite the existence of apparent archeological gaps, Charles DiPeso concluded that the residents of the San Pedro Valley had a continuous heritage from the mammoth hunters of the distant past to the residents of the *rancherías* (Native American seasonal settlements) found by the first Spaniards to enter Arizona.[31]

The survey done by Deal and D'Ascenzo did not produce evidence of prehistoric occupation in the mining areas of Montezuma Canyon compared to other areas within the Huachuca Mountains. To anyone standing at the site in 1987, it was evident that the State of Texas Mines had seen their last days. The debris supported the facts that the place had been occupied—from the Spanish colonial, Mexican, and early Anglo-American periods to the end of the 1970s. The material culture supported the modern occupancy of the property and the historical records bore witness that the mines had been worked intermittently during that long aforementioned period. The two archaeologists saw a slightly different scene, especially around the site of the State of Texas Mines, than what mining engineers and inspectors had seen in the past. Instead of prehistoric sites, they discovered a site littered with trash dumped by the miners who had lived there. Yet the forty acres surrounding the State of Texas Mines yielded a material culture left by prospectors and miners from the Mexican occupation of the area and by late-nineteenth-century Anglo-American miners.[32] Many of the so-called artifacts dated to the twentieth century as late as the 1970s. Still, given the appearance of the site, the archaeologists could not help but see it as an eyesore.

To begin, they described their westward drive up the canyon for over a mile to the first right-hand turn toward the north. The dirt and gravel road "goes uphill directly to the main workings, roughly 1/4 mile upslope."[33] Upon their arrival at the State of Texas Mines, they realized that they were looking at a historic site. Their notion of artifacts began to change.

Of the site and their changing attitude toward it, they noted, "A lead/zinc mine, with about 4 openings, situated on steep slopes. The tunnels are blasted into rock outcrops. Various prospects, isolated adits, stopes [steplike cuts in a mine where minerals are extracted] and workings are found in the surrounding area." They observed that the site was about 5,800 feet above sea level. Regarding the depth of the mine, they merely recorded "unknown." What they saw around them revealed a site that had been worked off and on, then neglected for periods of time. The so-called artifacts included "oil drums (openings cut in sides—secondary use), oil cans, rubberhose, lumber, roofing (tar) paper, metal pipe, wire, rubber boots, misc. tin cans, gloves, twisted cable, hand-pump sprayer, broom fragment, anti-freeze bottles, cloth, machinery, belts,. . . cut bone, concrete footings with bolts, stoneware," and other fragments of things strewn about the site. Vandalism, they wrote "has greatly diminished the site's value."[34]

Near a south wall of an opening on the southeastern side, they saw a metal box set into the rock that they surmised was used for storing blasting caps or powder. Toward the south on a down slope from the main workings about ten meters away, they saw a platform seven meters long. The southeast side of it was built up and retained by a rock wall about 30 inches high. The earthen platform had a concrete foundation where a diesel-fired air compressor was located. They described the foundation as 30.5 inches by 142 inches by 12.5 inches in height with a "lip at its foot 8 inches wide." Nearby, they saw a smaller platform of earth that was reinforced by piled rock at the north end of the concrete foundation. The rock was piled two to three courses, 11 inches high. They measured its dimensions as 101 inches by 84 inches in size. They noted that as late as March 1987, a thousand-gallon corrugated iron water tank sat on that platform. The second concrete platform was situated west of the concrete foundation. It measured 70 by 90 by 2 inches in size. It was a flat slab that was "currently mostly obscured by trash."[35]

Regarding the tailings, they said that a "stockpiled ore area" was located east on the down slope of the main works. They mentioned that the tailings lined the road along the north side. Near it, they noted the collapsed metal and wooden remnant of an ore chute and a loading bin "jumbled at the foot of the ore pile along the road." At the top of the tailings they noticed an adit with a log that reinforced it above and in front of the opening. They saw the remains of two small tracks for ore carts leading from the adit across the tailings. One led to the old chute or bin and the other along the length of the pile. Nearby, there were five long ore sample trays at the southwest end of the stockpiled area. Each tray was made of wood and measured 11.5 by 73 by 1¾ inches. On the east end of the pilings, there was a stope that had been dug into the ridge slope. A second stope had been dug into the slope halfway between the east end stope and the adit. The tailings line the road for approximately 50 meters from there. The area was strewn with sample bags, pane and bottle glass, leather, nails, wide-mesh screen, carpet, cans of WD-40, beer cans, cement bats, socket-set case and holder, and other debris.[36]

Deal and D'Ascenzo noticed that on a slope above the main workings was a "bulldozed flat, and a circular area which is 'lined' with rock perhaps a flat/platform for a tank?" Up slope from there, they saw a "series of cement collar[s] to keep it intact." About 80 meters above the main works, they saw an "area of tailings with three vertical shafts and a small test pit. The westernmost shaft was braced with timber and a rock cemented wall on the shaft's east side to brace it from collapsing." At the time they saw it, the shaft was partially collapsed. The tailings had a retaining wall of piled rock on the slope side near the middle shaft. Between there and the main workings, the terrain was rather steep.[37]

The archeologists once again referred to the road that led past the main workings and veered to the right at a fork along a small spur that went up the bulldozed flat and skirted an adit. From the fork, the road went straight to a ridge past a vertical shaft on the east side of the road and tailings on the west side of the road. The road led to another "rather large adit." The adit was full of water and had a wooden bulkhead across it about 35 meters from the entrance. A wooden fence lined the front of the adit. A few meters from the adit, workers had placed a spigot on a metal pipe where water could be turned on or off. Near there, they found a piece of penstock almost a foot in diameter and rubber boots. Just to the right (or east) of the adit was a dryfall. The adit appeared to have been blasted into a rock outcropping that had begun to seep.[38]

At the top of the ridge, in the center and at its head, where the main workings with the three vertical shafts were situated, was a small prospect. A second prospect could be seen on the adjacent ridge to the west.

Above the water adit were three other adits. One adit was directly above; the second adit, an open stope, was west of it. Nearby was a "good-sized" tailings pile. The third one was about 10 meters upslope and east of the first and had a small pile of tailings.[39]

Deal and D'Ascenzo continued down the road from the main workings. There, they noticed more holes "from the mining endeavor." One of them was an adit that was dug under the road. It had collapsed. The adit was located on the south side of the road. Down slope from there was a large pile of tailings that ran down to the foot of the spur from the main road. That adit, despite being filled, "could be entered." To the north of the road, an open stope "cut up the ridge."[40]

Farther down the road they could see "an obvious rock outcrop" that was used as a "storage room (powder magazine)." It had been blasted into the rock. They believed that it was originally a prospect, "a small hole outside of it indicates the possibility." They said, "The room is not very deep (about 6 ft) & the opening has been closed-in with cement and rock to form a door-jam for a double-thick wooden door which is still intact & fits snugly into the opening."[41]

Proceeding a few meters down the road from the powder magazine, they encountered "a small prospect & obligatory tailings" close to the curve in the road. It was located about 10 meters south of the road. On the east side of the road, in a deep drainage along the first curve in the road, they noticed "a grand collection of garbage appearing as if an entire house had been pushed down the slope." They recorded some of the items in the heap: "wood—2 x 4 and plywood—part of the walls, stove, table, water, washing machine, roofing, miscellaneous machine and metal parts, chair & bed springs, outdoor grill, wheel barrow, rubber tires, tin cans, electric xmas lights, electric coffee pot, polaroid camera, 'VLM exerciser,' BB gun, wire form for a lampshade, pie tin & rope."[42]

Deal and D'Ascenzo observed one last feature in their survey. They wrote, "Above the dump, E-NE about 40 meters is a prospect with a stockpile of rock from it piled neatly on the SE edge of the shallow hole. A few meters away from this prospect to the NE is a 'mine claim marker' or perhaps a marker for the property corner. This marker is the standard cairn, or pile of stacked rock."[43] The completed survey of Coronado National Memorial (CORO) 87B-1 was completed and submitted on September 29, 1987, to George Teague.

Other artifacts in the area were not necessarily associated with mining. For example, one report at CORO Site 13 indicated, "A clearly defined slab metate was noted at one end of the utilized face is a 'dimple' or small depression 2 cm. in diameter and 1 1/2 cm. deep. This artifact is similar to the two 'dimpled' artifacts described at CORO 6 and CORO 3. One unutilized chert flake was also found. The only temporally diagnostic artifact discovered was a chert projectile point with the tip broken off."[44]

Standing on the threshold of the twenty-first century and looking back in time, the archeologists, in 1987, could see that much had happened in Montezuma Canyon. Indeed, Montezuma Canyon was a window to the past and a work in progress. Archeologists Krista Deal and Lynne D'Ascenzo had done their job. They had looked at a site that told a different story of human occupancy at Montezuma Canyon and left a vivid description in their report about that place and those times. After Deal and D'Ascenzo had identified the mines and their attendant material culture in Montezuma Canyon, Superintendent Joe Sewell ordered the mines sealed in 1988 for safety and conservation purposes.[45] Thus, in all of its efforts, Coronado National Monument has aimed to protect all of the resources within its boundaries and incorporate them within its historical themes.

Notes

1. Hugo H. Huntzinger, "Boundary Adjustment—a Radical Proposal," n.d., WACC, Folder L 1417: Boundary Adjustments—Surveys & Reports F1.

2. For a comprehensive history of Coronado National Memorial, see Joseph P.

Sánchez, Bruce A. Erickson, and Jerry Gurulé, *Between Two Countries: A History of Coronado National Memorial, 1939–1990* (Albuquerque, NM: Rio Grande Books, 2007).

3. Presidential Proclamation, 2995—Establishment of the Coronado National Memorial Arizona, November 5, 1952, signed by President Harry S. Truman. Also see Public Law 478, 82nd Congress, approved July 9, 1952, amending the Act of August 18, 1941, 55 Stat. 630 (16 U.S.C. 450y); untitled, n.d., congressional debate on bill H.R. 7553, Western Archeology and Conservation Center (hereinafter WACC), Folder H 18: Biographical Data, General F11.

4. Senator Carl Hayden to Grace Sparkes, Washington, DC, July 2, 1954, Hayden Papers, AC, Arizona State University Document 537 folder; Luis A. Gastellum, Assistant General Superintendent, Southwestern National Monuments (SWNM), NPS, to Sparkes, Globe, October 15, 1954 D18, Master Plans [1954] F2.pdf, WACC archives, CD box 3.

5. Elizabeth A. H. John, ed., John Wheat, trans., *Views from the Apache Frontier. Report on the Northern Provinces of New Spain by José Cortés, Lieutenant in the Royal Corps of Engineers, 1799* (Norman: University of Oklahoma Press, 1998), 27.

6. See Oakah L. Jones, *Pueblo Warriors and the Spanish Conquest* (Norman: University of Oklahoma Press, 1966). Also see "Juan Bautista de Anza's Campaign of 1779 against Cuerno Verde," in Joseph P. Sánchez, ed., *Early Hispanic Colorado, 1678–1900* (Albuquerque, NM: Rio Grande Press, 2015), 111. Anza, for example, had 259 Queres Indian allies with him as well as several hundred Ute warriors against Comanche raiders.

7. David J. Weber, *Bárbaros: Spaniards and their Savages in the Age of Enlightenment* (New Haven, CT: University of Yale Press, 2005), 195, fn126.

8. Ibid., fn127.

9. Ibid., 195–96.

10. Angie Debo, *Geronimo: The Man, His Time and Place* (Norman: University of Oklahoma Press, 5th printing, 1989), 420.

11. Colin G. Calloway, *First Peoples: A Documentary Survey of American Indian History* (Boston: Bedford/St. Martin's Press, 2005), 35.

12. For a discussion on historical and present political, economic, and cultural trends and events that have shaped the ways that Mexicans and Americans have regarded each other over the centuries, see W. Dirk Raat and Michael M. Brescia, *Mexico and the United States: Ambivalent Vistas* (Athena: University of Georgia Press, 4th ed., 2010). The authors provide perspectives regarding the borderlands where the two countries share a common history and heritage.

13. Robert Spude, "The Federal Presence: Boundary Commission, U.S. Forest Service and the CCC" (unpublished manuscript); Robert R. Humphrey, *90 Years and 535 Miles, Vegetation Changes Along the Mexican Border* (Albuquerque: University of New Mexico Press, 1987), 5, 22.

14. Robert Spude, "The Federal Presence: Boundary Commission, U.S. Forest Service and the CCC" (unpublished manuscript); J. Evetts Haley, *Jeff Milton, a Good Man with a Gun* (Norman: University of Oklahoma Press, 1948), 171–72.

15. "Invasión Mexicana a Bisbee, Arizona, EEUU=Guardas aduanales mexicanas que rodearon la estación de Bisbee y aprehendierón a otro mexicano" 1892, Archivo Histórico Diplomático de la Secretaria de Asuntos Exteriores, Mexico City 11-9-194, also see 15-7-14.

16. Robert Spude, "The Federal Presence: Boundary Commission, U.S. Forest Service and the CCC" (unpublished manuscript); Humphrey, *90 Years*, 6–10.

17. Anonymous, "History of Coronado Activity," ca. 1995, Coronado National Memorial files, WACC, p. 5; Grace Sparkes to Margaret Rockwell, Prescott, April 11, 1940, Sparkes Collection, Arizona Historical Society (AHS), Box 23, Folder 956. Sparkes refers to work done on the road two years earlier from the date of her letter.

18. Anonymous, "History of Coronado Activity," ca. 1995, Coronado National Memorial files, WACC, p. 5.

19. Superintendent Joseph L. Sewell to Superintendent, Death Valley National Monument, Subject: Mine Closures, Hereford, November 17, 1987; Archeologist, Division of Archeology, WACC, Subject: Trip Report, Coronado Mine Safety Project, Tucson, January 12, 1988, WACC, Folder L 3023: Mining General F 39.

20. Interpretive Prospectus, State of Texas Mine Site, Coronado National Memorial, 1988, WACC, Folder K 18: Interpretive Prospectus F2.

21. Annual Statement for Interpretation and Visitor Services, Coronado National Memorial, 1988, WACC, Folder K 1817: Annual Statement for Interpretation F2.

22. Krista Deal to the chief, Division of Archeology, Tucson, September 29, 1987, memo file code H2623 CORO (WR) RWI, CORO WACC Archives.

23. Data Control Card: Coronado, Project #: CORO 1987B, George A. Teague, CORO WACC Archives.

24. E. B. Sayles, *The San Simon Branch: Excavations at Cave Creek in the San Simon Valley*, I. Material Culture, Medallion Papers, No. 34 (Globe, AZ: Gila Pueblo, 1945), iv; Jay J. Wagoner, *Early Arizona: Prehistory to Civil War* (Tucson: The University of Arizona Press, 1975), 11–13.

25. Harold Sterling Gladwin, *Excavations at Snaketown,* IV. Reviews and Conclusions, Medallion Papers, No. 38 (Globe, AZ: Gila Pueblo, 1948), 127–31.

26. Yvonne G. Stewart, "Montane Cochise Culture Sites in Coronado National Memorial," in ed. Robert M. Linn, *Proceedings of the First Conference on Scientific Research in the National Parks,* vol. II, New Orleans, LA, November 9–12, 1976, sponsored by National Park Service and American Institute of Biological Sciences, Washington, DC: United States Department of the Interior, National Park Service Transactions and Proceedings Series, Number 5, 1979, CORO MAX 1 - Archeology, Folder 75a: Archeological Survey, CORO Files.

27. Carr Tuthill, *The Tres Alamos Site on the San Pedro River, Southeastern Arizona* (Dragoon, AZ: The Amerind Foundation, 1947), 15, 83–86; Charles C. DiPeso, *The Babocomari Village Site on the Babocomari River, Southeastern Arizona* (Dragoon, AZ: The Amerind Foundation, 1951), 224–41; Charles C. DiPeso, *The Sobaipuri Indians of the Upper San Pedro River Valley, Southeastern Arizona* (Dragoon, AZ: The Amerind Foundation, 1953), 1–4.

28. Archeologist, Division of Archeology, Western Archeological and Conservation Center (WACC), to Chief, Division of Archeology, WACC, Tucson, December 10, 1990, CORO MAX 1 - Archeology, Folder 90a: Montezuma Cave Artifacts, CORO Files.

29. Harold Sterling Gladwin, *A History of the Ancient Southwest* (Portland, ME: Bond Wheelwright, 1957), 337.

30. DiPeso, *The Babocomari Village Site*. Recently, Deni J. Seymour, *Where the Earth and Sky Are Sewn Together: Sobaipuri-O'odham Context of Contact and Colonialism* (Salt Lake

City: University of Utah Press, 2011), demonstrates the longevity and continuity of native cultures in southeastern Arizona and northeastern Sonora.

31. DiPeso, *The Sobaipuri Indians,* 263–68.

32. Data Control Card: Coronado, Project #: CORO 1987B, George A. Teague, CORO WACC Archives.

33. D'Ascenzo and Deal, Archeological Site Record, September 24, 1987, CORO 87B-1, p. 1, CORO WACC Archives. The following discussion is based on this document.

34. This paragraph, including all but final quote, ibid., p. 1; final quote, ibid., p. 2.

35. This paragraph, including quotes, ibid., p. 3.

36. This paragraph, including quotes, ibid.

37. This paragraph, including quotes, ibid., p. 4.

38. This paragraph, including quotes, ibid.

39. This paragraph, including quotes, ibid., p. 5.

40. This paragraph, including quotes, ibid.

41. This paragraph, including quotes, ibid.

42. This paragraph, including quotes, ibid., p. 6.

43. This paragraph, including quotes, ibid.

44. CORO Site 13, CORO WACC Archives.

45. Ron Cron, Resource Maintenance Work Leader, Death Valley National Monument, to Superintendent, Coronado National Memorial, Subject: Coronado Mine Safing Project—9/12/88—10/1/88, Death Valley, November 21, 1988; David L. Sharrow, Environmental Protection Specialist, Mining and Minerals Branch, to Chief, Environmental Assessment Section, Mining and Minerals Branch, Land Resources Division, Subject: Trip Report for Abandoned Mineral Lands, Trip to Arizona, Denver, November 29, 1988, Superintendent Joseph L. Sewell to Superintendent, Death Valley National Monument, Subject: Mine Closures, Hereford, November 17, 1987; Archeologist, Division of Archeology, WACC, Subject: Trip Report, Coronado Mine Safety Project, Tucson, January 12, 1988, WACC, Folder L 3023: Mining General F 39.

CHAPTER 1

Montezuma Canyon, the Coronado Expedition, and Historians

A Historiographical Conundrum

We know, of course, that Coronado climbed the highest peak in order to survey the vast territory to the north and to the south, in his search for the 'Seven Cities of Cibola'. Nothing lower than the highest vantage point would have satisfied him, and when honoring him we should build at the point that is actually hallowed by his footsteps.

—Mrs. J. M. Keith, 1940[1]

Centuries after Francisco Vázquez de Coronado and a large expeditionary force trekked through a large area stretching northwest from Compostela, Nayarit, to places that today are clearly known as Sonora, Arizona, New Mexico, Texas, Oklahoma, and Kansas, his exact pathway is still a mystery. In 1940 Congress sought to commemorate the epic expedition by creating the Coronado Cuarto Centennial Commission. The commission had hoped to establish an international memorial to commemorate the first European explorers into the greater Southwest and the north Mexican states. In so doing, they wished to affirm historical ties that bind the United States and Mexico. Seeking to pinpoint the spot where the Coronado Expedition crossed the present international boundary from Mexico into the United States, the commission contracted historians to find the route or, at least, a corridor. The search for the route resulted in a flurry of academic publications that brought the state of knowledge about the expedition to its high point. Their conclusions tied the Coronado Expedition to Montezuma Canyon. In the same way, the Coronado Cuarto Centennial Commission inadvertently abetted the creation of a historiographical tradition tied to the Coronado Expedition of 1540.

In 1990, when the 450th anniversary of the Coronado Entrada (entry) once again came into view, a renewed interest in that expedition among scholars unfurled. Symposia, publications, reenactments, and other commemorative activities abounded. Since 1992 there has been interest in regard to the expedition of 1540, and a few archaeological publications have expressed new finds. Published in 1997, one book, however, brought the state of knowledge about the expedition to a reasonable level: *The Coronado Expedition to Tierra Nueva: The 1540–1542 Route across the Southwest,* edited by Richard Flint and Shirley Cushing Flint. The book contained a series of essays, penned by well-known historians and archaeologists, that summarized the state of knowledge dealing with archaeology and history about the Coronado Expedition. The publication included a historiography of the Coronado Expedition written by Joseph P. Sánchez. He identified at least thirteen general geographical issues that historians and archaeologists have explored and pondered. They included segments between points, such as,

Compostela to the Abra [The Valley of Sonora]
Suya and the Sonora–Arizona connection
The location of Chichilticale
From the Despoblado to Cíbola: The Arizona–New Mexico riddle
Vázquez de Coronado's tiguex: The Albuquerque/Bernalillo campsite
From Tiguex to pecos and beyond: Spring 1541
The search for Coronado's bridge
with the main army from the bridge on the Rio Cicuye to the Llano Estacado and back
Mysterious Cona: place or event?
The main army returns to the Rio Grande
north by the needle through Texas and Oklahoma
Quivira—at last
The expedition heads home[2]

To a degree, the historiography of the expedition represented a starting point for those who would dare tread across Coronado's path.

Some of the contributing authors of the Flints' book did not stop their research into Coronado's *entrada*. The Flints, for example, continued their tireless search for new information regarding the expedition and have published several new books and articles on the subject. Archaeologist Donald Blakeslee, meanwhile, made a new discovery at Blanco Canyon, in the Texas Panhandle, of material cultural items associated with the Coronado Expedition. Over the years, crossbow points related to the expedition have been found at Hawikuh (Zuni), Santiago and Piedras Marcadas Pueblo (Albuquerque), and Yellow Lake Canyon (Lubbock), among other places.

Since the late nineteenth century, a long list of historians and archaeologists have carried out their own search for the Seven Cities of Cíbola. With few exceptions, theories about the route have been presented as fact by several researchers, but proof for hypothetical conclusions concerning the actual line of march by the expedition will never be satisfactorily attained. In the first place, no maps of the expedition exist. Second, the documents are too vague with regard to distance between points, place names that no longer exist, and lack of detail to define exactly where the expedition camped or traveled. The historiography of the expedition demonstrates that only a handful of sites can be identified, but how the expedition got to them is fraught with hypothetical examples.

The expedition of Francisco Vázquez de Coronado is significant because it was the first major European exploration to penetrate the interior of the continent to its heartland in present Kansas. Exploring from Compostela on the west coast of Mexico, northward through Sonora, eastern Arizona, and across central New Mexico to the Rio Grande, the expedition moved eastward across the Texas Panhandle, marched through Oklahoma, and reached the great bend of the Arkansas River in central Kansas.

Narrative accounts of the expedition, the first written by Europeans, describe its many encounters with the native inhabitants and contain a wealth of information about certain societies and their cultures while they were still pure of European influences. Likewise, Coronado and his men wrote descriptions of the flora and fauna and other natural resources they encountered. They were the first Europeans to describe the Grand Canyon of Arizona and the large herds of buffalo on the Great Plains, the name we give today to the vast treeless plains that stretch from the Arctic coast to South Texas and from eastern New Mexico almost to the Mississippi River. The expedition members noted mountains, valleys, rivers, salt beds, lakes, forests, and other topographical features, including the Continental Divide, the watershed that separates rivers flowing toward the Pacific Ocean or the Gulf of Mexico and the Atlantic.

The traditional consensus regarding the route, however, is that it lies close to that proposed by A. Grove Day and Herbert Eugene Bolton.[3] Both men popularized portions of the route through western Mexico, Arizona, New Mexico, Texas, Oklahoma, and central Kansas. Although the route they proposed is not the object of this analysis, it plays an important role in the historiography of the expedition led by Francisco Vázquez de Coronado. The Bolton–Day route, particularly as it crossed through northern Sonora into present Arizona, became the accepted route on which Congress based the location of Coronado National Memorial in 1941–52.

In recent years, nonetheless, researchers have debated portions of the route proposed by Day and Bolton, and some have even gone as far as to propose new routes. There are reasons for the disparities between some of the hypotheses: Day and Bolton dealt with the larger picture of the route. They were able to connect known places visited by the expedition with theories explaining how it reached them. Later researchers, concerned only with portions of the route, began to discover other hypothetical alternatives by concentrating on specific topographical and cultural features in certain areas believed crossed by the expedition. It should be noted that Day and Bolton actually tested their hypothetical routes on the ground, as have other researchers. Unlike Day and Bolton, who visited the Spanish colonial archives in Spain and Mexico and who read the original manuscripts of the expedition, some of the early writers of the route lacked access to the documentation and used translations that precluded certain perspectives about what the expedition had seen. Other writers, it is apparent, lacked geographical knowledge about the areas traveled by the expedition or did not read carefully the sources available to them.

When the Coronado Cuarto Centennial Commission was formed in 1935, the members focused their attention on the United States–Mexican border where Coronado could have entered the United States. Throughout the fall of 1940 and into the summer of 1941, Congress entertained the possibility of creating the Coronado International Memorial on the Arizona–Sonora border. Answering a question regarding the proposed monument, in the *Congressional Record* for that day, Congressman John Robert Murdock of Arizona commented that the monument would be established "at the point on the international border where Coronado crossed into Arizona 400 years ago this spring."[4] Earlier, on March 26, Congressman John M. Houston addressed the House of Representatives in a *Washington Post* article entitled "Southwest to Celebrate Four Hundredth Anniversary of Coronado's March" dated two days prior.[5] Reading from that article, Houston told the House, "the exact spot where Coronado entered the territory of what is now the United States has long been a matter of controversy." Supporters of the memorial argued for the Naco entry point with a focus on Montezuma Canyon and its high points.

To reach a solution, the matter was referred to the NPS; early in January 1940 a special party of historians, headed by Herbert E. Bolton, director of the Bancroft Library at the University of California, drove to Compostela, Nayarit, Mexico. They retraced, mile for mile, what they believed to be the original route of the Coronado Expedition of 1540. In the end, they determined that the explorers had entered the United States at Naco, Arizona, which is on the east slope of the San Pedro Valley, about ten miles south of Bisbee, Arizona.[6] In his book *Coronado: Knight of Pueblos and Plains,* Bolton reiterated his position that the entry point, in the vicinity of Naco, was somewhere south of Benson, Arizona.[7]

The acceptance of the vicinity of Naco as the point of entry by the Coronado Expedition gained popularity among the Arizona proponents of the Coronado International Memorial for a variety of reasons. Some of the conclusions regarding the Coronado entry point were speculative, and others went beyond reason. For example, in a letter dated May 9, 1940, from Mrs. J. M. Keith to Charles M. Morgan, executive secretary of the Coronado Cuarto Centennial Commission, Mrs. Keith complained that the proposal for a memorial containing 2,900 acres "is too large a tract to be effective or practical." Instead, she suggested a smaller tract, consisting of one section along the north and one section along the south side of the Arizona–Mexico international line, that would include a museum at the "very highest point" along the border. What would be the highest point, and why would it be important? Mrs. Keith explained, "We know, of course, that Coronado climbed the highest peak in order to survey the vast territory to the north and to the south, in his search for the 'Seven Cities of Cibola'. Nothing lower than the highest vantage point would have satisfied him, and when honoring him we should build at the point that is actually hallowed by his footsteps." Mrs. Keith, undoubtedly, referred to a high point at Montezuma Canyon called Lookout Peak, which was later renamed Coronado Peak. Still, it would be left to historians, archaeologists, and other researchers to validate the history of the Coronado Expedition's entry into Arizona from Mexico.[8]

There was another alternative to the Naco area point of entry by Coronado. In his autobiographical notes, Morgan mentions that there was a push to have the Coronado International Monument located in Nogales, Arizona. "For many years," he wrote, "there has been continuous controversy [about where the Coronado Entrada came out of Mexico into what is now Arizona]. As a casual student of southwestern history I was well aware that they went down the San Pedro River—but a lot of very influential people seriously contended that he came down the Santa Cruz, crossing the present line near Nogales."[9]

To quell the Nogales proponents, Morgan claimed he influenced a study to be made. "We put a suitable resolution through the commission," he wrote, "So an imposing historical commission, headed by the famous southwestern historian, Dr. Herbert Bolton, from the University of California at Berkeley, with members from the Universities of Arizona and New Mexico, representatives of the Park Service, photographers, etc. all equipped [*sic*] with special high-wheeled cars for rough country, carrying all the known data along; took off from Compostela and retraced the route of the Coronado Entrada to the border." The Bolton group, wrote Morgan, "came out along the San Pedro, any other route would have been quite impossible."[10] Apparently, Bolton presented his preliminary findings to Congress in November 1939.[11]

In his letter to Congressman John R. Murdock in 1939, Clinton P. Anderson, managing director of the New Mexico Coronado Commission, wrote that the people of Nogales raised the question regarding Coronado's route. They did so because, wrote Anderson, they wanted "a monument in that City for Coronado as a step toward the realization of their dream of making Nogales the great International Gateway. I believe that Mr. Morgan feels that Coronado came into the State 160 miles East of Nogales, and that the Park Service will so decide."[12]

Other historians such as R. K. Wyllys at Arizona State Teachers College in Tempe emphatically argued in favor of the San Pedro Valley point of entry and against the Santa Cruz Valley route.[13] Renowned New Mexico historian J. Manuel Espinosa supported Coronado's entrance along the San Pedro River into Arizona near the Palominas–Naco area as the corridor, which led to the Arizona entry point.[14]

On February 6, 1940, G. R. Michaels, secretary of the Bisbee Chamber of Commerce, announced to Dr. Vernon Aubrey Neasham, regional historian, NPS, and the NPS Santa Fe Regional Office, that the last hurdle toward gathering a consensus about the whereabouts of Coronado's entry into the United States had been overcome. "Needless to say," he wrote, "all of the people in this area were delighted with the announcement from Albuquerque, Sunday. Coronado entered what is now the United States via San Pedro Valley. We wish to assure you that we are ready and willing to do everything possible to assist your committee in getting this memorial project under way."[15]

In an undated printed letter to the minister for foreign relations in

Mexico, the United States Coronado Exposition Commission appeared ambiguous about Coronado's point of entry. The commission wrote, "The point at which Coronado's expedition passed into what is now Arizona from Mexico is generally believed by historians to have been in the vicinity of the San Pedro and Santa Cruz River valleys."[16]

Acknowledging the significance of the Coronado Expedition, the commission appended a historical statement that read, "Coronado's expedition was one of the outstanding achievements of a period marked by notable explorations. It made known the vast extent and the nature of the country that lay north of central Mexico, and from the time of Coronado, Spaniards never lost interest in the country. In no small measure their subsequent occupation of it was due to the curiosity so created."[17]

In 1952, during the congressional hearings to change the name from Coronado International Memorial to Coronado National Memorial, Representative Murdock, who had supported the original 1940 legislation, again believed it was important to reassert that the location of Coronado National Memorial was correct. "I might say to those of you who are students of history," he remarked, "that there has been some discussion as to where Coronado entered what is now the United States, but that I think was very definitely determined by a board of historical authorities headed by Dr. Herbert Moulton [*sic*], of the University of California, who in my judgment, is the best student on the Spanish phases of American history that we have. We feel certain that we know almost exactly the spot which was entered by Coronado in 1540."[18] Indeed, the February 1952 issue of the *Arizona Highways* announced that it, too, could prescribe the exact route: "Coronado's route from Mexico crossed the southern peak of the Huachucas across the valley and San Pedro where recently an old Spanish spur was found buried in the sand. Their route also trailed over the Bisbee mountain near Lime Peak and across the divide to the valley below."[19] Despite the apodictic quality of such statements, questions regarding Coronado's entry point persisted and would continue to be raised time and again throughout the next fifty years, especially when the 450th anniversary of the expedition rolled around in 1990–92.

Significantly, Day, in 1940, was among the first to propose that the expedition entered Arizona through a point near Naco, not far from the present Coronado National Memorial. The Bolton–Day route is presented herein with the historiographical perspectives of other researchers who have promulgated theories, hypotheses, and issues related to the expedition's travel through a large portion of North America. The collective conclusion about the location of portions of Coronado's route among historians and other researchers has taken the form of consensus. Although historians continue their research of Coronado's route, the general consensus of the route along the San Pedro River as known in the 1940s and 1950s influenced the location of Coronado National Memorial.

Historians agree that the Coronado Expedition was the first major European exploration to penetrate the interior of the present United States. Exploring from Compostela on the west coast of Mexico, northward through Sonora and Arizona to a point near Coronado National Memorial, the expedition moved northeastward to New Mexico and eastward across the Texas Panhandle, through Oklahoma until it reached the Great Bend of the Arkansas River in central Kansas.

Narrative accounts of the expedition describe its many encounters with the native inhabitants and contain a wealth of information about certain societies and their cultures at the time of contact.

During the period 1539 to 1545 two other expeditions, aside from that led by Coronado, explored lands within present-day United States. One expedition was led by Hernando De Soto, whose men explored from Florida to Texas. The other expedition, commanded by Juan Rodríguez Cabrillo, sailed up the California coast, discovered San Diego Bay, and reached as far north as Cape Blanco in Oregon. The information gathered by these expeditions aided Spanish officials in evaluating the widest geographic expanse of North America from coast to coast. Indeed, the Spaniards were the first Europeans to leave a written record of their deeds in North America, thus beginning a literary heritage about a large geographic area from California to Florida and the lands between them. That heritage includes the diaries, reports, correspondences, and later historical documentation referencing the expedition. Equally important to that heritage is the literature generated by modern writers about the expedition: that body of literature is extensive. Many writers tried their hand at determining the route of Coronado's men, especially where it crossed from Mexico into the United States.

Where did the expedition leave Sonora to explore northward? Most historians agree that the single most important leg of the expedition is that from Compostela through Sonora. Without a fundamental understanding of that portion of the route it is impossible to determine exactly where the expedition entered present Arizona and what direction it took beyond that point. The literature suggests two viable points through which the expedition passed upon entering present Arizona: the San

Pedro and San Bernardino River valleys. Because Coronado's route from Compostela to either of those two points is vague, a third line of march, one farther east, is possible. In recent years scholars have discounted a fourth alternative: a western route through the Santa Cruz valley. In any case, finding the location of the expedition's entry into the present United States depends wholly on determining the route taken through Sonora.

Although Bolton and Day, independent of one another, presented a route through Sonora based on observation and analogy of their readings of the documents and what they perceived to be on the ground, Charles DiPeso approached the problem in 1974 by utilizing available archaeological data and pertinent historical documentation. The historical problem lay in part with the lack of identity of rivers in Sonora for the early Spanish period. Of that dilemma, DiPeso wrote, "When modern historians attempt to correlate present-day names, such as Yaqui or Sonora River, with names used by early explorers who had no maps and often were inconvenienced by a lack of interpreters, and who used such terms as Yaqui and Senora, then distances and travel times are sacrificed and misconceptions are bound to arise. As just mentioned, a league was accepted as being a specific distance, and wherever possible was used to determine distances between points."[20]

By comparing accounts of various sixteenth-century expeditions, DiPeso arrived at a certain determination of place names in Sonora. The variations of place names mentioned by explorers, explained DiPeso, were inconsequential because their singular locations were determined by Indian settlements along them, and their names were constant. Besides, he argued, the distance between them was a controlling factor, because the explorers had given estimated figures of time taken to travel between them and/or measurements in leagues. Additionally, Coronado kept a record of distances by having one of his men count the steps between the expedition's daily campsites.[21]

DiPeso's analysis could very well be a key to the historical conundrum concerning Coronado's route through Sonora. By following the documentation almost to a fault, DiPeso determined that the route of Coronado veered northeastward to the Bavispe River and its confluence with the Batepito River, which he followed to the San Bernardino River that originates in southeastern Arizona considerably east of the San Pedro River. DiPeso made a strong case for the expedition crossing into Arizona at present Slaughter Ranch not far westward from the

Arizona–New Mexico border. He concluded that the expedition entered New Mexico crossing into the Animas Valley through Antelope Pass and then straddled the Arizona–New Mexico boundary until reaching Zuni Pueblo.

Earlier, in 1872, Brigadier General J. H. Simpson, one of the first to attempt to trace Coronado's route in southern Arizona, had assumed that the Spaniards had entered the present United States through the Santa Cruz Valley. Simpson believed that the expedition visited Chichilticale, which he reckoned to be Casa Grande on the Gila River, and then turned northeast across the Pinal and Mogollon Mountains to Zuni. Simpson's account, filled with errors, suggested the westernmost theory of the expedition through Arizona. His discussion of the route through the Mogollon Rim, however, lacks substantive detail.[22] The notion persisted for almost seventy years. In 1939, for example, archaeologist Charlie Steen suggested that Fray Marcos de Niza's preliminary expedition in 1539 had entered Arizona through the Santa Cruz River valley and turned northwestward somewhere between Tucson and Phoenix, entering the mountains probably beyond Florence near the Salt River.[23] In 1540 Niza served as a guide of the Coronado Expedition.

Other scholars have contended that the expedition entered Arizona through the San Pedro River Valley because it was most compatible with Spanish documentation and topography, being the easiest route northward. In 1895 Frederick W. Hodge argued that the expedition traveled north along the Sonora River and entered Arizona through the San Pedro River Valley. From there, he suggested they crossed the Pinaleño Mountains over Railroad Pass, following the San Simeon valley to a point near present Solomonsville and the Gila River, south of the present White Mountain Apache Reservation.[24] Hodge's route took the expedition directly on a northeastward path to the Zuni River. Of this portion of the route, Hodge's explanation, likewise, lacks sufficient detail for analysis. The debate over the location of the expedition's crossing into Arizona from Sonora was only beginning. Hodge had raised a point that would cause much speculation concerning the San Pedro River Valley hypothesis.

In 1947 George J. Undreiner reexamined Fray Marcos de Niza's journey to Cíbola. He proposed that Niza had entered Arizona on April 13, 1539, by following a route north along the Pima road about fifteen miles east of Lochiel soon after which he reached Quiburi, a Sobaipuri village on the San Pedro River. Three days later, Niza visited Baicatcan, another village on the San Pedro, which DiPeso had dated pre-1698. Herein was the conundrum: Pedro de Castañeda, chronicler of the Coronado Expedition, stated that after visiting a certain Indian town the expedition described a four-day *despoblado* (an uninhabited area) north of there. Undreiner pointed out that, in his preliminary expedition of 1539 Niza, probably at Baicatcan or at least at Quiburi, learned that two more days of travel would take him to a *despoblado,* which would take four days to cross. He contended that Niza, after two days of travel, had reached the northernmost Sobaipuri village on the San Pedro and that it was probably near Aravaipa Creek.[25]

On that same point, Albert H. Schroeder responded to historians who had suggested that Coronado's expedition went down the San Pedro River in southeastern Arizona. Additionally, on the basis that Juan Jaramillo, chronicler of the expedition, had indicated that the expedition turned east, Schroeder routed Niza and Coronado either up Aravaipa Creek or east from the Tres Alamos region.[26] Schroeder wrote, "If the former route is accepted it would imply that that portion of the middle San Pedro River, more than two days travel south of the junction with the Aravaipa, would not have been occupied, since it would then be the four-day despoblado."[27]

Seeking to validate Niza's whereabouts on his route, Schroeder's thesis pointed to the very area where DiPeso, basing his conclusions on archaeological evidence, had suggested. DiPeso argued, "Occupation may have been unbroken from late prehistoric into historic (1690s) times. Thus, the old routes appear to be in error." In support of Hodge's hypothesis, Schroeder defended Niza, commenting, "The evidence presented herein not only indicates the good father was telling the truth, but that Coronado and his chroniclers knowingly supported much of his relation pertaining to the trip through this area."[28] Thus, Schroeder, in the end, cast his lot with the San Pedro River Valley entrance hypothesis.

The debate surrounding the San Pedro River Valley entrance is tied to the location of Chichilticale (sometimes spelled Chichilticalli). Of Chichilticale, Coronado wrote, "I rested for two days at Chichilticale, and there was no chance to rest further, because the food was giving out." In his account, Pedro de Castañeda reported, "The land changes again at Chichilticale and the thorny trees disappear. The reason is that since the gulf extends as far as that place and the coast turns, so also the ridge of the sierra turns. Here one comes to cross the ridge and it breaks to pass into the plains of the land."[29]

What was Chichilticale? At times the documents refer to it as a valley, other times it appears as a mountain range, a bay, or even a *despoblado*, and finally, as a place or a village. Coronado and Melchior Díaz mentioned the *"people of Chichilticale."* After careful consideration, DiPeso concluded that it was south of the Arizona-Sonora border, closer to the Batepito River and the San Bernardino valley. He wrote, "Ruins which might be ascribed to those of the 'red house' of Chichilticale occur up and down the San Bernardino Valley, and the Stevens Ranch site contains pottery fragments which indicate a trade relationship with the N[orth] and the Little Colorado." By placing Chichilticale in that area, DiPeso suggested that north of the confluence of the San Bernardino River valley was a fifteen-day *despoblado*.[30]

Schroeder correctly surmised the critical need to define the location of Chichilticale because, for one of many reasons, it determined where the expedition went next. He countered any argument that suggested that Chichilticale lay south of the Arizona-Sonora border. Schroeder stated that, "The ethnological traits reported by the early Spanish who recorded their travels of 1539 and 1540 through Arizona point to the Yavapai as the people who occupied the area on the north side of the fourday *despoblado*, where Chichilticale was located. Internal evidence within these early documents also indicates that Fray Marcos and Coronado followed the San Pedro to its mouth, not just to Tres Alamos or Aravaipa on the San Pedro, and that from there they crossed the Gila and went over to the Salt River as Undreiner suggests." Schroeder was emphatic about the significance of this point, writing, "Thus, the Yavapai remain as the only possible group, separated by four days' travel that bordered the Sobaipuri on the north in 1539 and 1540."[31]

In contrast to DiPeso's and Hodge's routes from Arizona to New Mexico, Schroeder proposed that after departing the mouth of the San Pedro River, the expedition proceeded down the Salt River. He suggested that they reached "almost to the mouth of Tonto Creek, then up Salome Creek and over the north end of the Sierra Anchas and then generally northeast over the Mogollon Rim across to Zuni. There is little or no evidence to indicate they went east from the San Pedro at Tres Alamos or via Aravaipa Creek and then across the present-day San Carlos Apache country to Zuni. Such a trail would necessitate a route directed to the north or northnortheast [*sic*], rather than northeast as the documents state."[32]

Writing in 1983, Carroll L. Riley and Joni L. Manson also agreed, without specifying their argument that Chichilticale was in southern Arizona or New Mexico.[33] Riley, on the basis of historical, anthropological, and botanical evidence revolving around linguistics, argued that the location of Chichilticale was at one of two probable locations: one on the lower Salt River, the other on the upper Gila River.[34]

Having crossed the *despoblado*, the anonymous sixteenth-century writer of the *Relación del Suceso* commented, "The entire route up to within fifty leagues of Cíbola [New Mexico] is inhabited, although in some places at a distance from the road."[35] This and other commentary by the members of the expedition are open to interpretation. The route to Cíbola from the *despoblado* is fraught with a dearth of information, leaving the researcher often with little more than his imagination.

The most accepted route of the expedition through Arizona is that proposed by Herbert E. Bolton. Since 1949 the Bolton route has gained in venerability, partly because of his scholarly influence and partly because his fieldwork almost rivaled that of Coronado's epic march across a large portion of North America. Bolton built on the work of earlier researchers, and was probably influenced, although he denied it, by A. Grove Day's *Coronado's Quest: The Discovery of the American West*, which was published a few years earlier, in 1940.

Day favored the Sonora Valley as a probable point from which the expedition reached Arizona. Furthermore, he opted for the San Pedro River route, specifying that Coronado had entered Arizona through a plain extending to the headwaters of the San Pedro River near present-day Naco. Somewhere near there, he explained, was the point of departure for crossing the *despoblado*. Day went on to propose that the expedition crossed the Gila and Salt Rivers by means of an old Indian trail, and then proceeded through the White Mountains to the upper drainage of the Little Colorado near St. Johns to the Zuni River. Although Day did not specifically tell how the expedition crossed the area, he deferred to the work by Sauer and Winship for his information.[36]

In 1954 the NPS revisited the question regarding the expedition's entry into the United States. The authors of the master plan for Coronado National Memorial called for additional research to "determine the location of San Heronimo (Gerónimo), the site founded for the main portion of Coronado's army, believed to have been located close to international border."[37] They also knew that their question could not easily be answered.

On the other hand, the accurate determination of each segment of the route is essential toward understanding each succeeding segment.

The location of San Gerónimo de los Corazones is predicated on where the expedition was previous to getting there; and, by the same token, once the explorers left San Gerónimo, where did they go?[38]

Other writers had attempted to answer that question. In 1907, Frederick Hodge and Theodore H. Lewis had identified San Gerónimo as present-day Ures, some distance from the border.[39] In 1940 George P. Hammond and Agapito Rey wrote that San Gerónimo was located "at Corazones in the Sonora valley, about where the river emerges from the canyon known locally as La Tescalma, the army settled down to await orders from Coronado. There in the distant new land the Spaniards constructed dwellings and established a town, naming it San Gerónimo de los Corazones.

Pedro de Castañeda, a member of the 1540 expedition, recalled that Coronado's men had, after considerable difficulty, "reached, by stages, a province which Cabeza de Vaca [1536] had named Corazones, because there the natives had offered him many hearts of animals. Without delay [Tristán de] Arellano proceeded to establish a town there, naming it San Hierónimo de los Corazones, and began at once to settle it. Later, seeing that it could not be maintained, he moved it to a valley called Persona—I mean Señora—and the Spaniards called it Señora, and so I shall call it from now on."[40] Thus, the first site of San Gerónimo is not necessarily a mystery, as it is identified with present Ures. Therefore, it is considered a spot on Coronado's route that pointed toward the San Pedro River as part of the places the expedition passed through in its trajectory to Cíbola.

The subsequent history and the attendant historiography of San Gerónimo, which had been moved to a place called Suya (40 leagues from Corazones), however, presents a different story to that of Ures. Thus, San Gerónimo likely had three locations: the site at present Ures, the site at Señora, and the site at Suya.

At Suya, the second or third site (depending on which historian one reads) of San Gerónimo, trouble brewed. Concerned that the main body of the expedition that had gone forward would reap the benefits derived from the conquest of another rich civilization, the men at that outpost mutinied. The remaining men, under Captain Diego de Alcaraz, were too few to defend themselves against the natives of the area. Already, there had been conflicts and warriors had hit some of his men with poisoned arrows. The poison was deadly, and the natives knew that the Spaniards were becoming too weak and too few to defend themselves.[41]

On one occasion the warriors attacked, killing three Spaniards, one of them Captain Alcaraz, several servants, and more than twenty horses in the melee. The day after the attack, the Spaniards decided to abandon the area and return to Culiacán, which they reached.[42] The location of Suya as the second or third site of San Gerónimo remains a mystery.

Castañeda wrote, "The town was situated near a small river."[43] The "small river" and the fact that the second site of San Gerónimo was forty leagues closer to Cíbola could have placed it within 120 miles to 200 miles depending if the factor is a three-mile league or a five-mile league. Both measurements were used during that period.

Where was Suya? Historians have argued and hypothesized about its location. It is possible that present Bacoachi, at the northern end of the Sonora River, is a candidate for consideration as San Gerónimo in the Suya Valley. If so, then, Coronado's expeditionary force could easily have been within reach of the headwaters of the San Pedro River. The question regarding the location of Suya, however, opened a historical Pandora's box.

Charles DiPeso argued that a different hypothetical model for the location of Suya is possible. He concluded that there were three San Gerónimos. DiPeso suggested that Corazones (San Gerónimo I) was the first base camp for the expedition. He argued that it was located in the middle Cedros Valley. Accordingly, DiPeso posited that the second base camp in the Señora Valley (San Gerónimo II) was actually in the Nuri Chico Valley. Slightly north and westward from there, DiPeso argued, was the third base camp (San Gerónimo III) in the Suya Valley, not far from the confluence of the Batepito and Bavispe Rivers—near present Colonia Morelos. In so arguing, DiPeso departed from the San Pedro River hypothesis and concluded that Coronado, upon leaving Suya, continued toward the San Bernardino River, then crossed over Antelope Pass on his way to Cíbola. Of the route leading to Cíbola from Suya, DiPeso wrote,

> Padre de Niza, Melchior Diaz, and Coronado's troops all traveled along this section of the old Acoma road seeking Cíbola. From the Río Batepito junction the army may have gone N by NW up this river to the San Bernardino junction, 43 km, and then up the San Bernardino in a northerly direction, keeping the Sierra de San Luis on the right (E), to the vicinity of the modern Slaughter Ranch another 17 km. Next they would have continued up the San Bernardino Valley, traveling NE past the site of present-day Rodeo, New Mexico, and keeping the Chiricahua Mountains

on the left (W) and the Peloncillos on the right (E), finally arriving at what is now called Antelope Pass in the latter range, an additional 65 km.[44]

Still, scholars concurred that the expedition entered Arizona through the San Pedro River Valley because it was most compatible with Spanish documentation and that the topography was the easiest route northward.[45] The writers of the master plan had, indeed, grasped the significance of their questions: Where was San Gerónimo? Where did the expedition go after leaving San Gerónimo and after leaving the San Pedro Valley? Part of the question lies in the location of Chichilticale: Did the expedition arrive there before or after the San Pedro Valley exploration?

Just as it is paramount to understand the expedition's whereabouts through Sonora in order to determine where they entered Arizona, it is equally important to learn about their route from Arizona to New Mexico. In that way, it might be possible to backtrack to the Arizona point of entry. Each leg of the expedition's trek through a given area links with its previous leg and the one that follows it. Like Day, Bolton relied on Winship's translation of Castañeda's account and other sources to define his proposed route, which he then set out to prove through his fieldwork. Generally, Bolton's route has the expedition leaving the traditionally mentioned Compostela to Culiacán where they followed the coastal plain, veering northeastward between the Gulf of California and the Sierra Madre Occidental, crossing rivers until they reached the Sonora River valley. From there, deduced Bolton, the expedition entered Arizona through the San Pedro River Valley. The Bolton route placed the expedition's point of departure through the *despoblado* near Benson, Arizona, from where it marched northeast through the Galiuro Mountains and crossed the Arivaipa Valley, passing through Eagle Pass between the Pinaleño and Santa Teresa Mountains.

Bolton surmised that the expedition's line of march through the *despoblado* ran along the Gila River, crossing it at present-day Bylas, after which it forded the Salt River near Bonito Creek. He proposed that Coronado continued northward, crossed the White River near Fort Apache, and ascended the Mogollon Rim by following small streams before emerging on the Little Colorado River near its confluence with the Zuni River. Shortly, the expedition reached Hawikuh.[46]

The route has been accepted by some historians, modified by others, and contested by yet other researchers who offer their own conclusions that are markedly different from Bolton's. Researchers, namely R. M. Wagstaff, have criticized the Bolton proposal by noting that the distances traveled by the expedition do not conform to Bolton's conclusions. Also, Bolton's identification of rivers, which often appear to be juxtaposed to fit the narrative, are misleading. Although Wagstaff did not adequately support the discrepancies he cited, DiPeso attempted to propose an alternative route in which he accounted for rivers and distances. Employing the same methodology as he had on the rivers in Sonora, DiPeso suggested that the expedition traveled from Antelope Pass to Cíbola, meandering in and out of Arizona and New Mexico until they reached Zuni.[47]

Preceding Bolton, Carl Sauer's interpretation of the route through Arizona is traced from the San Pedro River to a point north of Benson, around the Galiuro Mountains into the upper basin of Arivaipa Creek north to the Gila River by way of Eagle Pass between the Pinaleño and Santa Teresa ranges. Following the San Carlos River, the expedition turned northeast, crossing the Natanes Plateau and the Black River to a point on the White River near present-day Fort Apache from where Coronado passed near present-day McNary. From there, they crossed the Colorado Plateau to the Little Colorado River, thence to the Zuni River before reaching Hawikuh.[48]

The consensus among historians is that the San Pedro River served as the passageway to Arizona on the last leg of Coronado's march through Sonora. They mostly agree that from a point along the San Pedro River the expedition veered northward, entering Arizona somewhere along the present border. Day suggests that Coronado crossed into Arizona where the valley broadens, near Naco, not far from Bisbee. As the exact entry point cannot be ascertained, historians have debated the hypothesis and added their own conclusions. From its strategic location, Coronado National Memorial overlooks the panoramic view of the San Pedro River Valley which, the legislators of 1940 surmised, the expedition crossed in 1540, and commemorates the Francisco Vázquez de Coronado expedition as part of our national story. The wise creators of the master plan for Coronado National Memorial in 1954 astutely recognized the purpose of the memorial. They began the master plan development outline with the words:

> Though this area was set aside as a memorial to commemorate the first large scale Spanish expedition into the Southwest, no physical remains of historic features or trails pertaining to this event exist within the area . . . from high on the southern end of the Huachuca Mountains, one looks over the San Pedro and Santa Cruz Valleys, either one of which, depending on the historian consulted, may represent the actual route of

travel over which Coronado passed in the spring of 1540 when he with his advance guard, and later his main army, came through this region. There also is a view out over a wide expanse of the Sonora Valley region through which Coronado approached Arizona from the south.[49]

These words ring as true today as when they were written.

Notes

1. Mrs. J. M. Keith to Mr. Chas. M. Morgan, May 9, 1940, Phoenix, AZ, Coronado National Memorial Collection, Box 4.

2. Sánchez, Joseph P. Sánchez, "A Historiography of the Route of the Expedition of Francisco Vázquez de Coronado: General Comments," pp. 31-35. Other topics include "Compostela to Cíbola," pp. 138-148; "Cíbola to Río de Cicúye," pp. 215-225; "Río Cicúye to Quivira," pp. 281-301, in Richard and Shirley Flint, editors, *The Coronado Expedition to Tierra Nueva: The 1540-1542 Route Across the Southwest* (Niwot: Colorado University Press, 1997).

3. Herbert Eugene Bolton, *Coronado: Knight of Pueblos and Plains* (Albuquerque: University of New Mexico Press, 1949); Arthur Grove Day, *Coronado's Quest: The Discovery of the Southwestern States* (Berkeley: University of California Press, 1940).

4. Congressional Record—Senate, November 1940, 13645.

5. Southwest to Celebrate Four Hundredth Anniversary of Coronado's March. Extension of Remarks of Hon. John M. Houston of Kansas in the House of Representatives, Tuesday, March 26, 1940. Includes article by Martelle W. Trager, *Washington Post* of March 24, 1940 in appendix to the Congressional Record, 1677.

6. Martelle W. Trager, "Southwest to Celebrate Four Hundredth Anniversary of Coronado's March—Traveling Pageant to Follow Trail Spaniard Blazed in Quest for Riches," *Washington Post,* March 24, 1940 in appendix to the Congressional Record, 1677.

7. Bolton, *Coronado*. The Herbert Eugene Bolton Papers at the Bancroft Library, University of California, Berkeley, contain correspondence related to his study on Coronado. Actually, Arthur Grove Day in 1940, nine years before Bolton, had suggested Naco as the entry point. See Arthur Grove Day, *Coronado's Quest: The Discovery of the Southwestern States,* for his full account of the Coronado Expedition.

8. This paragraph, including quotes, from Mrs. J. M. Keith to Mr. Chas. M. Morgan, May 9, 1940; letter originates from Phoenix, AZ, Coronado National Memorial Collection, Box 4.

9. Charles M. Morgan, "Autobiographical Notes, 1960," Coronado National Memorial Collection, WACC, Folder H 14: Area and Service History (1939) F1.

10. Paragraph to here, including quotes, ibid.

11. Charles M. Morgan to Herbert E. Bolton, November 4, 1939, Coronado National Memorial Collection, WACC, Folder H 14: Area and Service History (1939) F1.

12. Clinton P. Anderson to Congressman John R. Murdock, October 10, 1939, University of New Mexico Archives, Box 1.

13. Comments of Dr. R. K. Wyllys, History and Social Studies Departments, Arizona State Teachers College, Tempe, AZ, in Karl E. Kilby to President Zimmerman and Gilberto Espinosa, Albuquerque, NM, University of New Mexico Archives, Box 7.

14. Comments of J. Manuel Espinosa, St. Louis University, in Karl E. Kilby to President Zimmerman and Gilberto Espinosa (n.d.), University of New Mexico Archives, Box 7.

15. G. R. Michaels to Aubrey Neasham, Bisbee, AZ, February 6, 1940, Hayden Papers, AC, ASU Box 591, folder 2.

16. United States Coronado Exposition Commission to the minister for foreign relations, the Republic of Mexico, 1940, Coronado National Memorial Collection, WACC, Folder H 14: Area and Service History (1939) F1.

17. Ibid.

18. An Act to provide the establishment of Coronado National Memorial in the State of Arizona, House of Representatives, Committee on Interior and Insular Affairs, Subcommittee on Public Lands. H.R. 7553, June 16, 1952, unpublished U.S. House of Representatives Committee Hearings, 1947–54.

19. Quoted in Tolson to Sparkes, Washington, DC, February 21, 1952, Hayden Papers, AC, ASU, Box 201, folder 3.

20. Charles DiPeso, *Casas Grandes* (Dragoon, AZ: Amerind Foundation, 1974), 39.

21. George P. Hammond and Agapito Rey, eds. and trans., *Narratives of the Coronado Expedition* (Albuquerque, University of New Mexico, 1940), 240.

22. James H. Simpson, "Coronado's March in Search of the 'Seven Cities of Cibola' and Discussion of their Probable Location," in *Annual Report of the Board of Regents of the Smithsonian Institution* (Washington, DC: Government Printing Office, 1872), 329.

23. Charlie R. Steen, "The First European Explorers of the Southwest," Article VI, U.S. Department of the Interior memorandum for the press, on file, Coronado National Memorial, Arizona.

24. Frederick Webb Hodge, "The First Discovered City of Cibola," *American Anthropologist* 8 (1895): 142–252.

25. This paragraph George J. Undreiner, "Fray Marcos de Niza and his Journey to Cibola," *The Americas* 3, no. 4 (April 1947): 415–86.

26. Adolph F. Bandelier, "Historical Introduction to Studies among the Sedentary Indians of New Mexico," in *Papers of the Archaeological Institute of America* (Boston: American Series I, 1881), 1; and "An Outline of the Documentary History of the Zuni Tribe," *Journal of American Archaeology and Ethnology* 2 (1892): 407; George P. Winship, *The Coronado Expedition, 1540–1542* (Washington, DC: Fourteenth Annual Report of the Bureau of Ethnology, 1896), 387; Bolton, *Coronado*, 949, 105; Carl Sauer, "The Road to Cibola," Ibero-Americana, Berkeley, 1932, p. 36.

27. Albert H. Shroeder, "Fray Marcos de Niza, Coronado and the Yavapai," *New Mexico Historical Review* 30 (1955), 265.

28. DiPeso quote in ibid., vol. 4 265; Schroeder quote in ibid., 267.

29. Coronado quote in Hammond and Rey, *Narratives*, 166; Castañeda quote ibid., 251.

30. Melchior Díaz quote in ibid., 165; DiPeso quote in DiPeso, *Casas Grandes*, 100.

31. First Schroeder quote in Schroeder, "Fray Marcos de Niza," *New Mexico Historical Review* 31 (1956), 31–32; second Schroeder quote in ibid., 33.

32. Ibid., 32.

33. Carroll L. Riley and Joni L. Manson, "The Cíbola-Tiguex Route: Continuity and Change in the Southwest," *New Mexico Historical Review* (October 1983): 349.

34. Riley, "The Location of Chichilticale," in *Collected Papers in Honor of Albert H. Schroeder*, ed. Charles H. Lange (Santa Fe, NM: Ancient City Press, 1985), 153.

35. Quoted in Hammond and Rey, *Narratives*, 284.

36. Arthur Grove Day, *Coronado's Quest: The Discovery of the Southwestern States* (Berkeley: University of California Press, 1940), 339.

37. Hammond and Rey, *Narratives*, 2.

38. For a historiographical view of the route of Coronado's Expedition, see Joseph P. Sánchez, "A Historiography of the Route of the Expedition of Francisco Vázquez de Coronado: General Comments," in *The Coronado Expedition to Tierra Nueva: The 1540–1542 Route Across the Southwest*, ed. Richard and Shirley Flint (Niwot: Colorado University Press, 1997). Sánchez discusses each segment of the route as follows: "Compostela to Cíbola," 138–48; "Cíbola to Río de Cicúye," 215–25; "Río Cicúye to Quivira", 281–301.

39. Frederick Hodge and Theodore H. Lewis, eds., *Spanish Explorers in the Southern United States, 1528–1543* (1907, reprinted 1984), 301, fn1. Also see Bolton, *Coronado*, p. 150.

40. Pedro de Castañeda, "Narrative of the Expedition to Cíbola, Undertaken in 1540, in Which Are Described All Those Settlements, Ceremonies, and Customs; Written by Pedro de Castañeda of Náxera," in Hammond and Rey, *Narratives*, 209.

41. Ibid., 269.

42. Ibid.

43. Ibid.

44. Charles C. DiPeso, John B. Rinaldo, and Gloria J. Fenner, *Architecture and Dating Methods, Casas Grandes: A Fallen Trading Center of the Gran Chichimeca*, vol. 4 (Dragoon, AZ: Amerind Foundation), 100.

45. Sánchez, "A Historiography of the Route," 141.

46. Bolton, *Coronado*, 108–17.

47. Charles DiPeso, *Casas Grandes* vol. 4 (Dragoon, AZ: Amerind Foundation, 1974), 102.

48. Sauer, "The Road to Cibola," 36–37.

49. Master Plan Development Outline, Coronado National Memorial, November 1954, D18, Master Plans [1954] F2.pdf, WACC, Archives CD Box 3.

CHAPTER 2

After Coronado

Spanish and Mexican Mining Interests in the Huachucas

It is our pleasure and will that all persons from whatever station, condition, rank, or dignity, Spaniards and Indians, our vassals may extract gold, silver, quicksilver, and other metals, by themselves, or through their servants or slaves in all mines that they may find wherever they may wish.

— King Felipe II of Spain, June 19, 1568[1]

We came to a pueblo called Chinapa; five leagues from there are the mines at Bacanuchi, and eight leagues beyond there toward the northeast are the mines of Cananea.

— Father Juan Nentvig, 1764[2]

In time this would facilitate and encourage work in the mines in the adjacent mountains, especially in the Guachuca Mountains, which are now producing good silver.

— Nicolás de Lafora, 1766[3]

Property was worked by Spaniards.

— Grace Sparkes, 1959[4]

Arizona and Sonora historically contain significant mineral deposits. For most of the twentieth century, Arizona produced half the nation's copper and appreciable amounts of gold and silver. From atop Montezuma Pass, within Coronado National Memorial, the breathtaking view to the south is sometimes marked by the haze from smoke rising from copper smelters in Cananea, Sonora. To the east are the Mule Mountains and Bisbee. Both played a role in Arizona's mining history. To the north are the remnants of the legendary Tombstone silver district. Ghost towns abound in the mountainous terrain throughout Arizona. They are stark reminders of the boom-and-bust mining strikes that left remnants of mining operations and mine sites, some dating to the seventeenth century.[5] Still, Mexico's aura is easily perceived in the land, the architecture, and the people, for, historically, Mexicans were the first modern settlers, ranchers, farmers, and miners of the area.

In writing the historical background portion of her report concerning the State of Texas Mines within Montezuma Canyon in 1959, Grace Sparkes, with a matter-of-fact attitude, noted that her "property was worked by Spaniards and early drill holes may be seen [as well as] old antiqua [*sic*] on property."[6] Earlier, in his report on the State of Texas Mines in 1951, Axel L. Johnson, an engineer for the State of Arizona Department of Mines and Minerals, concluded that Spanish–Mexican period miners had extracted five hundred tons of ore from that site.[7] A 1905 mining publication stated, "The lands include at least one Antigua, worked for silver-lead ores by the Spaniards, probably as early as 300 years ago."[8]

Anglo-American miners working claims in Montezuma Canyon in early 1877 noted ancient mine shafts, called *antiguas,* with remnants of crumbling adobe furnaces, collapsing stone dwellings, and other Spanish period workings. As the story goes, early Anglo-American miners believed some of the workings were made by the Aztecs and, therefore, gave the name Montezuma to the canyon. Location notices filed with the county recorder reveal examples of Mexican or Spanish period workings.

David B. Rea, who filed one of the first mining claim notices in Montezuma Canyon, on May 20, 1877, noted an old shaft adjacent to his claim stake and a *cupel* (furnace camp) three quarters of a mile southeast from his claim. The *cupel* was probably a small Mexican adobe furnace used to smelt ore. Not far from Rea's claim stood the old Elías hacienda, said to be ten miles away toward the southeast. Rea, who knew the Elías family and their abandonment of their landholdings, apparently also knew about the mines or prospects they had worked over the years in Montezuma Canyon. Other sources indicated that the Elías family mine was "fifty feet from old house ruins." They made reference to the Old Elías Mine and the Mission Mine at the mouth of the canyon, which other prospectors later sought to claim. Curiously, the authors of the documents also noted, "There is an old Fort built of stone near the entrance to the shaft or opening to the mine." It is possible that Mexican miners used the stone fort, if indeed it was a defensive structure, to defend themselves against Apache raiders. Rea's claim included the earlier Hispanic workings, then called the Wade Hampton. Subsequent owners patented it as the State of Texas mines, complete with the differently spelled Antiqua [*sic*] mentioned by Grace Sparkes.[9]

Such sources and tales show that Spanish and Mexican period mining occurred in the Montezuma Canyon, especially at the State of Texas Mine site. In the seventeenth and eighteenth centuries, northern Sonora and southern Arizona were known for their silver mines. Hispanic miners were interested in high-grade deposits of silver and gold, and toward the end of the period, their interest extended to lead and copper. The Spanish and Mexican mining tradition in the region and within the boundaries of Coronado National Memorial, particularly at Montezuma Canyon, commenced when Sonoran settlers came into the area in the 1600s.

The settlement of Pimería Alta, present southern Arizona, was spurred by mining exploration. The first mines in Sonora date to the 1640s.[10] As early as 1680, José Romo de Vivar settled and founded the town of Bacanuchi. He also claimed land in Cananea, Cocóspera, and at the southern end of the Huachuca Mountains.[11] The business of Romo de Vivar's settlers combined subsistence farming with stock raising and mining in the area. Contrary to historians who claim that the Jesuit Francisco Eusebio Kino was the first cattleman in Pimería Alta, his contemporary Romo de Vivar had, by 1680, introduced the first cattle herds into Bacanuchi and Cananea on the south bank of the San Pedro River. It should also be noted that Romo de Vivar and his settlers were probably the first serious miners in the area.

During the seventeenth century Spanish settlements sprang up along the Santa Cruz and San Pedro River valleys. In the 1680s and 1690s Bacanuchi and Cocóspera served as bases for the expansion of missions northward along the San Pedro River Valley.[12] On both sides of the present United States–Mexico border in that area, the Jesuits established missions at places like Cocóspera, Terrenate, Cananea, San Joaquín de Basosucan (also known as San Joaquín de Huachuca), Santa Cruz de Gaybanipitea (Jauanipicta), and Quiburi. The latter two missions were along the San Pedro River north of the memorial. San Joaquín de Basosucan was at the north end of the Huachacas along Babocómari Creek (today Rancho Babocómari). Later, a fortification was constructed nearby to protect the area. Near Indian villages and missions, Spanish settlers often established towns and introduced ranching, farming, and mining in northern Sonora and Pimería Alta. In the eighteenth century the region was known for its silver mines.

By 1700 the Spanish frontier had advanced to places just below the present border between present Mexico and the United States. In the eighteenth century, Apaches and other warlike tribes continued to raid Spanish settlements in Chihuahua and Sonora, carrying off herds of sheep, horses, mules, cattle, and sometimes Spanish captives. Some Apache plunder trails emanated from their Huachuca Mountains strongholds.[13] Although Apache raiders forced the temporary abandonment of many places, a defensive line of presidios was established along the northern Sonoran frontier that served to prevent the permanent abandonment of the entire region. As a result, settlements were reestablished and new mines were constantly discovered and worked under occasional military protection. Rich placers of gold had been found in Sonora and in Chihuahua, attracting settlers into the area.

One of the most famous mining settlements was a place called Arizonac; it was active in 1736–41. The name Arizona probably originated from the name Arizonac, which was east of modern Nogales, just below today's international boundary. In 1736, miners discovered what came to be known as the famous *bolas* or *planchas de plata* or nuggets or slabs of silver.[14] The heretofore unparalleled claim to untold riches created a rush to the area. Word about the find of the silver of Arizonac soon reached Madrid where the king reasserted his claim as sovereign to subsoil mineral rights. If the find were, indeed, a mine, then the king would collect 20 percent of the income from it. If it were a treasure, then the king's cut would be 50 percent. Thus, when a royal mine inspector, Juan Bautista de Anza, visited the site, he declared it to be a treasure. In a few years, the silver at Arizonac had all but been played out. The discovery, however, encouraged further prospecting, eventually leading to Sonora becoming the richest mining region in Mexico's northern frontier. Arizonac represented the northernmost mining area in the mid-eighteenth century and was the beginning of significant, major European mining traditions in Pimería Alta.

In his *Descripción Geográfica,* Father Juan Nentvig, S.J. wrote that after he had reached the pueblo of Chinapa, in northeastern Sonora, he traveled to the mines of Basochuca. Four leagues (about ten miles) from there, he arrived at Bacanuchi, another mining settlement. He wrote, "Eight leagues [about 20 miles] toward the northeast are the mines of Cananea."[15] The area along the San Pedro River leading north past the

Huachuca Mountains and beyond were not only areas worked by Jesuit missionaries, but were also areas of interest to settlers and miners living in the Cananea area. Jesuit missionaries also worked at Quiburi and Santa Cruz along the San Pedro. Since the 1680s settlers had moved into northeastern Sonora and established settlements that had, since the days of Romo de Vivar, introduced cattle, horses, mules, sheep, and goats into the area. From these settlements, especially Cananea, the Spanish could have easily explored Montezuma Canyon in the Huachuca Mountains.

In 1766 the Marqués de Rubí led an expedition to inspect military conditions on the north Mexican frontier. Nicolas de Lafora, an engineer on the expedition, remarked about the advancing settlements along the San Pedro River, and the silver mines in the Huachuca Mountains, most likely in Montezuma Canyon. Lafora recommended moving the fort at San Felipe de Jesús de Guebabi northward to the San Pedro. He justified his proposal:

> Its [San Felipe de Jesús de Guebabi] climate is unhealthy and the water is not at all good, nor are there any farm lands nearby. For this reason and despite the danger, settlers plant on the banks of the San Pedro River in the Sobaipuris valley, five leagues away [roughly ten miles]. They maintain a storehouse there which has been burned two or three times by the enemy. This valley [San Pedro] is very suitable for settlement and it would be well to move the presidio there so that settlers might gather under its protection. Undoubtedly they would be attracted by the good and abundant land there. In time this would facilitate and encourage work in the mines in the adjacent mountains, especially in the Guachuca Mountains, which are now producing good silver, notwithstanding the scarcity of people and the excessive risk.[16]

Mining activities during the Spanish and Mexican periods in Arizona along the Huachuca Mountains date to the second half of the eighteenth century. Lafora's description leaves little doubt about the location of mining activities in that area. He also wrote, "One league from the San Pedro River, we crossed the Terrenate River at the place called Las Nutrias. The latter forms a lagoon one league above the said crossing. The river resumes its course and gushes out again lower down. A creek coming from the northern part of Guachuca sierra three leagues away also empties into the lagoon. Here there are many silver mines producing very good ore."[17] Thus the history of mining in that area, while little known heretofore, dates from this period and explains the antiguas found during the early Anglo-American period, particularly in the late nineteenth century.

The gold strike of 1771 at La Cieneguilla, near present Altar in northwestern Sonora, attracted a new migration to the north. Many of the settlers—ranchers and miners—who went there eventually moved northward in 1776 to the newly established settlements and presidio at Tucson.[18] Settlers from Tubac and Tucson explored for mineral wealth in the surrounding mountains including the Santa Ritas, Santa Catalinas, and Huachucas.

In 1777 Manuel Barragua, Francisco Castro, and Antonio Romero from Tubac reported to Captain Pedro de Allande Saavedra about "watering places, land for cornfields, pastures for horses and cattle, and minerals of the region." They also mentioned "routes taken by the Apaches for their attacks and escapes and places where they camp."[19] Regarding mining in the area in the vicinity of Tubac, they wrote,

> There are many mines of very rich metals some of these mines are especially productive. One yields eight ounces of pure silver to every twenty-five pounds of ore. . . . Ten to fifteen miles further on, in the Babocómari Valley, there are excellent gold placers. These were examined by José Torres and all of the Tubac settlers. . . . Ten miles east of Tubac, in the Santa Rita Mountains, two silver mines have been worked with smelters and three more with quicksilver, all with a tolerable yield. Though these mines are common knowledge to all of the Tubac settlers, they cannot be worked on a permanent basis because of the Apaches, who have pastures and encampments in that vicinity.[20]

The mining traditions in Pimería Alta were already old in 1777, as Tubac was founded in 1752 and the mines at Cananea were known since the 1680s. For twenty-five years Tubac's settlers explored the entire area and continually opened new mines. They would have been more prosperous had not Apache raiders intermittently forced them away from the mines.

Throughout the 1780s Apache raiders disrupted the daily lives of Spanish settlers along the Santa Cruz and San Pedro rivers and undoubtedly miners in the Huachuca Mountains. Tucson was attacked in 1782, as were other settlements in the area. In March 1785 Pedro de Allande y Saavedra, commander of the Royal Presidio of San Agustín de Tucsón, led a force against the Apache in the mountainous terrain of Babocómari, Huachucas, Santa Catalina, and Santa Rita.[21] His victories resulted in the recovery of horses and mules from mining settlements, including those from as far as west as La Cieneguilla, as well as in the surrender of an appreciable number of Apache warriors.

From the 1790s and continuing for twenty or thirty years, there was intermittent peace between Spanish settlers and Apache raiders in Pimería Alta. Doubtless, during that period, many mines were opened from time to time. Mines in the area stretched south from Tucson to Tubac, Arivaca, Santa Rita (about eleven miles from Tubac), and Babocómori near the north end of the Huachucas. Mine inspectors verified the existence of gold, silver, and copper mines in claims throughout the region. Some claims were made as far west as the Colorado River. Quicksilver mines were discovered as far north as Oraibi in northern Arizona, which then was considered part of New Mexico. Iron was discovered in the Madre Mountains between Tucson and Tubac. Certainly, in present Pima County, many mines were found and worked.[22] The Huachuca Mountains and general vicinity in present Cochise County are similarly dotted with sites worked by Spanish and Mexican period miners.

The history of mining in southern Arizona, nonetheless, generally supports the lore of lost mines and treasures surrounding nearly every place where Hispanic miners trod in present southwestern United States. Similarly, lost mine stories have, over time, flitted along the mountains of Arizona. In 1736, for example, the find of *planchas de plata* (slabs of silver) and *bolas de plata* (balls of silver) were discovered.[23] The find sparked a small rush to the area. Still, the lost mines of Arizonac became a part of the lore revolving around lost treasures. Indeed, the location of Arizonac has never been in doubt, but similar traditions are likely responsible for exaggerated stories of lost Spanish and Mexican mines in the area. The Huachucas are no different.

More importantly, the mining traditions, technology, and laws of Spain and Mexico are evident in the greater Southwest. Indeed, the Spanish crown owned all topsoil and subsoil rights to the parts of the Americas under its claim. Thus, during the Spanish colonial period ownership of land and mines, as were other resources, were greatly regulated. The long arm of Spanish law reached every nook and cranny of the empire, including those in New Spain's remote frontiers stretching from California to Florida, and including the Huachuca Mountains of Pimería Alta.

Spanish and Mexican mining law in North America predated, and later influenced, those of the budding United States in the late eighteenth and early nineteenth centuries. Based on ancient Spanish legal traditions, the Ordenanzas de Minería [mining ordinances] of 1783, submitted by the

Tribunal General de la Minería [General Tribunal of Mining] in Spain, revised mining law throughout the Spanish empire.[24] The Ordenanzas de Minería of 1783, compiled by Don Joaquín de Velázquez Cárdenas de León and Don Lucas de Lessaga, president of the tribunal, consisted of nineteen titles and many other sections to support and explain the law.[25] The Ordenanzas de Minería also dealt with the reorganization of the Tribunal General de la Minería.

The laws covered many topics, including the appointment of judges and inspectors of mines, the legal processes in adjudicating disputes, and the rights of mine owners, mine operators, and miners. More specifically, the Ordenanzas de Minería of 1783 explained the process for claiming a mine, making new discoveries, and registering lodes. The laws provided guidance in dealing with abandoned and lost mines, defense of mines, mining companies, inundated mines, as well as water rights pertaining to mines. Additionally, the laws covered land grants and *demasías* (excess lands outside of but contiguous to the land grant) and mines, the sale of minerals, the education and teaching of mining techniques, and the operations of mills and processes. As with all countries, the sovereign's ownership of subsoil and topsoil rights form the basis of mining practices, tradition, and law since time immemorial.

Spain's sovereign title to all rights dealing with land and resources was explicit and resided within the absolute powers of the monarchy. Only the king of Spain, as the sovereign, had the power and authority to grant to his vassals the privilege of using the land and/or extracting minerals from the land within Spain and the Empire. The age-old prerogatives of the sovereign were detailed in the earlier codes of the Laws of the Indies. Book 4, Title 19 of the laws is entitled "Concerning the discovery and labor of the mines." In royal terms, the sovereign explained the written law that had been promulgated for use in the Americas on December 9, 1526, by King Carlos V, and reiterated on June 19, 1568, by King Phillip II. Emphasizing the royal prerogative, the law stated, "It is our pleasure and will that all persons from whatever station, condition, rank, or dignity, Spaniards and Indians, our vassals may extract gold, silver, quicksilver, and other metals, by themselves, or through their servants or slaves in all mines that they may find wherever they may wish. And so that they may well possess and hold, and work them freely without any kind of impediment, having given an account to the governor and royal officials in accordance with the law. . . [they] have been confirmed by us."[26]

Thus, the law clearly stated that the king's vassals could discover and work mines using whatever labor was available to them, provided they register the locations of their mines.

The law also reinforced the tradition and practice that prohibited civil officials—that is, ministers, governors, mayors, scribes working for mines, or lesser officials—from participating in mining ventures or enterprises whatsoever. This practice carried over into the post-Spanish period following Mexican independence in 1821. Mexican laws naturally built on earlier Spanish laws, particularly in regard to mining and other land uses.

Similarly, Title V of the Ordenanzas de Minería of 1783 explicitly stated, "The mines are rightfully the property of the Crown." The Ordenanzas took their precedence from laws of Spain, specifically the Nueva Recopilación (new compilation), as follows: "(Art. 2) Without alienating them from my Royal Patronage, I grant to my vassals in both ownership and possession, in such a way that they may sell them, modify them, donate them, bequeath them. . . . (Art. 3) They are granted under two conditions: First that they contribute to my Royal Treasury and second, that the mines are worked and enjoyed in complement to the conditions stated in these Ordinances."[27]

The Ordenanzas de Minería covered many situations concerning the mining industry. Education was a priority, and the Ordenanzas provided legislation for the establishment of a school of mines called the Real Seminario de Minería. Potable water was a concern to mining communities who complained about miners dumping pollutants into nearby streams. Among the regulations, therefore, the law prohibited the pumping of water from mines into arroyos, aqueducts, or streams leading to settled areas. Among other issues, security and safety at mines were provided by *peritos* (trained surveyors), also known in New Spain (Mexico) as *mineros* (miners) or *guardaminas* (guards).[28]

The law stated that it was "prohibited to construct mines without the direction and continued assistance of one of the learned and practiced peritos."[29] The *peritos* were given special privileges enjoyed by miners in terms of education and training in mineralogy. They were permitted to mine and keep what they found. They were allowed to use mining tools, mills, vats, and other facilities of the mine. In general, the mining laws of the late eighteenth century awakened interest in mining. Spanish mining laws passed into Mexican law after 1821.

Although the Spanish legal tradition pertaining to mining influenced that of the Mexican nation, the laws applied to situations as they occurred. In areas where full-scale mining operations were evident, the traditions, practices, and laws served those communities. In areas where new mines were starting up, the sovereign exercised its power in reminding claimants to follow all procedures in registering their claims. Indeed, an entire section of the Ordenanzas de Minería was dedicated to the acquisition of mines. Of specific interest to claimants in the remote northern areas of Mexico, one chapter of the Ordenanzas is entitled *"Concerning the Manner of Acquiring Mines, New Discoveries; Registration of Veins, and Denouncements of Mines Abandoned and Lost."*[30] Similarly, the laws of the Indies spelled out procedures for the acquisition of land, particularly land grants that contained mineral wealth. During the early years of Mexican nationhood, bureaucrats adhered to earlier legal traditions based on Spanish law, and worked through newly revised versions of the same as Mexico instituted new procedures regarding the acquisition of land and mines.

The Ordenanzas de Minería would have pertained to small-scale mining that took place in the Huachucas during the Spanish and Mexican periods. Indeed, the Ordenanzas de Minería were quoted and used as a source in the litigation of land grants in southern Arizona by the Surveyor General in the nineteenth and early twentieth centuries.[31] Such mining ventures were limited by many factors including distance, technology, few laborers, and danger from Apache raiders, which tended to discourage mining in the area. Owners of the San Rafael del Valle and San Pedro land grants, discussed in chapter 3, worked mining sites in the Huachucas and in the area of the State of Texas Mines. Given their times, technologies, and economies, Spaniards mined for silver and copper and whatever gold ores they could find. In all, they pointed the way for future mining in that area, and they influenced, in many ways, where later mines would be located.

Mining traditions between the Gila River and the present international boundary with Mexico continued into the Mexican period, 1821–53. Near present Nogales, for example, the San Rafael de la Zanja grant contained mines and minerals.[32] During the Mexican period large land grants were established in and near the area of Coronado National Memorial. In 1827 the San Juan de las Boquillas y Nogales grant and the San Rafael del Valle grant operated ranches in the area. A third, the San Pedro land grant, ran between the Huachuca Mountains and Bisbee along the border in the southwestern part of Arizona. The San Pedro grant was issued in 1833 to Rafael González, the owner of the San Rafael del Valle grant.[33] Within a regional context, the Elías family, as owners of the grant, also considered the lands within Montezuma Canyon as part of their property. Without the discovery of specific records or documents, likely in Mexican archives, the extent of their mining activities is unknown at this time. That they, like many speculators in northern Sonora, operated the mines is highly probable. The smelter, stone houses, and mine works mentioned by Anglo-American miners in 1877 might date from the Mexican period, especially the workings they staked as the "Old Elías" mine. Increased Apache raids in the later 1830s and 1840s also caused abandonment of their claims in Montezuma Canyon and other places in Pimería Alta.

Appendix 2A

El siguiente día, que se contaron 5 de referido mes, después de haver celebrado missa el dicho Padre Kino, salimos de aquí, llevando la derrota al mismo rumbo que el día de San Lázaro, que dista como 6 leguas a las orillas del río de Santa María, guarnexido de mucha alameda, con lindas vegas para mantenencia de ganados y fértiles tierras de lavor, todas devajo de riego; por cuyos contornos, a poc distancia, ay más de 20 casas con sus familias que se pueden agregar para componer un mediano pueblo.

Aquí tomamos un refresco y proseguimos el mismo rumbo, que hera al norueste, hasta llegar al pueblo de Santa María que dista de San Lázaro 6 leguas; ambos pueblos pertenezientes el de Cocóspera. Haviendo caminado, este día, como 12 leguas, hicimos noche aquí, viniéndonos a saludar toda la gente con mucha afavilidad, haviendo barrido la casa de terrado que tienen hecha para el Padre ministro. Y, asimismo, nos pusieron cruzes y arcos por los caminos, ofreziéndonse dos justicias el acompañarnos, como lo hicieron, hasta tres jornadas.

Toda esta tierra es fértil para sembrar de todas semillas, de hermosas vegas para ganados y cavalladas. Tiene el río de Santa María desde aquí, el origen y nacimiento, de cuyo pueblo tiene la deribación. Al principio, corre como 5 leguas, al sur y luego, va declinando, haciendo un medio círculo; y lleva su rorriente, al norte, más de 100 leguas, hasta juntarse su caja con el Río de Jila, que es el río grande que sala para la mar de Californias, como, adelante, diré en su lugar.

El día 6 del referido mes de nobiembre, después de haver celebrado misa el Padre, a la qual asistió la gente con atención, salimos de este pueblo de Santa María, llevando el rumbo siempre al norueste; y, a puestas del sol, llegamos a la ranchería de San Juachín de Basosuca, que dista 14 leguas, donde hallamos la casa de terrado que tienen hecha para el Padre ministro, muy barrida y compuesta, con petates en el suelo, para ospedarnos aquella noche; haviéndonos puesto, en el camino, arcos y cruzes, concurriendo toda la gente a saludarnos.

Desde esta ranchería empezamos a contar todos los naturales, contando, en ésta, como 12 casas y, en ellas, 60 almas, a las quales predicó el Padre en lo que estriva la salvación; a cuya plática asistieron contoda atención y admiración.

El día del corriente, después de misa, nos despedimos de los naturales y proseguimos nuestro viaje, caminando para el oriente, y llegamos a la ranchería que se llama Santa Cruz de Jauanipicta, que dista 6 leguas, donde nos hicieron el mismo rezivimiento que los antezedentes, de cruzes y una dezente casit de palos y petates, donde nos opedaron. Y el Padre les habló de su heterna salvación y de la gran gloria que se alcaça por medio del santo baptismo; los quales respondieron: quieren Padres para que los ynstruyan y, desde luego, dieron 6 párbulos a baptiçar.

Esta ranchería se compone de 20 casas y, en ellas, 100 almas, todas lavorías; y nos dieron de todos sus bastimientos contoda liveralidad. Ay hermosas tierras de lavor, por correr, por ellas, el río del Terrenate que lleva su corriente al norte (otras tantas leguas como el referido de Santa María). Sacan eél lindas azequias, en cuyas riveras tiene puesta le Padre Kino una estançuela de ganado mayor, que lo guardan los naturales, con todo cuydado, para el Padre ministro que esperan rezevir. Y, en dicha ranchería, hallamos, también, dos cavelleras y otros despojos de golpe que estos sobahípuris dieron a 16 enemigos, hocomes y janos, matando los 13 dellos, y los tres restantes se les escaparon mal heridos; cuyos despojos estavan vaylando (que es la costumbre, entre estas entes, de festejar así sus triunfos). Con los qual verificamos lo my de nuestr parrte que está toda esta de estos pimas y sobaípuris, emos de esperimentar, en adelante, algún descanso en esta provincia de Sonora que, tantos años, ha, la están ymbadiendo, con tantas ostilidades y rovos, los dichos enemigos hocomes." (Burrus, Kino and Manje, 358–60)

Appendix 2B

Es Nuestra merced, y voluntad, que todas las personas, de qualquier estado, condicion, preeminencia, ó dignidad, Españoles, é Indios, nuestros vassallos, puedan sacar, oro, plata, azoque, y otros metales por sus personas, criados, ó esclavos en todas las minas, que hallaren, ó donde quisieren, y por bien tuvieren, y los coger, y labrar libremente sin ningun genero de impedimento, haviendo dado cuenta al Governador, y Oficiales Reales para el efecto cotenido en la ley siguiente, por manera, que las minas de oro, plata, y los demás metales sean comunes á todos, y en todas partes, y terminos, con que no resulte perjuizio á los Indios, ni á otro tercero, ni esta permission se estienda á los Ministros, Governadores, Corregidores, Alcaldes mayores, y sus Tenientes Letrados, Alcaldes, y Escribanos de minas, ni á los que tuvieren especial prohibición: y cerca de señalar, tomar las minas, y estacarse en ellas, se guarden las leyes, y ordenanças hechas en cada Provincia, siendo po no confirmadas.

Notes

1. "Del descubrimiento y labor de las minas", Book IV. Title XIX, First Law, which allows to discover and benefit the mines to all the Spaniards, Indians, and vassels of the king, in Compilation of Laws of the King of the Indies. Published by the Catholic Majesty of King Don Carlos II, Julian de Paredes, Madrid, 1681.

2. *Juan Nentwig, S. J. Descripción Geográfica, Natural y Curiosa de la Provincia de Sonora 1764*, ed. Germán Viveros (Mexico City: Archivo General de la Nación, 1971), 148.

3. Lawrence Kinnaird, *The Frontiers of New Spain: Nicolas de Lafora's Description, 1766–1768* (Berkeley, CA: The Quivira Society, 1958), 107.

4. Horace J. Stevens, *The Copper Handbook*, vol. V (Houghton, MI 1905), 559. See also Mine Owner's Report, Department of Mineral Resources, May 26, 1959, signed by Grace Sparkes, Arizona State Department of Mines and Minerals, Phoenix, AZ.

5. See Charles K. Hyde, *Copper for America: the United States Copper Industry from Colonial Times to the 1990s* (Tucson: University of Arizona Press, 1998); Grace McCool, *Sunday Trails in Old Cochise: A Guide to Ghost Towns, Lost Mines and Buried Treasure in Cochise County, Arizona* (Tombstone, AZ: Tombstone Epitaph, 1967), 48–55.

6. "Mine Owner's Report," Department of Mineral Resources, May 26, 1959, signed by Grace Sparkes, Arizona State Department of Mines and Minerals, Phoenix, AZ.

7. "State of Texas Mines, Field Engineers Report," by Axel L. Johnson, 1, Phoenix, September 11, 1951, Arizona State Department of Mines and Minerals, Phoenix, AZ.

8. Horace J. Stevens, *The Copper Handbook*, vol. V (Houghton, MI 1905), 559.

9. This paragraph is based on information provided by Dr. Robert, historian, NPS. See also "Doredor Mine, National Register of Historic Places eligibility report," copy at Technical Information Center, National Park Service, Denver. Also see "Location of Mines," Record Books, book 1, 95, 1623, 2556, Cochise County Recorder.

10. Alfredo Jiménez Núñez, *El Gran Norte de México: Una frontera imperial en la Nueva España, 1540-1820* (Madrid: Editorial Tébar, S.L., 2006), 120.

11. Francisco Almada, *Diccionario de Historia, Geografía, y Biografía Sonorenses* (Chihuahua, Mexico, DF: Ruíz Sandoval, 1952), 612.

12. Ernest J. Burrus, S. J, ed., *Kino and Manje: Explorers of Sonora and Arizona—Their Vision of the Future* (Rome: Jesuit Historical Institute, 1971), 198–99. This portion of

Juan Manje's Journal of the Fourth Expedition begins on November 4, 1697. Manje and Father Francisco Eusebio Kino leave Remedios, south of Magdalena. Note that on November 11, 1697, Kino and Manje leave Quiburi and go ten leagues (about twenty-five miles) north along the San Pedro to Los Alamos (*Kino and Manje*, 362). Please see appendix 2A at the end of this chapter for the text in Spanish of this journal.

13. Regarding one stronghold within Coronado National Monument there is mention of a cave. NPS literature states that the "cave has been called by several names including Montezuma's Treasure Vault and Geronimo's Cave. Legends claim that it was used by the Apaches as a hide-out when being pursued by the U.S. Army and in the late 1800's it was not uncommon to find arrowheads in the cave." Coronado Cave Brochure, Coronado National Memorial, National Park Service, 1.

14. For a general reading of the mines at Arizonac, see Hubert Howe Bancroft, *Arizona and New Mexico, 1530–1888* (San Francisco: The History Company, 1889), vol. 17, 374, 401, 420, 578, passim.

15. Juan Nentvig, S. J., *Descripción Geográfica, Natural y Curiosa de la Provincia de Sonora 1764*, ed. Germán Viveros (Mexico City: Archivo General de la Nación, 1971), 148.

16. Lawrence Kinnaird, *The Frontiers of New Spain: Nicolas de Lafora's Description, 1766–1768* (Berkeley, CA: The Quivira Society, 1958), 107.

17. Ibid., 106.

18. Kieran McCarty, OFM, compiler and translator, *Desert Documentary: The Spanish Years, 1767–1821* (Tucson, AZ: Arizona Historical Society, 1976), 19.

19. Ibid., 32.

20. Ibid., 32–33.

21. Ibid., 46. Also see Joseph P. Sánchez, "Pedro Fages in Sonora, 1767–1768 & 1777–1782," *New Mexico Historical Review*, 51 (1976): 281–94 for eighteenth-century Spanish military efforts to control the area from the Colorado River to the San Pedro River.

22. Bancroft, *Arizona and New Mexico*, 399–401.

23. Patricia Roche Herring, "The Silver of Real de Arizonac," *Arizona and the West* 20, 3 (1978): 245-58.

24. The official title of the Mining Ordinances of 1783 is "Reales Orenanzas para la dirección, régimen y govierno del importante Cuerpo de la Minería de Nueva España, y de su Real Tribunal General."

25. Don Joaquín de Velázquez Cárdenas de León and Don Lucas de Lessaga began the compilation of mining laws in 1778 and completed their work in 1783. Modesto Bargalló, *La Minería y la Metalurgía en la America Española durante la Epoca Colonial* (Mexico–Buenos Aires: Fondo de Cultura Economica, 1955), 307.

26. "Del descubrimiento y labor de las minas," Book IV. Title XIX, First Law, which allows to discover and benefit the mines to all the Spaniards, Indians, and vassels of the king, in Compilation of Laws of the King of the Indies. Publish by the Catholic Majesty of King Don Carlos II, Julian de Paredes, Madrid, 1681. See appendix 2B, end of this chapter, for the complete Spanish text of this law.

27. Ordenanzas de Minería of 1783, law 4, title 13, book 6, articles 2 and 3; quoted in Bargalló, *La Minería y la Metalurgía* 311.

28. Re: Real Seminario de Minería, ibid., 313; re: *peritos*, ibid., 311.

29. Ordenanzas de Minería, "Titulo IX, art. 2: se prohibe labrar minas sin la dirrección

y continua asistencia de uno de los Peritos inteligentes y prácticos, que en Nueva España llaman Mineros o Guarda-minas, el cual ha de estar examinado, calificado y aprobado por alguno de los Facultativos de Minería que se deberá haber en cada real o asiento," Bargalló, *La Minería y la Metalurgía*, 311.

30. Ibid., Chapter 6.

31. See the Report of the Surveyor General in Juan Pedro Camou vs. the United States, December 1891, Santa Fe, New Mexico, Case No. 3 in which the Ordenanzas de Minería of 1783 are noted. Also see the San Rafael de la Xanja Grant, which documents the mining operations on that land grant. San Rafael de la Xanja Grant, "Mines and Minerals," in Court of Private Land Claims (PLC) Microfilm Roll B. Microfilm Collection, Arizona State Archives and Records, Phoenix, AZ.

32. San Rafael de la Xanga Grant, "Mines and Minerals," in the court of Private Land Claims, Microfilm Roll B, Microfilm Collection, Arizona State Archives and Records, Phoenix, AZ.

33. San Pedro Land Grant, in Court of Private Land Claims, Microfilm Roll A., Microfilm Collection, Arizona State Archives and Records, Phoenix, AZ.

CHAPTER 3

The San Rafael Del Valle and the San Pedro Land Grants

About 50 years ago, he [Rafael Elías Gonzales] was driven from those estates, leaving behind him thousands of heads of cattle and large bands of horses.

—*Arizona Daily Star*, 1878[1]

Around 1720 Francisco Elías González de Zayas left Spain for the New World, and eventually made his way to the colonial silver town of Alamos, Sonora. Twenty years later, in 1740, an older and widowed Elías González outfitted a militia force of one hundred armed men at his own expense to quell a Yaqui uprising in Sonora. His exploits earned him a commission in the Spanish army. In 1751 Captain Elías González was the commander of the Terrenate presidio. By then he had remarried and settled in Arizpe. He died in El Paso del Norte in 1790. His children and grandchildren and succeeding generations of descendants lived and still live in the Arizona–Sonora border country. Some of them live in Tucson. The family achieved prominence because some of its members served as governors or military officers in Sonora and others pioneered the economic development of the region.[2] One of his descendants, Rafael Elías González, developed two large properties—the San Rafael del Valle and the San Pedro land grants—in southeastern Arizona and northeastern Sonora.

Land grants in the San Pedro Valley south of Boquillas are significant because they led to the subsequent development of present southeastern Arizona. Rafael Elías González's land grants are part of the historical process that bridge the Spanish colonial period and the early Anglo-American period in southern Arizona. Francisco's grandson, Sonoran governor José Florentino Rafael Elías González, who signed his name simply as Rafael Elías González, petitioned for both grants of four *sitios* (individual grant of a square league of land) each.[3]

Although the livestock industry, introduced by Mexican land grant owners, determined a large part of land usage, ranchers not only grazed their herds within the land grant, they also became involved in exploring for copper or silver. In time, by the early 1800s, the Elías González family claimed that they had over 200,000 head of cattle proportioned over large districts of their land.[4] Other animals, horses and mules in particular, also grazed on their large estate in southeastern Arizona. In 1869, José Elías González and other ranchers on the United States side of the international boundary presented testimony before the legislature of the Arizona Territory (created 1863), enumerating the number of livestock, horses, mules, cattle, and oxen they had lost to Apache raiders.[5] In 1878 a reporter for *The Arizona Star* wrote, "About 50 years ago, he [Rafael Elías González] was driven from those estates, leaving behind him thousands of heads of cattle and large bands of horses."[6] Such accounts demonstrate the presence of livestock introduced by first Spanish and later Mexican ranchers and owners of land grants, such as the San Rafael del Valle and San Pedro land grants.

Abandonment of land grants occurred largely because of warfare between the settlers and Apaches in the area, particularly during the 1820s and 1830s. Among the major ranches abandoned along the San Pedro River were San Juan de las Boquillas y Nogales and San Rafael del Valle. Their owners were forced out after a major Apache offensive in the mid-1830s.[7]

In spring 1832, for example, Apache warriors hit villages in Sonora. In retaliation, settlers of northern Sonora organized a militia unit to reinforce presidial soldiers in the area. The settlers met at Cocóspera, about thirty-five miles southwest of the Huachuca Mountains. They called their force the Sección Patriótica (patriotic section). Their elected leader was Joaquín Vicente Elías. By May 1832 the Sección Patriótica, made up of one hundred volunteers, had joined with a larger force commanded by Captain Antonio Comadurán, a veteran regular army officer. In early June 1832 the Mexican force clashed with Apaches at Arivaipa Canyon north of Tucson. The defeated Apaches were routed, leaving behind their dead and wounded as well as animals and captives.[8] The Apaches, however, were not beaten; they turned their attacks on the settlements of Pimería Alta.

After another Apache offensive in the middle 1840s, other punitive expeditions sallied forth to apprehend the raiders. In 1845 Colonel José María Elías González called a council of war at the Tucson Presidio. He proposed a major military campaign against the Apaches who had been raiding from the Huachucas and Mule Mountains southward beyond

Cananea. Nearly four years later, in 1849, he led a punitive expedition against the Apaches. This time, Colonel Elías González commanded 191 soldiers with a supply train of eighty-four pack mules guarded by eighty militiamen. Marching westward from Fronteras to Mule Mountains under cover of night between September 23 and 25, 1849, they covered eighty miles. Peering into the distance, they could see the Huachucas, which served as an Apache stronghold. Meanwhile, a detachment was sent toward the northeast to reconnoiter the Cajon de las Alisas (present Chiricahua Mountains). Their scouting reports suddenly pulled the expedition toward and beyond the Chiricahuas, Puerto del Dado (Apache Pass) and into Sierra de las Burras in New Mexico as far as Doña Ana.[9] After a series of skirmishes the expedition returned to Fronteras. In the end, a captured informant told Elías Gonzales' men that they had been successful in driving out the Apaches. The history of the area, however, indicates that several more decades of warfare followed.[10]

Eight years after Elías González's expedition, in 1854, a year after the United States' acquisition of southern Arizona, Chiricahua warriors mounted another offensive in their war against the settlers on both sides of the new borderline. One of the leading warriors, Mangas Coloradas, was relentless in his attacks against settlements near Santa Cruz. A combined force of Anglo-Americans and Mexican volunteers from Santa Cruz, tracked Mangas Coloradas and his men into the Huachucas.[11] Their attack forced Mangas Coloradas eastward to New Mexico. The area between Tucson and the Mule Mountains, meanwhile, had become a no-man's land.

By December 1858 Mangas Coloradas had returned. Accompanied by Cochise and Geronimo, he led more than a hundred warriors in a series of raids against northern Sonoran settlements. They crossed southward into Sonora from the Huachuca Mountains. Meanwhile, José Juan Elías had departed Ures for Fronteras with a complement of troops and a piece of artillery. His march was northeastward. Both Apache warriors and Mexican troops were bound to clash. Elías passed by deserted settlements at Chinapa and Bacoachi as he moved toward Fronteras below the present Arizona–New Mexico line. Everywhere he stopped settlers told him of the devastation left by the Apaches. Some settlers volunteered to serve under Elías.[12] Others provided the troops with food and water. Although some fighting occurred, the clash between Elías and the Apaches did not take place.

Apache raids throughout southern Arizona and northern Sonora became ever more aggressive in the 1860s. Between 1862 and 1865, the Civil War reached as far west as the Colorado River. The Confederate occupation of Arizona, which began with the invasion of the New Mexico Territory and the creation of the Confederate Territory of Arizona, was short-lived. Union forces engaged the Confederates in New Mexico and forced them out. The Confederate goal was to create a gateway from Texas through New Mexico to California, valued for its ports and mineral wealth. Although the Confederates were driven out of New Mexico Territory by spring 1862 following the battles at Apache Canyon and Glorieta Pass near Pecos, New Mexico, the Confederates weakly held Tucson. The response to drive out the Confederates from Arizona came from California. Aside from Colonel James Carleton's California Column, which lost a skirmish at Picacho Pass and later occupied Tucson as the Confederate forces abandoned Arizona, little is known about California's participation in the Civil War. By 1863 the Arizona Territory came into being with the stroke of a pen by President Abraham Lincoln.

Once Union troops abandoned forts in Arizona, miners and cattlemen found themselves defenseless against Apache raiders. The Confederate occupation of Arizona, meanwhile, did not provide protection against the Apaches. The Confederate occupation began with the invasion of the New Mexico Territory and the creation of the Confederate Territory of Arizona. Union forces engaged the Confederates in New Mexico and forced them out. The Confederate goal was to create a gateway from Texas through New Mexico to California, valued for its ports and mineral wealth. Early responses from California were lackluster at best. Col. James Carleton's California Column, for example, fought a skirmish, and lost, at Picacho Canyon, and later occupied Tucson as the Confederate forces abandoned Arizona.

Meanwhile, as the Civil War raged in the United States, France invaded Mexico to collect its debt and occupied it until 1865. French imperialist backers moved into Sonora, creating a new threat to Arizona. Once Carleton and his California troops had moved west to New Mexico, Arizona was left virtually defenseless against Apache raiders and a possible threat from pro-Confederate French Imperialists on the Arizona–Sonora border.

Within a year from Carleton's departure, however, the First Regiment of Native Cavalry, as the Californio Lancers were called, occupied Arizona. Their story began in 1862 when Senator Romauldo Pacheco of California, a staunch Union loyalist from San Luis Obispo and Santa

Barbara Counties, proposed that Native Hispanic Californians would make excellent cavalry recruits because of their prowess as horsemen, and because they were accustomed to living and working in the harsh outdoors. Pacheco believed that his fellow Californios would prove their patriotism. To that end, he proposed the formation of a regiment of native cavalry to serve in the New Mexico Territory, Arizona Territory, and Texas. His proposal was accepted and, in January 1863, the California War Department authorized creating a four-company battalion.[13]

The First Battalion of Native California Cavalry, comprising Companies A, B, C, and D, was inducted into federal service in 1863 at San Francisco. Their weapons were pistols, daggers, and lances, to which the U.S. Army added carbines. To most Californians the nonpareil lancers were impressive. Indeed, in 1846, during the Mexican War, General Andres Pico and his lancers defeated the Army of the West and even wounded its commanding officer, General Stephen Watts Kearney, at the Battle of San Pasqual. At the outbreak of the Civil War, General Pico chaired the Committee on Militias. He was confident that, if used correctly, these units would prove their valor in battle against the Confederates and later against the Apaches in southern Arizona. Aside from assignment in southwestern Texas and the New Mexico Territory, the First Battalion of Native California Cavalry virtually covered a portion of Arizona Territory ranging from Fort Barrett, Pima Villages to Fort Bowie, Camp Goodwin, Camp Lowell, Fort Mojave, Camp McDowell, Camp Verde, Fort Whipple, and Fort Stanford (formerly Fort Breckenridge). In so doing, they brought some relief for ranchers and townspeople from Apache raids.

In March 1865 the First Battalion of Native Cavalry moved east to fight Apaches in Arizona. They were assigned to the military District of Arizona under the command of Brigadier General John S. Mason. The First Battalion of Native Cavalry prepared to march nearly a thousand miles to camps south of Tucson. Company A assembled at Benicia Barracks on the mouth of the Sacramento River in early April, where it began preparations for the nearly thousand-mile march. Meanwhile, Major Cremony and Captan Porfirio Jiméno in command of Company B arrived at Camp Low where they set up headquarters before departing for Arizona. The move was delayed a few weeks because of the assassination of President Abraham Lincoln. Memorial services for the fallen president took place throughout California.[14]

Moving from their bases in California, the Californios mustered at

San Juan, then moved to Drum Barracks, and finally to Tubac in Arizona Territory. In their march the troops suffered from lack of water and extremely high desert temperatures reaching above 117 degrees Fahrenheit.[15] They found Tubac in ruins and abandoned. The military camp was moved to Calabasas then south from there to Fort Mason (named for its commanding officer).

Strategically located for action in southern Arizona and northern Sonora, Fort Mason was, nevertheless, more of a camp than a fort. Construction of the fort began almost immediately. Meanwhile, the Californios were exposed to accidents and disease. More than 40 percent of the troops were ill from malaria, which commonly assaulted the troops. After the monsoons hit in summer and fall, five enlisted men of the Native California Cavalry and two officers, First Lieutenant Crisanto Soto of Company A and Captain Thomas A. Young of Company D, fell ill and eventually died of malaria.[16]

Major Cremony, Captan Jiméno, and Company B arrived at Tubac in early November 1863. They moved on to Fort Mason; as they were setting up their camp there, a courier from Patagonia hurriedly arrived with word that a large force of warriors under Colonel Refugio Tanori, an Opata chieftain who had been commissioned and armed by the French imperialists in Sonora, had entered Arizona. The courier told them that Tanori had attacked San Rafael, a ranching and mining community on the Santa Cruz River. Quickly ordering a detachment of soldiers from companies B, C, and D, they rode hard all night across the Patagonia Mountains to San Rafael, arriving there early in the morning. Turning south, the Californians followed the tracks of the raiders. Crossing the United States–Mexico border into Sonora, Cremony and his men were within sight of Santa Cruz. Ten men under Lieutenant Edmund W. Coddington entered Santa Cruz and spoke with French imperialists who told them that Tanori had likely gone to Imuris, more than forty miles away. By then Tanori and his warriors had faded into the desertscape. With that information, Cremony turned his men around and returned to Fort Mason.[17]

Threats from Apache warriors and from French imperialists who favored the Confederacy plagued the Californios at Fort Mason. Eventually, they would very effectively take to the field against the Apaches. For example, in the campaign against the Chiricahua Apaches, led by Cochise, little if any contact was made, yet the command in California praised the Californios for driving the tribes away from the border and into Mexico. Some of their actions had taken them within view of the

Huachuca Mountains. It appeared that Cochise wisely chose to avoid a confrontation.[18]

As for the French imperialist sympathizers in Sonora, the presence of the Californios and their aggressive attitude likely made the imperialists think twice about whether it was worth a fight for southern Arizona. After all, the Confederates had been driven out three years before, and in 1865 Benito Juarez's army vanquished the French and executed Maximilian. Meanwhile, at Appomattox Courthouse, General Lee had surrendered his troops to General Grant. When word reached the western territories, the Californio Lancers were, within weeks, ordered back to California where they were mustered out.[19]

The participation of the Californio Lancers in the occupation of the Arizona Territory had been important, because it preserved the region for the Union and it eliminated the intrusion of French imperialist backers to invade the land. In the time the Lancers served in Arizona, they brought a modicum of relief from Apache raids to the area.

Thus, between the late seventeenth and late nineteenth centuries, Apache warriors had from time to time forced Hispanic, and later, Anglo-American settlers and miners to barricade themselves and brace for punishing attacks, or to abandon their homes or land grants for a safer place to live. Although the word *abandonment* can have relative meanings, it appears that Hispanic settlers merely chose not to reside on their land grants, but rather in the settlements of northern Sonora, inclusive of areas such as Tubac, Tucson, Tumacacori, and Santa Cruz. Largely they left their cattle to roam and increase over the expanse of their boundaries. Periodically the Mexican landowners would return to brand or round up their herds to move them closer to home. The first Americans to enter the region found large herds of unattended cattle in the areas of the two land grants in southeastern Arizona.[20]

Related to Coronado National Memorial, one of the most significant land grants is the San Rafael del Valle grant that lies on both sides of the San Pedro River north of present Hereford. Rafael Elías González petitioned for both the San Rafael del Valle and San Pedro grants. Elías González requested four *sitios* for the purpose of raising cattle and horses.[21] In 1827 Elías González acquired the San Rafael del Valle grant for $240. Although the grant was confirmed in 1828, Elías González waited five years to receive official title to the land in 1832. Before he was driven out by the Apaches, he developed a cattle ranch with some cultivation of fields within it.

The boundaries of the grant fell within the present Coronado National Memorial and included Montezuma Canyon. The boundary survey evolved when, on March 12, 1827, Rafael Elías González petitioned Nicolas María Gaxiola, treasurer general of the State of Sonora, to denounce a tract of public land adjacent to Rancho de San Pedro for ranching purposes. Nearly four months later, on July 1, 1827, Gaxiola ordered Pablo Fraijo, *alcalde* (mayor) of Santa Cruz, to survey and appraise the referenced tract and solicit bids for the sale of the property in accordance with the Act of May 20, 1825.[22]

After presenting public notice of the planned survey, Fraijo appointed a counter, and hired two measurers and two markers as his assistants. On August 21, 1827, Fraijo went out to the tract he called San Rafael del Valle and selected the center point as the reference to his survey. From there, he measured southward two hundred *cordeles* to the north boundary of Rancho de San Pedro in the San Pedro River Valley. A cordel was a cord or rope usually made from the waxed fiber of the pita plant. Generally, a cordel measured 50 varas and a vara was 32.9 inches.[23]

Rancho de San Pedro comprised land for which Jesús Pérez had, in 1821, made a petition. Later, Pérez sold the land to Rafael Elías González who attached it to his lands at San Rafael. At that point in the survey, Pérez met the surveyors and acknowledged that they had correctly surveyed the northern limits of his grant.

Fraijo resumed the survey by running a line up the valley two hundred *cordeles* from the center point to a small limey hill. He ran another line measuring fifty *cordeles* from the center point that terminated at the foot of Sierra de las Mulas. A final line of fifty *cordeles* ran from the center point to a point below the Sierra de Guachuca. The survey was complete and Fraijo completed his report. After Elías took possession of the land, he agreed to erect permanent boundary monuments east of the five points established by Fraijo, within the present memorial.[24] Thus, Elías's land grant spread across the entire San Pedro Valley from the Huachucas to the Mule Mountains.

Meanwhile, Fraijo appointed two appraisers, Manuel Soto and Carmilo Arvisa. Their evaluation of the land indicated that it had a worth value of 60 pesos for each of the four *sitios* totaling 240 pesos. The value was easily ascertained because the Act of May 20, 1825 required a value of 6 pesos per *sitio* for lands having a stream of water.[25] A *sitio* equaled 4,428.4 acres.[26] Once the evaluation was completed, Mexican law required that a public solicitation be made for bids to purchase the property. The bid was published at Santa Cruz for thirty days beginning on August 30, 1827. As no bids were made, Fraijo then referred the matter to Gaxiola, who, on February 7, 1828, submitted the matter to Concepción de Alamos, the *fiscal* (fiscal administrator) for an opinion regarding the validity of the procedures taken to that point.

Having reviewed the *expediente* (file) and the steps taken in the survey, Alamos expressed his findings. First, he remarked that he was surprised that Fraijo had not used a compass to make his survey. Of all the instruments used in the survey, Alamo opined that the compass was the most indispensable tool to determine the course or direction of the survey. He could have produced a well-grounded challenge to the survey on that basis alone, but because it would cast a cloud over Elías's ownership of the land, Alamos chose to allow the omission and continue with the proceedings.

Once Alamos had rendered his opinion, Gaziola ordered that the land be sold at public auction. According to the Act of August 4, 1824, Article 11, and the Act of May 20 1825, Article 11, the sale was publicized.[27] For three days, April 16, 17, and 18, 1828, offers were solicited, but none was forthcoming. Because no one had bid against Elías, the land was sold to him for the appraised amount. Quickly, on April 18, Elías paid for the land and the sale was recorded in the *Toma de Razón* (*recording of the land*). Nearly four years later, on December 25, 1832, Elías received title to Rancho de San Rafael del Valle. The Act of August 4, 1824 and the Act of May 20, 1825, also provided that the sale of the land to Elías was subject to certain terms. First, he must occupy and develop the property. Second, should he abandon the land for a period of three years for any reason other than being forced out by Apaches, the land could be taken away and granted to another interested party. Predictably, as had happened with other settlers, Apaches did eventually force Elías off the land.

On October 28, 1878, Francisco S. León gave testimony to the surveyor general of Arizona, John Wasson, about the abandonment and cause of the abandonment of the San Rafael del Valle grant. Wasson asked him, "Do you know when the possession of said Rancho was abandoned by Don Rafael Elías?" León answered, "I cannot remember the date, but it was before the time of the war with the United States [1846–48]." Wasson then asked, "What was the cause of said abandonment?" Leon's answer was precise. He said, "It was abandoned on account of the Apache Indians, who attacked his rancho . . . killing the people, burning the ranch house, and running off the stock." To the question whether

León thought Elías González could have returned to the land at any time of his choosing, Leon gave a definitive answer. "It would have been impossible and I know that. . . from years past depredations have been constant at this Rancho at San Rafael del Valle."[28]

When Elías González died, his widow, Guadalupe Pérez de Elías, and their three sons, José Juan, Manuel, and José María, inherited the property. Despite the abandonment of the land, the law had protected his ownership, which was passed on to his heirs.

In 1861 France had invaded Mexico, which was subsequently ruled by Maximillian until his defeat and execution in 1865. Meanwhile José Juan Elías, the eldest brother, was killed in battle defending Sonora against French loyalists. The Camou brothers, Joseph Pierre and Pascual Camou, on the other hand, were French citizens who sided with the invaders. In 1862 the Elíases, owing $12,000 to the Camou brothers on loans taken on the land, transferred the land in lieu of payments to Joseph, Pierre, and Pascual Camou of Hermosillo, Sonora. Thus the San Rafael del Valle grant has a greater history beyond the litigation that attended it.

Seeking confirmation of the validity of their grant, the Camou brothers, on February 26, 1875, petitioned John Wasson, surveyor general, to commence the necessary procedures. The surveyor general launched an investigation of the Camou brothers' claim. Special Agent Rufus C. Hopkins found the *expediente* in the archive at Hermosillo, Mexico, verified that it had been written on stamped paper, and confirmed that the survey, the appraisal, and the sale were all proper. He saw that a certificate demonstrated that the title had, indeed, been issued. Because Hopkins had not found any procedural anomalies, Wasson issued his report authenticating the original title issued in good faith under Mexican law. On October 29, 1879, Wasson confirmed the grant to the Camou brothers not to exceed four square leagues granted to Rafael Elías González and later "purchased" from the Elías family.[29]

A discrepancy was discovered and quickly challenged by the Camou brothers. In 1879 Deputy Surveyor Solon M. Allis surveyed the land and determined that it comprised 17,360.6 acres. The Camou brothers contracted George J. Raskruge to survey the property in 1891. The Raskruge surveyed indicated that the 1828 survey reported that the size of the tract was actually 20,034.62 acres.[30] By the end of the year the Camou brothers' estate, represented by Juan Pedro Camou, as petitioner, pressed the U.S. Court of Private Land Claims for the confirmation of the grant. He presented his case before the Court of Private Land Claims. The case progressed to the United States Supreme Court, which rendered its decision in 1898.[31] In the end, it had taken twenty years to resolve the issues and included two court cases in the Court of Private Land Claims and two before the Supreme Court.

Despite Raskruge's report that all procedures were in order, the United States argued to the contrary. The United States lawyers argued that even though all the papers were in order, the claim had been invalidated by the Colonization Law of August 18, 1824, which required the Mexican federal government, not the state of Sonora, to confirm the grant.[32] They argued that, in this case, the San Rafael del Valle grant, even if originally valid, had been annulled by subsequent decrees.

Both sides in the case reviewed Mexican laws and policies that occurred after 1821. The Colonization Law of 1824, for example, provided that lands "within twenty leagues of the boundaries of any foreign nation, or within ten littoral leagues, cannot be colonized without the previous approval of the supreme general executive power."[33] The grant, however, had been made before the United States had acquired the territory in present southern Arizona. Other provisions of the law reiterated the principle that, after 1853, the Mexican federal government reserved the right to approve concessions of land and revoked the power of states to do so.

The issue was further complicated by historical events that occurred in 1853. Needing money, the dictator Antonio López de Santa Anna sold a large swath of land stretching from Mesilla (in present New Mexico) to the Colorado River running along the Gila River as its northern boundary. A binational survey commission would determine the southern boundary along the resulting present-day line. The Gadsden Purchase Treaty provided that Mexico be paid $18 million for the land that encompassed the San Rafael del Valle grant and other grants within the ceded territory. A new international boundary was surveyed, and those grants now lay on the north side of the border. Thus, the Gadsden Purchase Treaty, borrowing language from the Treaty of Guadalupe Hidalgo of 1848, provided that the United States would protect the property of Mexican citizens within the territory prior to the Gadsden Purchase Treaty just as it protected the property of the U.S.

Just as the Gadsden Purchase Treaty was being negotiated and ratified (in 1854), Santa Anna issued the Decree of July 7, 1854. This decree required that all concessions of land made in Mexico after September 1821 be approved by the Mexican national government, as Article 1 of the decree clearly stated: "The titles of all the alienations of public lands made in the Territory of the Republic from September 1821 till date, whether by the general authorities or by those of the extinguished States and Departments, shall be submitted to the revision of the Supreme Government, without which they shall have no value and shall constitute no right of property."[34] Article 2 stipulated that all previous concessions of land be authenticated by the commissioners of the Ministry of Public Works residing in all the departments and territories to review titles of acquisition within six months of receipt and publication of the law in each area.

One provision permitted a slight reprieve to landowners, who had received concessions since September 1821. Article 6 provided, "Those made by said authorities in the epochs of the extinguished Federation are likewise void; provided, they were not made for the purpose of extending and promoting colonization, which was the purpose proposed by the law of August 18th, 1824."[35] Article 14 provided that the law of November 25th remained in force as long as it did not conflict with the present decree. Article 1 in the Decree of November 25th, 1853 stated "It is declared that the public lands, as the exclusive property of the nation, never could have been alienated under any title by virtue of decrees, orders, and enactments of the legislatures, governments or local authorities of the States and Territories of the Republic."[36]

Finally, on May 21, 1898, the U.S. Supreme Court issued its opinion. Although there were other legal markers in Mexican history that had revoked the power of the states to make grants, it was undeniable that the Act of August 4, 1824, had provided that the states could collect revenues from the sale of vacant lands located within their respective boundaries. The intent by the Mexican national government, argued the Supreme Court, allowed the states to sell such lands, and the states themselves had made laws authorizing the sale of public lands. Therefore, a Mexican state did have the right and authority to make valid sales of vacant lands and had these rights prior to 1836. The United States, furthermore, was obligated to recognize those concessions under the terms of the Gadsden Purchase Treaty. Perhaps the most significant fact in the entire process was that Elías had followed all required terms of acquiring land. He had not exceeded the four square leagues requirement and had obtained possession of the property without being challenged by the Mexican government. In the end, he sold his land to the Camou brothers. One issue remained regarding the amount of land claimed by

Elías and that claimed by the Camou estate. The Camou family argued that the land they purchased was larger by some 2,460 acres. There was one inescapable historical fact that the Supreme Court unequivocally agreed on: a definite grant was in place prior to the Gadsden Purchase Treaty.

In May 1899, the Court of Private Land Claims met in Tucson, Arizona, and heard testimony on behalf of the Camou family. They argued that the area contained 20,034.62 acres of land. Their discussion focused on the location of the center point laid down by Fraijo in the survey of 1827. Oddly, it could not be located. In the end, the Camou family lost its case and the final determination of the size of the property was 17,474.93 acres.

On November 6, 1903, the Court of Private Land Claims confirmed and patented the San Rafael del Valle grant as the one originally granted to Rafael Elías, his heirs, successors, and assigns. The question of ownership had run its course from 1827 when Rafael Elías González first received the land to 1903 when the Camou brothers received its patent.

The subsequent history of the San Rafael grant is equally as interesting. In 1905, the Camou family sold the land to William Cornell Greene, then of Bisbee. He attached it to his estate holdings as part of the Cananea Land and Cattle Company, which he developed. In 1912, after his death, the Greene Family sold it to the Boquillas Land and Cattle Company, which owned the San Juan de las Boquillas y Nogales land grant downstream. The remaining portion of the land grant went through several transfers until 1967 when Tenneco, Inc. and the Kern County Land and Cattle Company merged and acquired the land.

A second land grant associated with Coronado National Memorial is the San Pedro grant, along the river to the east. In 1821, José de Jesús Pérez, a citizen of Arizpe, Mexico, petitioned Governor Antonio Cordero for four *sitios* of land on which he would raise livestock. Pérez reported that he had acquired the cattle through his own hard work while in military service. He had no place to keep them and that was the reason for his petition. Under the provisions of the cedula of February 14, 1805, Pérez would have one year "to settle and cultivate those uncultivated and vacant" lands, otherwise they would revert to the Crown.[37] The land Pérez requested was south of the present international boundary near the ancestral home of the Elías family known as San Pedro. The house was two or three miles northeast of an abandoned place known as Las Nutrias. On March 12, 1821, Governor Cordero ordered Nazario Gómez, the *alcalde* of the Presidio of Fronteras, to notify the adjoining landowners that the land would be surveyed, appraised, and sold. In preparation for the sale, Gómez returned the *expediente* of the actions ordered by Cordero.

Meanwhile, Gómez's term expired. His successor, Miguel Terán, insisted that as the new *alcalde*, the authority to complete the sale was his responsibility. Gómez claimed that Cordero's original order had conceded him a special appointment as judge commissioner, and that Terán was to assist him. Unbending, Terán got his way, and Gómez gave him the *expediente*. Terán appointed his assistants: he chose Lúcio Gómez to serve as the treasurer, Ramon Benítas and Teodoro Aros as the appraisers, and Luis Aragon as the compassman. Until then, none of the adjoining landowners had complained that the petition included land that would encroach on their properties. Therefore, Terán issued a public notice of the survey to commence on May 6, 1821.

As it turned out, however, another person had already claimed that land, and a dispute ensued in which the lands were divided between the claimants. Asserting his right to the land, Manuel Antunes, a claimant to the land, informed Terán that he had plans to register a tract within the area to be surveyed. His claim was based on his usage of the land as pasturage for his herds. Antunes was given until May 18, 1821 to show that his claim was within the lands petitioned by Pérez. Having made his point, Antunes agreed that Pérez could have the lands downriver from the house at San Pedro as long as the survey did not include the lands upriver from that point. Pérez's agent, Rafael Salas, objected to the proposal because his client would be deprived of water from a cienega that was the source of water for that area. An agreement was made by which Pérez would be entitled to half of the water. Although Pérez purchased the land, he eventually sold the land to Rafael Elías González, the owner of the San Rafael del Valle grant.[38] On October 25, 1832, proceedings commenced to transfer the land to Elías González. Seven months later, on May 8, 1833, a title deed was issued to Elías under Article 11 of the Act of August 4, 1824 and the Act of May 20, 1825.[39] Elías now owned the land.

After the death of Rafael Elías González, his family petitioned that Surveyor General John Wasson survey the grant for the purposes of confirming the property lying within the United States. Earlier, Rufus C. Hopkins, Wasson's assistant, had been in Hermosillo and examined the *expediente* of the grant. Hopkins read through fifty pages of documents and concluded that the proceedings of the survey, appraisal, and the sale were in order. He assured Wasson that the documents were authentic.

Based on Hopkins's report, Wasson appointed Thomas A. Barton to investigate the boundaries of the grant and prepare instructions for the new survey that would be undertaken. Barton rode over the area of the grant looking for landmarks indicated in the documents. He found a good number of monuments, but he could not determine their significance in regard to the previous survey by Mexican surveyors. Natural markers mentioned in the documentation were likewise located, but there were so many that Barton was not able to determine which ones marked the boundary. Place names were problematic. For example, three mountains in the area appeared to have the same name: Pecacho. Therefore, it was difficult to pinpoint which mountain could be the reference point for the grant. Then there was the issue of the town of San Pedro, where the Elías family lived. It was located several miles south of the international boundary. Just south of there was Las Nutrias. Barton was so confused by the many monuments and natural boundaries that he concluded that the descriptions fit almost any point in the San Pedro Valley for a distance of more than twenty-five miles.

Agitated by the report, Wasson sent G. C. Wharton to Sonora to locate the initial point of the boundaries so that a survey of the grant could be made. The most notable fact about the grant was its reference point: "the house of San Pedro."[40] The town of San Pedro was about eight miles from the border and the house was the ancestral home of the Elías family where some of them still resided. Wharton concluded that because the size of the original grant was four square leagues, it was too small to stretch into the United States. The entire grant, in his opinion, was located in Sonora.

One fact stood out, however, to contradict Wharton's seemingly absolute conclusion. The documents at Hermosillo revealed that the grant had been extended sometime after the death of Rafael Elías González by his grandson, Manuel Elías. In 1880 Manuel Elías purchased the surplus lands (*demásias*), beyond the northern boundary of the grant. At that time, the Mexican portion of the grant containing 68,243.09 acres had been surveyed. Of those acres, 50,889.24 acres of surplus land had been sold to the Elías family on June 22, 1886. Wharton concluded that the Elíases had therefore obtained the full amount of land allowed under the *cabida legal* (right to legal standing) in Mexico. Therefore, contended Wharton, they had no legal claim for the additional land within the United States.

At that point in the investigation of the San Pedro grant boundaries, the Elías claim became increasingly complex. Based on Wharton's conclusion, the new surveyor general, John Hise, disapproved the survey request. In a letter dated October 14, 1887 to William A. J. Sparkes, commissioner of the General Land Office, Hise explained his refusal for a survey by writing that if the San Pedro claim was questionable, then the accuracy of two other grants was doubtful. The two grants were the San Juan de Boquillas y Nogales grant and the adjoining San Rafael del Valle grant, of which the southern boundary joined the northern boundary of the San Pedro grant.

By 1885 the recently incorporated Reloj Cattle Company had been purchasing quitclaim deeds within the *demasías* from the Elías González family for two years.[41] The Reloj Cattle Company quickly challenged Hise's decision. The upshot was a suit filed on March 1, 1893, in the Court of Private Land Claims by the Reloj Cattle Company officials, who claimed that they had acquired the Arizona portion of the land from the Elías family.[42] A new survey of the Reloj Cattle Company property by H. G. Howe and Philip Contzen covered 52,232.3 acres on both sides of the boundary. The U.S. portion of the Reloj Cattle Company's holdings totaled 38,622.6 acres. The lawyers for the United States argued that the property in question was entirely in Mexico.[43] Thus no claim on the U.S. side could be considered valid.

The case dragged on for six years. In the hearing held on June 2, 1899, the Reloj Cattle Company lawyers produced grant papers demonstrating the correctness of the survey. In the closing arguments, however, the Reloj Cattle Company's claim was disallowed. Quickly, the Reloj lawyers petitioned for and were granted an appeal. Finally, on March 27, 1903, the United States Supreme Court affirmed the judgment of the Court of Private Land Claims.[44] As the gavel fell, so too did the hopes of the Reloj Cattle Company to retain its land.

As an epilogue to the San Pedro grant story, there were many complications and events that obscured its ownership, boundaries, and extent of the *demásias*. Over the years, the sons of Rafael Elías González had acquired lands beyond the grant. Those lands, considered to be *demasías*, ranged beyond the international line in the United States and exceeded thirty-six square miles, or more than 18,000 acres. In 1887 the Mexican department of public works denied the claim on the Mexican side, given that a survey to the land could not be made because no monuments could be located that could determine the limits of the ranch. Thus, a cloud was placed over the grant and its *demasías*.

Politically influential, the Elías González family appealed to President Porfirio Díaz in 1888 for title to the land and it was granted on the Mexican side. According to Mexican authorities, the entire grant, with the exception of the *demasías* lands, was entirely within the northern portion of the state of Sonora.[45] They recognized that the *demasías* were on the U.S. side of the international boundary. Historically, at least, it seems that the Reloj Cattle Company, that had purchased *demásias* lands north of the border, did have a claim.

Throughout the Spanish colonial and Mexican periods, settlement patterns followed the Santa Cruz and San Pedro River valleys. The San Pedro River settlements moved northward from Bacanuchi and Cananea, then followed the San Pedro northward to Santa Cruz and Quiburi. Another line moved eastward from the Tubac and Tucson settlements to the north end of the Huachucas. Cattlemen, miners, and farmers moved into the settled areas. Traditions for stock raising and mining emerged throughout both periods. Finally, during the Mexican period land grants, particularly the San Rafael del Valle and San Pedro grants, influenced the development of the area. Doubtless, the land grant owners and their workers were probably the miners referred to by Grace Sparkes and Axel Johnson in the twentieth century when they wrote their reports about early Spanish mining within the State of Texas Mines claims.

Notes

1. "The Mule Pass Mines," *Arizona Star*, November 14, 1878. Copy available at Arizona Historical Society, Tucson, AZ.

2. James E. Officer, *Hispanic Arizona, 1536–1856* (Tucson: University of Arizona Press, 1987), 317–23.

3. Ibid., 323, fn2.

4. "Reminiscences of Rafael Elias, 81-Year-Old Pioneer," *Bisbee Daily Review*, July 29, 1934. Copy available at the Arizona Historical Society, Tucson.

5. Memorial and Affidavits Showing Outrages Perpetuated by the Apache Indians in the Territory of Arizona for the years 1869–1870. Published by Authority of the Legislature of the Territory of Arizona, San Francisco: Francis & Valentine, Printers, 517 Clay Street, 1871, Arizona Historical Society, Tucson.

6. "The Mule Pass Mines," *Arizona Star*, November 14, 1878. Copy available at Arizona Historical Society, Tucson, AZ.

7. San Rafael del Valle Grant A, Case No. 3, U.S. Department of the Interior/Land Department, Spanish Land Grants 10.1.11A, Case No. 3. Copy can be found at Arizona State Library, Archives and Public Library, Microfilm (hereafter San Rafael del Valle Grant A, Case No. 3). On October 28, 1879, Francisco S. León presented a deposition regarding the abandonment of the San Rafael del Valle grant.

8. Edwin R. Sweeney, *Mangas Coloradas: Chief of the Chiricahua Apaches* (Norman: University of Oklahoma Press, 1998), 47.

9. Diario de las operaciones practicadas por el Señor Comandante General del Estado José María Elías Gonzales (December 30, 1849), Archivo Histórico de Hermosillo, folio 1 and 4, Reel 15, Arizona Historical Society, Tucson, AZ. For modern place name designations, see Diana Hadley, "Inter-Ethnic Contacts in the Borderlands: The Apache Campaign of José María Elías Gonzales," unpublished manuscript (1986), Arizona Historical Society, Tucson, AZ, 3.

10. Apache raids into and throughout Sonora continued to the end of the nineteenth century. See "Invasión al Estado de Sonora por indios barbaros, 1885. Nueva envasión al estado de Sonora," Archivo Diplomático de Asuntos Exteriores, Mexico City, ms. 17-21-94.

11. Edwin R. Sweeney, *Mangas Coloradas: Chief of the Chiricahua Apaches* (Norman: University of Oklahoma Press, 1998), 303.

12. Ibid., 377.

13. See the section on the First Battalion of Native Cavalry in Richard H. Orton, *Records of California Men in the War of the Rebellion* (Sacramento, CA: State Office, 1890).

14. Orton, *Records of California Men*. Tom Prezelski covers the history of Companies A, B, C, and D in "Lives of Californio Lancers: The First Battalion of Native California Cavalry, 1863–1866," *Journal of Arizona History* 40 (Spring 1999). Also see Aurora Hunt, *The Army of the Pacific: Its Operations in California, Texas, Arizona, New Mexico, Utah, Nevada, Oregon, Washington, Plains Region, Mexico, etc. 1860–1866* (Mechanicsburg, PA: Stackpole Books, 1951). Also see Joseph P. Sánchez, Carol Shively, Ted Alexander, and Robert Spude, *Hispanics and the Civil War: From Battlefield to Homefront* (National Park Service, 2011).

15. See Tom Prezelski, "Lives of Californio Lancers: The First Battalion of Native California Cavalry, 1863–1866," *Journal of Arizona History* 40 (Spring 1999).

16. See Prezelski, "Lives of Californio Lancers."

17. Ibid.

18. Ibid.

19. Orton, *Records of California Men*.

20. Officer, *Hispanic Arizona*, 148–49.

21. San Rafael del Valle Grant A, Case No. 3, Testimony of Manuel de la Brena, Pedimento Fiscal, Concepción de Alamos, Sonora, February 7, 1828. This is an extract from the original petition and confirmation of the grant. Brena noted that the granting of the four *sitios* of land was for raising cattle and horses.

22. Mathew G. Reynolds, *Spanish and Mexican Land Laws*, Buxton & Skinner Stationery Company: St. Louis, Missouri (1895), 129-31. See Laws of the State of the West (Sonora and Sinaloa), Part I, 66, No. 30. Provisional Law for the Regulation of the Purchase of the Lands of the State.

23. Betty Eakle Dobkins, *The Spanish Element in Texas Water Law* (Austin: University of Texas Press: 1959), 72. Dobkins explores the measurements for Texas land and water rights and uses figures that applied to the north Mexican states during the eighteenth and nineteenth centuries. Measurement of the *vara* in New Spain (Mexico) during the Spanish colonial and Mexican periods varied from 32.5 inches to 33.33 inches.

24. Testimony of Manuel de la Brena, Pedimento Fiscal, Concepción de Alamos, Sonora, February 7, 1828; San Rafael del Valle Grant A, Case No. 3.

25. Provisional Law for the Regulation of the Purchase of the Lands of the State in Reynolds, Spanish and Mexican Land Laws, 129.

26. Dobkins, *The Spanish Element*, 76–77.

27. Mathew G. Reynolds, *Spanish and Mexican Land Laws*, Buxton & Skinner Stationery Company: St. Louis, Missouri (1895), 118–20 and 129–31.

28. This paragraph, including quotes, from San Rafael del Valle Grant A, Case No. 3. On October 28, 1879, Francisco S. León presented a deposition regarding the abandonment of the San Rafael del Valle grant.

29. San Rafael del Valle Grant A, Case No. 3, ibid.

30. Ibid.

31. Camou v. United States, 171 U.S. 277 (1898).

32. The Colonization Law of August 18, 1824, in Mathew G. Reynolds, *Spanish and Mexican Land Laws*, Buxton & Skinner Stationery Company: St. Louis, Missouri (1895), 121.

33. Ibid.

34. Annuls Sales of Lands Made by States, Department, etc. Decree of July 7th, 1854, in Reynolds, *Spanish Mexican Land Laws*, 326.

35. Ibid.

36. "Decree of November 25th, 1853," in Reynolds, *Spanish Mexican Land Laws*, 324.

37. "Decree of February 14, 1805," in Reynolds, *Spanish Mexican Land Laws*, 76.

38. Jay J. Wagoner, *Early Arizona: Prehistory to Civil War* (Tucson: University of Arizona Press, 1975), 224.

39. Reloj Cattle Company v. United States, copy in Court of Private Land Claims, Arizona District; Act of May 20, 1824, in Reynolds, *Spanish and Mexican Land Laws*, 129–31.

40. Reynolds, ibid.

41. Jay J. Wagoner, *Early Arizona: Prehistory to Civil War* (Tucson: University of Arizona Press, 1975), 225. In 1899 the Reloj Cattle Company appealed to the Court of Private Land Claims for confirmation of 38,622.06 acres of *demasías* lands. The exaggerated claim was more than double the acreage of the actual *demasías* lands purchased from the Elías González family and was already of doubtful claim, given the cloud over the claim by the Mexican survey of 1887.

42. Reloj Cattle Company v. United States, No. 10 in Court of Private Land Claims, Arizona District.

43. Reloj Cattle Company v. United States, 184, U.S. Reports, 624–49. Although the Court of Private Land Claims entertained the question in 1893, the U.S. Supreme Court, in Reloj Cattle Company vs. United States, reasserted that the claim would not be honored because the Court of Private Land Claims should never have taken up the question of *demasías* lands with questionable validity, especially because the entire grant lay within Mexico.

44. Reloj Cattle Company v. United States, 184 U.S. 624 (1902).

45. Jay J. Wagoner, *Early Arizona: Prehistory to Civil War* (Tucson: University of Arizona Press, 1975), 225.

CHAPTER 4

The Crown of Montezuma Canyon

A History of the State of Texas Mines

The State of Texas group of claims... is located on the west slope of the southern end of the Huachuca Mountains, in Parker Canyon (formerly called Montezuma Canyon)...24 miles from Bisbee.... There are other ore showings besides those on the Texas groups—along and near the contact on both the westerly and easterly flanks of the mountain. Along the contact to the northwest are a group of 7 patented claims, and to the southeast a group of 6 patented claims.

—J. S. Coupal, 1940[1]

Following the Gadsden Purchase Treaty of 1853, settlers from the United States poured into southern Arizona Territory. They had been part of a westward expansion that, in the 1760s, crossed the Appalachian Mountains from the coastal regions of North America. Almost unabated, Anglo-American settlers reached the Mississippi River within a few years and encountered Spanish settlements at San Luis (present St. Louis, Missouri) and other places southward to New Orleans. Anglo-American settlements quickly expanded across the continent in the next few decades. By 1848 the United States had acquired much of the present southwest and had established the New Mexico Territory. By mid-1850 southern Arizona had also been incorporated into the United States, which, in 1863, established the Arizona Territory. Meanwhile, Anglo-American and Hispanic settlers clashed on many issues including law, property, and mineral and water rights. Anglo-American cattlemen, farmers, and miners, among others, reestablished their politics and economies on this new land. Throughout the territory, mining attracted many who saw the possibilities of untold wealth. In time, they came to possess mines that had been worked by their Hispanic predecessors and, with a new technology, opened up new mining areas. By the late nineteenth century Montezuma Canyon was hosting a new wave of people who had come to stay. A new history was about to unfold.

In 1940 J. S. "Sam" Coupal, director of the Arizona Mineral Resource Board, surveyed a number of mining sites, particularly the State of Texas Mines in Montezuma Canyon within present Coronado National Memorial. Coupal was a trained mining engineer who not only directed surveys, but also participated in their analyses. In his "Synoptic Report of State of Texas Mine," he wrote, "The State of Texas group of claims, consisting of one patented claim, two full size and one fractional unpatented claim and a 5 acre mill site claim, a total of about 70 acres, is located on the west slope of the southern end of the Huachuca Mountains, in Parker Canyon (formerly called Montezuma Canyon) a distance of 6 miles from the Bisbee Huachuca highway, Number 92, at a point 24 miles from Bisbee."[2] Coupal's "Synoptic Report" revealed that there were many mines in the area, but the State of Texas one appeared to be potentially the richest.

David B. Rea had originally staked what would become the State of Texas Mines on May 20, 1877, as the Wade Hampton, the name of a popular, fiery southern politician.[3] Rea knew Juan Elías, the *alcalde mayor* of Tucson, and had come to the mining area shortly after the removal of the Chiricahua Apache to a new reservation. However, Rea abandoned his Wade Hampton claim before working it when he became a partner in opening what proved to be the phenomenally rich Copper Queen Mine in future Bisbee.[4]

Under the 1872 mining law,[5] miners could acquire title to mineral lands following a set procedure. A prospector would "locate" a mineral vein, mark off a mining claim of 600′ by 1500′ along the vein, and place a location notice on the claim. They then recorded, for a filing fee, a "location notice" at the county recorder's office. The prospector had "possessory" title to the claim as long as he or she performed $100 worth of work each year (the equivalent of digging a ten-foot shaft or prospect pit). If the work was not performed the claim was considered forfeited and another prospector could lay claim to the "abandoned" ground. After proving they had found minerals, the prospector could have his or her claim surveyed by a recognized U.S. Mineral Surveyor and then request a patent to the land after paying a filing fee ($1.25 per acre). After the requirements were met, the U.S. government's General Land Office [now Bureau of Land Management] issued a patent. This was the process used for gaining title to the State of Texas mine, though after several convoluted efforts.

The restaking of the State of Texas claim appears to have occurred in the summer of 1878. The *Arizona Citizen*, January 4, 1878, noted that U.S. deputy surveyor John L. Harris and party were surveying lands along the San Pedro River. In an era when conflict of interest was not a concern, Harris had information about David Rea's claim. When the one-year time had elapsed, he jumped Rea's Wade Hampton claim and staked it as his own, renaming it the Lena. With Harris was longtime Pima County surveyor George A. Roskruge, who co-claimed with Harris the Lena on June 19, 1878. They also staked three additional claims, one of which, the Augusta Extension, was on what would later be part of the Doredor described in chapter 5. Harris also added to the location notice names of influential individuals who were not present, including John Wasson, the territorial surveyor general. From evidence at hand, Harris and Roskruge did little more than the annual assessment work before abandoning the claim in 1884.[6]

Meanwhile, silver had been discovered at Tombstone, forty miles northeast, causing a major mining rush to the area during 1878–80. Prospectors who had not been able to stake claims in the overcrowded Tombstone Hills turned to other areas, including the Huachuca Mountains. In August 1879 discoveries at the head of Cave Creek, over the divide from Montezuma Canyon, caused a small rush to the Huachucas. Over the next couple of years, the first serious opening of mines by Americans in the Huachuca Mountains occurred. During this period, the three miles of Montezuma Canyon was staked from one end to the other. Because of the old workings, miners named some claims the Montezuma, the Pizarro, or Coronado—prospectors had a penchant for naming claims after persons important in Mexico's history. Likely, Montezuma Canyon took its name from one of those mines.

Other investors with capital invested in the mines. William Gird, brother of one of the founders of Tombstone, invested in claims along Montezuma Canyon, including claims on what would later be property of the State of Texas Mines. Gird and partners used simple operations—hand windlasses and hand drills—to dig shallow shafts, thirty feet or less, to prospect a half-dozen claims looking for silver bonanzas. None of them panned out.[7]

A small community of prospectors built houses along the canyon floor. It appears Peter Conner, Charles Mansur, and Ambroise Chedal each staked or worked part of what would become the State of Texas claims as well. In 1880 Conner was thirty-six, a miner who lived in a house near the spring beneath the claims. He would stay in the area the next two decades. Among others, he restaked the Lena as the Chicago in 1885, and then restaked it again as the State of Texas in 1889. Conner built a house on the creek bed on his five-acre mill site, and made a living selling claims and receiving grubstakes, primarily from Bisbee saloon owner Charles Gerdes and Tombstone mining man August "Gus" Baron. Baron and Gerdes were partners with many of the prospectors in the Huachucas. Charles Mansur also arrived with the early crowd of prospectors. In 1880 the census taker found the 38-year-old Maine native living in Charleston, the mill town for Tombstone. Mansur moved to the mountains as a miner representing William Gird and later Baron: Baron had been mine superintendent for the Gird brothers' operations in Tombstone. During the 1880s Baron and his partners slowly bought up the State of Texas and adjoining claims.[8]

Of all places within Montezuma Canyon, the mining properties within Coronado National Memorial represent a number of site locations with a distinct material culture and chronology. Indeed, they define time and place within the historical crown of the memorial's story.

Although mines received new names during the early Anglo-American period in southern Arizona, many of them were well known and associated with towns south of the border in Sonora. As mining fever spread, a new lore emerged about old Mexican mines in southeastern Arizona and northeastern Sonora. In 1878, for example, *The Arizona Star*, then a weekly newspaper, ran a series of stories on mines in Sonora that related geographically or, at least, historically, with those mines north of the border. The story, "The Mines of Cananea," recounted the relationship between mines on both sides of the international line. Miner David B. Rea, author of the article, wrote, "In crossing the low divide between headwaters of the San Pedro and Sonora rivers, on the eastern slopes of the Cananea Mountains, a continuation of the Huachucas, we come to these mines."[9] Rea associated the mines in the Huachucas with those in the Sierra de la Marquilla that, he wrote, are "a continuation of the Huachuca range just across the border."[10]

The *Arizona Star* ran another story, this one entitled "The Mule Pass Mines," on November 14, 1878. The anonymous reporter described "old silver smelting works" near the Huachucas. He wrote, "The immense piles of old slag heaps lying around this old Real would indicate that mining had once been carried on in this vicinity of an extensive scale;

and that the mines that supplied these old works must lie somewhere near either in the Dragoon or Huachuca mountain ranges; the bits of ore picked up around the old works were black sulphurets of silver and copper silver glance of a high grade."[11] The area north of the mines of Cananea, that earlier had inspired mining in the Huachucas and the Dragoons, intrigued speculators; newspaper stories excited them about the prospects of striking it rich.

The *Arizona Star* continued to run stories about mines into December of 1878. The writer of the San Rafael Mines story began, "We have just met some parties from the Huachuca Mountains. They bring encouraging news and plenty of good mineral. Some fine discoveries have just been made, the most prominent among which are the mines composing the San Rafael group, near the old San Rafael mine." According to the writer, "these mines are located in the Huachuca Mountains, about twenty-five miles from the Aztec mill, and about thirty miles from the location of the Gird & Shefflin [*sic*] Mill at Tombstone."[12] Thus, the Huachucas were associated with the lore of mining that grew out of the Spanish and Mexican period mining ventures.

By the mid-1890s the State of Texas Mine belonged to August Baron, the banker and miner from Tombstone. Baron had the claim surveyed in 1897 and the plat was approved in 1898.[13] According to reports, twenty-five tons of high-grade lead, silver, or zinc ores were shipped to Canon City, Colorado, in 1897. Forty-two tons were shipped in 1898–99.[14]

Baron had his claim surveyed and patented in 1898. In 1902 it was leased by the Mitchell Development Company of Ishpeming, Michigan. In 1904 the State of Texas Mines consisted of three tunnels, a shaft nearly 250 feet deep, and another shaft not quite as deep. Copper had been found in the main shaft at 300 feet and—in later, diamond-drilled holes—below 350 feet. In 1906 Mitchell Development Company liquidated its assets there and Gray Metals Company took over. (The Mitchell operation throughout the canyon is detailed in chapter 5.[15])

By 1914 the State of Texas No. 2, Extension, Bonita, Josephine, and New York Mines had been added to the operation.[16] A new 350-foot vertical shaft was dug near the main workings of State of Texas No. 1 around the same time.[17] Records indicate that ore was cut at varying depths, but do not indicate the quality of ore. Although that shaft had caved in at the twenty-eight-foot level, Sparkes believed it could be rehabilitated.[18] In 1920 C. F. Willis reported in the *Arizona Mining Journal* that Gray Metals Company had shipped ore containing silver, lead, and zinc.[19]

August Baron died in 1913 and his mine properties were passed on to his wife, Christine. She promptly sold them to Douglas Gray of Tombstone, the owner of Gray Metals Company. In 1920 Gray took on two partners, Maurice Clark of Douglas and William H. Stilwell of Phoenix, and incorporated a new incarnation of the Gray Metals Company as a publicly owned corporation. Gray sold his mines to the new corporation in 1920 for $20,000. Only two years later, the State of Texas, Texas No. 2, Extension, Bonita, Josephine, and New York Mines were sold at public auction as part of a court judgment against Gray. Nathan L. Amster bought them in August 1922 for $9,370.90.[20]

In September 1926 T. J. Sparkes of Prescott, Arizona, and Burdett Moody of Los Angeles, California, purchased several mining claims in the Hartford Mining District from Nathan L. and Estelle D. Amster for $5,000. The purchase included the State of Texas, State of Texas No. 2, Extension, Bonita, Josephine, and New York Mines.[21] The partners did little or no mining over the next fifteen years.[22]

Moody had been a longtime associate of Grace Sparkes's father. In the late 1880s, Moody directed the Surveying Department of the Homestake Mining Company at Lead, South Dakota. In 1903 he was a board member of the Black Hill's Mining Men's Association, and in that same year he was elected president of the board.[23] In a January 1939 letter, Grace Sparkes told Burdett Moody that her father, T. J. Sparkes, had recently died; she discussed her family's efforts to reopen the State of Texas Mine. She added that she had not visited the property in two years.[24]

Moody replied that he and T. J. Sparkes had been hoping to sell the property and that he still wished to do so. He estimated that he had $8,000 to $9,000 invested in the mine property. A few months later he wrote that his cost was "in around $5,000 to $6,000 altogether."[25] Given that the property had cost only $5,000 and had not been operated since its purchase, it can be surmised that Moody had put up the vast amount of the partners' investment. T. J. Sparkes, a mining engineer, supplied expertise for the failing enterprise.[26]

Over the next few years Grace Sparkes continued to pursue loans to reopen the mine and encouraged Moody to support her. She shared ownership of a half interest in the State of Texas property with her siblings as joint heirs to their father, T. J. Sparkes. She seemed, however, to be the most active partner.

In 1940 Sparkes wrote to J. S. Coupal to request that he survey her mine. Sparkes hoped to mine zinc that had been found in the State of Texas Mine. She wrote to Coupal, "We should be able to do something to move the Texas property which was owned by my father and Mr. Burdette Moody of Los Angeles."[27] She added that she had authority to act in behalf of Moody's and her father's interest. In order to further her mining interests, she invited Coupal to survey her property to help determine the extent of the mineral wealth. By mid-October Coupal had arranged to see the mine and to meet with Perry L. Bones, who had been contracted to drill in the mine to test for mineral wealth.[28] The meeting date to inspect the mine had been set for October 16, 1940.[29] Bones, as it turned out, was Sparkes's brother-in-law.

In his report of October 19, 1940, Coupal wrote, "The major ore showing on the State of Texas claim is a replacement deposit of zinc-lead sulphides in the limestone at a distance of about 100 feet from the lime-granite contact. This ore body outcrops on the surface and is opened up by irregular workings which show a general dip of 23 degrees toward the contact—an inclined depth of about 70 feet, a length along the general strike of the contact of from 100 feet to 150 feet and a stope within one place of some 20 feet."[30] Almost unwittingly, Coupal concluded, "The area and particularly the State of Texas group of claims warrant active development." Those words were enough to propel Sparkes to develop her mine.

At that point in time, the mine had been developed to a shallow depth. The stopes, or steplike excavations, were a necessary feature to take out the ore after the shafts had been sunk. The crosscut or passageway that cut across the course of a vein of ore at the time was one hundred feet and had not reached the contact deposit. A shaft of about 240 feet had been sunk close to the contact deposit, but it, too, had not reached the ore.[31] Sparkes knew that work to develop the crosscut and the shaft could be easily justified. It would, however, take more excavation, time, and money to explore the value of the mine.

Meanwhile, Moody persisted in his desire to divest of the State of Texas properties.[32] Grace Sparkes was not alone in seeing the potential for turning a profit from the State of Texas. She and Moody received many offers from miners wishing to lease the property. None was accepted, as Sparkes was determined to keep the property and make it pay off for her rather than have others make money off her claim.[33]

Sparkes saw threats to the property from other sources as well, including the idea of the Coronado International Memorial. [In April

1940 Sparkes wrote to Moody, "I have done a good deal of work also to protect the claims against the Coronado Exposition idea," meaning the memorial. She continued that this "has meant work with the Arizona Commission, The Forestry, U.S., Park and other officials."[34] During the same month, Sparkes wrote to Margaret Rockwell of the Arizona Commission, the Coronado Cuarto Centennial Commission. Although she assured Mrs. Rockwell of her support for the memorial, her primary concern was that it not threaten her mine holdings.[35] Two years later, she informed Moody that the "entire camp was stolen when the CCC [Civilian Conservation Corps] constructed the road through the canyon."[36]] Despite her hidden agenda, the name of Grace Sparkes first surfaced in connection with the memorial in a large way during World War II. As a promoter of southern Arizona, she had shown interest in the memorial at an earlier date.

In 1942 Grace Sparkes gained total control of the State of Texas Mine property. By June of that year Moody had quitclaimed his share with the stipulation that he would receive half of future net profits or half of the net proceeds of any future sale.[37] In September the other Sparkes's heirs quitclaimed their shares to Grace as well.[38] That year she finally obtained a loan from the federal government under the Strategic Metals Act of 1942 in connection with the World War II effort.[39] Sparkes's mine produced zinc, among other metals, from 1943 to 1946.[40]

Sparkes operated the mines seven days a week by scheduling three shifts of two men each. Perry Bones, her brother-in-law, supervised the work. The ore was taken to Shattuck Denn Mill in Lowell, which was the first mill nearby that could separate the zinc from lead ore. At one time, the State of Texas Mines had its own processing mill, albeit primitive, that closed in 1917.[41] Until World War II erupted, the mines had been idle.

The war was a boon to the State of Texas Mines. During the three-year period, the mill processed 1,784 tons that resulted in 330,000 pounds of zinc from Sparkes's mines. Operations at the mines were entirely shut down in 1947. By 1948, the mine consisted of one patented claim and six unpatented claims.[42]

Burdett Moody died in 1946. It is unclear what the relationship between Moody and Sparkes was at the time and whether his widow retained any interest in the property.[43] As the 1950s began, nonetheless, Sparkes controlled the State of Texas property, but mining ceased being her primary interest. She was also active in promoting the memorial.

Just what did the State of Texas Mines contain that compelled its owners to invest time, labor, and money to develop it? In the face of Apache raiders, nineteenth-century Mexican miners risked their lives for the paltry silver, copper, and gold ores they could excavate. Eventually, Apache raiders ran them out of the Huachucas. As time passed, so too did sovereignty over the land change their claim to the land. After 1853 the United States took over southern Arizona. New investors arrived and prospected areas once mined by Mexican miners. Then in the 1880s a new technology and a new demand for different ores created a new promise for mining in the Huachucas.

World War I brought a new demand for copper and lead, and World War II brought an additional demand for zinc. Those three minerals, along with the hope that gold and silver would also be plentiful in the Huachucas, attracted speculators into the area. Thus, the mining reports became a very important facet of the history of the State of Texas Mines. All of the reports indicated certain quantities and percentages of silver, gold, lead, copper, zinc, and willemite were present. The reports usually had one effect on speculators: it whetted their appetites and desires for immeasurable wealth. One of the earliest assessments of the State of Texas Mines was made in 1920.

Tonnage was a major factor in reporting the quantities of ores found in the State of Texas Mines. Extraction of ores derived from how far a vein of ore could be tracked and pulled out from the earth. C. F. Willis's report represents the repeated hopes of all the owners of the State of Texas Mines from 1880 to 1979. Yet an old French saying applied to the mines of southern Arizona: "The more things change, the more they remain the same." The reports on the State of Texas Mines from 1920 to 1959 exemplified that dictum.

The report of 1920 concerning Gray Metals Co. in the Huachuca Mountains explained the early pattern of assaying ore from the State of Texas Mines. That report, abstracted from an article written by C. F. Willis in *Arizona Mining Journal*, reflected the latest information about the ores that had been extracted.[44] The history of the Gray Metals Company, which operated the State of Texas Mine, indicated that the owners believed the mine could operate on a high margin of profit. Willis's article explained, "Over 500 tons of ore have been shipped which average 17 ozs in silver, 7.5% lead and 22 to 24% zinc. High grade ore shows 84 oz in silver, 40% lead and 18% zinc. The silver follows the lead and with an increase in lead there is a decrease in zinc content." The quantity and variety of ores produced by the mine undoubtedly showed promise. In his report of 1920 Willis described an early opening of the mine shaft and its contents and indicated that copper had been struck after drilling between 170 and 310 feet. Smaller amounts of gold and silver were also noted.[45]

Sixteen years later, on October 2, 1936, a report, "Mineral Claim: State of Texas Mine,"[46] indicated new owners. They were T. J. Sparkes and Burdett Moody, who had clear title to the property. That year, 1936, the State of Texas Mine claimed values based on one thousand tons of ore containing varying amounts of gold, silver, copper, lead, and zinc. The Mineral Claim presented an estimate demonstrating the character of the ore with a strong zinc–lead outcrop. The report, furthermore, stated that the mine "as in the 'Upper Zone'[had] a potential possibility of 20,000 tons of ore."[47]

The owners of the mine, T. J. Sparkes and Burdett Moody, proudly proclaimed, "Mines of this kind are better known in Mexico, where they have been in successful operation for many years." They estimated that it would take $30,000 to develop and equip the property "with at least a 25 ton pilot mill, thereby enabling the mine to pay a fair profit, and develop to a greater producing tonnage, ultimately developing a 'paying mine' and one of long life."[48]

In 1940 Harold Ferrin, a geologist and geophysicist, wrote Diamond Drilling Report of Radar Geophysical Service from a survey he had made of the mine.[49] Ferrin's report became the basis of other reports made by other inspectors who quoted from it. The notations in his report indicated that the first test took place at Hole No. 1, "S 20 E" at the "End N Drift in War Stope. The depth of the hole was 81 feet. 'Depth starter hole 47.' Used old diamond drill hole, which was not collared for standpipe and therefore difficult to get accurate sludge recovery."[50] The exact amount of ore cored was ten feet three inches. The dip, or downward slope from horizontal, was calculated at 52 degrees; mineral deposits were encountered between sixty and sixty-two feet.[51] The geology of the tested holes indicated that Ferrin and Perry Bones had drilled through one foot four inches of marble to blue lime, then three feet six inches of blue lime, and seven feet of garnet and garnetized lime. Ferrin and his team performed a second test "made at Hole No. 2 to a depth of 97 feet. Its dip was calculated at 63 degrees." They encountered minerals at "64 feet to 70 feet, and cored about 6 feet of it."[52] Indeed, Ferrin had, using modern engineering techniques, unlocked the mystery of the State of Texas Mines.

Following Ferrin's report, J. S. Coupal made a thorough reconnaissance of the mines and produced a highly technical report on October

29, 1940, entitled "Synoptic Report of State of Texas Mine."[53] His report showed that the assayed ores were very promising. His analysis demonstrated the following quantities and percentages of ores containing gold, silver, copper, lead, and zinc.

	Gold	Silver	Copper	Lead	Zinc
300 tons	0.08 oz.	13.22 oz.	0.80%	7.50%	24.00%
200 tons	0.02 oz.	6.60 oz.	54%	2.80%	16.50%

Coupal followed up with a second report: "Supplemental Report, State of Texas Mine," submitted on May 1, 1941. That report supplemented the Synoptic Report of the State of Texas Mine completed on October 29, 1940. Coupal again visited the property on April 13, 1941 in order to check former samplings and to "roughly sketch the underground workings of the silver-zinc-led deposit."[54] Along with his descriptions of the mine, he wrote, "A blueprint is attached showing the major workings on this deposit."[55] Of the State of Texas Mine, Coupal wrote,

> The plan and cross-section show an incline stope, sunk from the surface on the outcrop, which varies in width of from ten to forty feet: is about 80 feet in length on the slope and shows a thickness of ore of from four to six feet. The stoped area is cut by a tunnel, the elevation of which is 34 feet below the collar of the stope.
>
> The ore occurs as a lense, in the bedding plane of the limestone, which at this points [*sic*] dips about 23 degrees from the horizontal and to the north. There is a vertical winze near the end of the stope which is filled with gob and is only accessible to a depth of five feet below the tunnel level, with the collar set of the winze [an inclined passage connecting two levels below the surface] timbered and exposed. Two feet to the north of the winze an east–west fault, dipping about vertical, cuts off the major ore showing.
>
> Flat incline winzes from 25 to 30 feet in length have been driven as exploration work beyond the winze mentioned above. Another 15 foot inclined winze is driven to the east at a point about 10 feet south of the vertical winze.
>
> On the surface there are four cuts, or trenches, which vary from ten to 40 feet in length. These are shallow trenches and have not cut the extension of the ore body exposed in the major inclined stope.[56]

Coupal then included samples taken and assayed by H. C. Smoot, of

Prescott, Arizona. He attached the "Assay Certificate of H. C. Smoot."[57] Like Ferrin, Coupal had advanced the knowledge about the State of Texas Mines to reflect its potential production.

Other information corroborated Ferrin's and Coupal's findings. The smelter at Shattuck Denn Corporation released a series of ore reports in quick succession with varied and hopeful results that would suggest the need for further exploration. Two years after Coupal's report, on May 14, 1943, Shattuck Denn Corporation submitted an ore settlement report on ores that was received on May 3, 1943.[58] Nearly two weeks after the first report, Shattuck Denn Corporation submitted a second ore settlement report on ores that was received on May 25, 1943.[59] The following month, Shattuck Denn Corporation submitted another ore settlement report on ores that was received on June 2 and 5, 1943[60] Two weeks later, Shattuck Denn Corporation submitted one more ore settlement report on ores that was received on June 11, 1943.[61]

At the end of the 1940s Ferrin returned to survey the State of Texas Mines. His findings, submitted on July 4, 1948, entitled "Diamond Drilling Report—Radar Geophysical Service Survey Made by Harold Ferrin," were based on surveys on other areas of the mine. Regarding "Hole No. 3, located at the end north drift war stope," Ferrin reported that it "had a dip of 90 degrees and a depth of 102 feet." Oddly, he recommended that it would be "Necessary to drill this hole 25' deeper to hit ore body and footwall."[62] A later report, made by Axel Johnson in 1951, recommended that Ferrin should have drilled another twenty-five feet to hit the ore he sought.[63]

Meanwhile, a report dated August 1951 included "appended notes dated May 26, 1959." It contained a "Copy letter American Smelting & Refinding [*sic*] Company" in Tucson, Arizona, dated August 8, 1951.[64]

Finally, in September 1951, Axel L. Johnson made a reconnaissance of the State of Texas Mines. He submitted his report on September 11, 1951. Johnson confirmed that Miss Grace Sparkes of Hereford, Arizona, owned the patented claims. He listed the claims as follows: "State of Texas #1. State of Texas #2. State of Texas Mill Site #1, and State of Texas Mill Site #2."[65]

The samples he examined in the State of Texas #1 were determined "by geophysical methods," to extend 120 feet "on the strike." It was twelve feet wide and about four hundred feet deep. Johnson reported, "The dip was 63 degrees to the north." In his report, he confirmed Ferrin's report of August 1947. Johnson wrote that the geophysical work of April and May

1948 was "partially checked by 2 drill holes to a depth of about 100 feet below the surface." It was found to be accurate "to that depth."[66]

Johnson noted that a considerable amount of ore had already been mined from this area in the top 30 to 40 feet. He attributed the removal of ore by the following entities:

1. By early Spanish and Mexican miners—an unknown quantity of ore near the surface—probably not over 500 tons.
2. By Miss Sparkes, under Government Loan (1942–1946)—2000 tons was mined and shipped. This ore averaged 15.9% Zinc, 32.15% Lead, 1.74% Copper, 9.09 oz of silver, and 0.578 oz of gold.
3. By Miss Sparkes during the same period (1942 to 1946)—1500 tons placed on dumps for future milling. This is estimated by Miss Sparkes to contain approx. $35 per ton in values.[67]

In his survey, he included an assay report on the drill holes made during his reconnaissance of the State of Texas Mines that showed varying amounts of zinc, lead, copper, and silver.

D.H. No 1	60 to 68 ft.	Zinc 27.6%	Lead 0.2%		
D.H. No. 1	70 to 72 ft.	Zinc 45.2%	Lead 0.3%	Copper 4.16%	Silver 9.0 oz.
D.H. No. 2	64 to 70 ft.	Zinc 25.1%	Lead 0.1%		Silver 2.2 oz.
D.H. No. 3. This hole was drilled vertical, while the other holes were drilled at right angles to the dip. It was drilled to a depth of 102 ft. or more. Mr. Ferrin's report states, "Necessary to drill this hole 25 ft. deeper to hit ore body and footwall. This hole should have been continued 25 ft. further."[68]					

Next, Johnson reported on the ore deposit of State of Texas #1. He said that the caved-in areas were still notable, making it inaccessible for inspection. He stated, moreover, "No former records indicated the extent of the deposit, or the quantity of ore that had been mined from it." He added that no work was contemplated in the near future. As if whispering into his report, Johnson wrote, "According to hearsay evidence, about $250,000 worth of zinc and copper ore was mined from this deposit."[69] It was difficult for him to predict how much ore remained in that particular deposit, but he advised that extensive work would be required to reopen the caved-in shaft and drifts.

His thoughts on the State of Texas #2 ore deposits were a bit more knowledgeable. The deposit, determined by geophysical measurements, extended 72 feet in length and five to six feet in width. The depth reached about 300 feet. He predicted that the probable ore from that deposit could be 7,500 tons, but most of it would be classified as direct shipping ore. He noted that the old workings consisted of a 28-foot shaft and a number of open cuts scattered about the hillside. One of them contained ore that showed 55.7 ounces of silver. The ore also contained 14.83 percent of lead, 1.15 percent of zinc, and 1.61 percent of copper. He wrote, "No ore of any appreciable amount has been mined from this deposit, and no drilling has been done to prove up the geophysical work."[70]

Johnson's general remarks at the end of the report recommended a brighter future for the mine than the one Sparkes saw, although the report probably gave her renewed hope and vindication that her work had been worthwhile. Johnson wrote,

> From the evidence that I saw in the present working, and from the evidence I obtained from the geophysical report and from the subsequent drilling, I would consider this property well worth of further exploration by means of a Government Exploration Loan.
>
> Such an Exploration Loan would:
>
> (1) On State of Texas #1—prove up some 20,000 to 30,000 tons of ore indicated by the geophysical work, prove the depth, width and extent of the deposit below the 70 foot level, and develop the deposit for future mining operations that should prove profitable for the owner, and which would provide the Government with some badly needed ore supplies.
>
> (2) On State of Texas #2—prove up some 7,500 tons of ore indicated by the geophysical work, prove the depth, width, and extent of the deposit, and develop the deposit for future profitable mining operations. The proposed 835 ft. tunnel may possibly also intersect ore veins.[71]

It seemed that the State of Texas Mines had high profit potential. A report issued in May 1959 regarding the "State of Texas No. 1 Patented Lode" estimated that the ore sent to Shattuck Denn Custom Mill had a high value: "This basis estimated value of this ore block - $2,800,000.00." However, the "Immediate Known Ore Reserves" were reckoned to have a "Total Value 9500 tons–$552,500."[72]

The same report, "State of Texas Mine No. 2—Patented," included an evaluation of the lead content of the mine. It read, "Partial Geophysical Survey recorded mineralized zone 72' long—5 to 6' wide and 300' long along the incline. Indicated about 9,000 tons high grade lead. This claim has unusual copper showings, which are also on No. 1."[73] Still, a caveat was written to explain the high numbers in the report. It reads, "It should be noted that we only shipped our higher grade ore to the custom mill bearing in mind that our Serial No. would be withdrawn if we did not bring out the highest zinc possible. There are huge tonnages of low grade - mineral rock - on this property. (We know shippers sent 4% zinc to custom mill during war period and collected premiums.) With proper exploration, development and modern methods of treatment huge tonnages could be handled from our property."[74]

In the end, the State of Texas Mines never lived up to its promises of great wealth. Much work, sweat, and tears had been shed over the mining enterprises undertaken to develop the State of Texas Mines. Indeed, Grace Sparkes had devoted much of the last years of her life to the mine which, in the end, left her heavily in debt. Today, the mine lies fallow as if awaiting the dawn of a new day to beckon another optimistic, starry-eyed gambler—or a new world economy that needs its resources—a day that will never come as long as the NPS owns the property.[75]

Appendix 4A

The lead-zinc deposit has been opened up by an inclined shaft and tunnel, from both of which considerable stoping has been done. Then at intervals of about fifty feet, trenches have been cut on the surface which demonstrate the continuity of the deposit. Almost from the surface the sulphides show, and two layers of the ore have been shown, while the surface indicates a third layer. Little work has been done except on the second highest of these layers and this shows from 7-11 ft in thickness with an average assay of 16.5 oz silver, 10% lead, 21% zinc, while the ore on the dump extracted from this and other places, shows 11.5 oz of silver, 7.85% lead and 22.5% zinc.

The copper bearing contact of the lime-granite has been opened by 350 ft shaft with considerable drifting, with 1390 ft of diamond drill holes sent out from the 350 ft level. The first of these holes struck ore at 170 ft and ran 20 ft through ore running 4-6% copper. . . . The second hole, at about 300 ft ran through four layers of ore 3, 5, 6 and 7 ft thick respectively, the latter assaying 6% copper. The third hole showed blank with the exception of the first ten feet. No ore has been encountered outside the limestone. The contact deposits have been opened also by two 50 ft shafts following the contact. At 310 feet the shaft passed through 13 feet of copper ore running better than 4% copper and 3.3 oz in silver.

Supplemental Report, State of Texas Mine, Engineer J.S. Coupal, May 1, 1941, Arizona State Department of Mines and Minerals, Phoenix, AZ.[76]

Appendix 4B

Sample #1. Representative sample of a small pile of sorted ore located near the portal of the working tunnel and on top of the number 2 dump. Estimated about 3 tons. A 50 pound sample from about ten spots was taken, broken, mixed and quartered to a 3 pound sample which assayed as follows: 0.04 ounces gold, 13.0 ounces silver, 7.6% lead, 25.3% zinc.

Sample #2. The No. 2. Dump at the portal of tunnel, estimated at about 200 tons of ore. This sample was taken from about 20 shallow cuts at 5 foot intervals on the surface of dump and on the slope of dump. A sample of about 100 pounds was taken, crushed, mixed and quartered to about 10 pounds which assayed as follows: 0.05 ounces gold, 8.2 ounces silver, 2.2% lead, 9.6% zinc.

Sample #3. The No. 1 dump located at the portal of the inclined stope is estimated at [a]bout 300 tons of ore. Sample was taken in the same manner as sample #2 and assayed as follows: 0.05 ounces gold, 10.2 ounces silver, 4.9% lead, 20.9% zinc.

Sample #4. Located on the west side of vertical winze, about 3 feet below the collar of winze, tunnel level, across a three feet width of ore. A rough channel cut taken with a moil. About a 10 pound sample, assayed as follows: 0.05 ounces gold; 4.3 ounces silver; trace lead; 20.9% zinc.

Sample #5. Located on the East wall of tunnel, which at this point is really a part of the stope as it shows a width of 20 feet. Sample taken over a width of 3 feet. A rough channel cut taken with moil. About 10 pound sample which assayed as follows: 0.05 ounces gold, 14.4 ounces silver, 5.9% lead and 20.0 zinc.

Samples #4 and 5 were taken as merely representing two points on the ore exposed in the incline stope. Both walls of the stope show ore from the surface to the vertical winze.

The development suggested is to drift east and west on ore at a point near the vertical winze and to drive such raises as are necessary to block out a sufficient tonnage of ore so as to justify further exploration work by sinking, drilling, or by geo-physical work.

Notes

1. J. S. Coupal, "Synoptic Report of State of Texas Mine," October 19, 1940, Arizona State Department of Mines and Minerals, Phoenix, AZ.

2. Coupal, "Synoptic Report," ibid.

3. "Location of Mines" Record Books, book 1, pages 95, Cochise County Recorder.

4. For the Elías family, see Tom Sheridan's *Los Tucsonenses* (Tucson: University of Arizona Press, 1985); for the Copper Queen Mine, see Lynn Bailey, *Bisbee Queen of the Copper Camps* (Tucson, AZ: Westernlore Press, 1983).

5. The 1872 Mining Law, 30 U.S.C. §§ 22-42.

6. "Location Notices," book 1, 255–58, Cochise County Recorder.

7. Lynn Bailey, *Tombstone, Arizona* (Tucson, AZ: Westernlore Press, 2004); *Arizona Weekly Star,* September 5, December 2, 1879, January 14, February 7, 1880; *Tombstone Epitaph,* June 12, 1880.

8. County Recorders Office, Location Notices and Books of Deeds, and Great Register for 1886, and U.S. census for 1880 and 1900; Huachuca Mines file, Bisbee Mining and Historical Museum, Bisbee; Lynn Bailey and Don Chaput, *Cochise County Stalwarts* (Tucson, AZ: Westernlore Press, 2000), provides biographies of Baron and Gerdes.

9. David B. Rea, "The Mines of the Cananea," *Arizona Star,* November 21, 1878. Copy available at Arizona Historical Society, Tucson.

10. David B. Rea, "The Mines of the Cananea", *The Arizona Star,* Vol. II, Tucson, Thursday, November 21, 1878, Arizona Historical Society, Tucson.

11. "The Mule Pass Mines."

12. "The San Rafael Mines," *Arizona Star,* December 5, 1878. Copy available at Arizona Historical Society, Tucson.

13. Geoffrey T. Bohrer, "Siamese Triplets: Grace Sparks, The State of Texas Mine and the Coronado National Monument" (National Park Service, 1993), 1–2.

14. Gray Metals Co., Huachuca Mts. Abstracted from *Arizona Mining Journal* 3, no. 12 (1920): 21, by C. F. Willis in "Copy letter American Smelting & Refinding [*sic*] Company, Tucson, August 8, 1951 (appended notes dated May 26, 1959)," Arizona State Department of Mines and Minerals, Phoenix, AZ. Also see Robert D. O'Brien, "Appraisal of Mineral Interests Inherent in the State of Texas Mine Tracts No. 101-06, 101-07, 101-08 Coronado National Monument" (San Francisco: National Park Service, Western Region, 1979), 3, IPRPC Files.

15. Mineowners Report, May 26, 1959, signed by Grace Sparkes, Arizona State Department of Mines and Minerals, Phoenix, AZ.

16. Peter M. Van Cleve, "History of Mining in the Coronado National Memorial" (1997), Coronado National Memorial Files, 5–6.

17. State of Texas Mines, Field Engineers Report, by Axel L. Johnson, Phoenix, September 11, 1951, Arizona State Department of Mines and Minerals, Phoenix, AZ. The caved-in area was still notable in 1951.

18. Mine Owner's Report, Department of Mineral Resources, May 26, 1959, signed by Grace Sparkes, Arizona State Department of Mines and Minerals, Phoenix, AZ.

19. Gray Metals Co., Huachuca Mts. Abstracted from *Arizona Mining Journal* 3, no. 12 (1920): 21, by C.F. Willis in "Copy letter American Smelting & Refinding [*sic*]Company, Tucson, August 8, 1951 (appended notes dated May 26, 1959)." Also see O'Brien, "Appraisal of Mineral Interests," 4.

20. Peter M. Van Cleve, "History of Mining in the Coronado National Memorial" (1997), Coronado National Memorial Files, 6–7.

21. Sale Agreement, Nathan L. and Estelle D. Amster to T. J. Sparkes and Burdett Moody, September 1, 1926, Sparkes Collection, AHS, Box 12, Folder 464, Arizona Historical Society; Mining Deed, Nathan L. and Estelle D. Amster to T. J. Sparkes and Burdett Moody, September 27, 1926, Sparkes Collection, AHS, Box 12, Folder 470.

22. Peter M. Van Cleve, "History of Mining in the Coronado National Memorial" (1997), Coronado National Memorial Files, 8.

23. See Black Hills Illustrated, edited and published by George P. Baldwin under the auspices of the Black Hills Mining Men's Association, 1903.

24. Grace Sparkes, Burdett Moody, c/o The Bureau Light, Water and Power, Los Angeles, CA, Prescott, January 30, 1939, Sparkes Collection, AHS, Box 7, Folder 294.

25. Burdett Moody to Grace M. Sparkes, Los Angeles, February 1, 1939; Burdett Moody to Grace M. Sparkes, Los Angeles, May 4, 1939, Sparkes Collection, AHS, Box 7, Folder 294. The Sparkes papers contain sales contracts, never executed, from this period that confirm that the property was in negotiation for sale. See especially Box 12, Folders 465-467.

26. Peter M. Van Cleve, "History of Mining in the Coronado National Memorial" (1997), Coronado National Memorial Files, 7.

27. Grace Sparkes to J. S. Coupal, Prescott, September 27, 1940, Arizona State Department of Mines and Minerals, Phoenix, AZ.

28. Coupal to Sparkes, Phoenix, October 8, 1940, Arizona State Department of Mines and Minerals, Phoenix, AZ.

29. Sparkes to Coupal, October 7, 1940, Arizona State Department of Mines and Minerals, Phoenix, AZ.

30. "Synoptic Report of State of Texas Mine." Engineer J. S. Coupal, May 1, 1941, Arizona State Department of Mines and Minerals, Phoenix, AZ.

31. Ibid.

32. Burdett Moody to Grace M. Sparkes, Los Angeles, August 1, 1941, Sparkes Collection, AHS, Box 7, Folder 296, and others in the same folder.

33. See, in particular, Sparkes Collection, AHS, Box 7, Folder 294.

34. Grace M. Sparkes to Burdett Moody, April 22, 1940, Sparkes Collection, AHS, Box 7, Folder 295, and others in the same folder.

35. Letter, Grace M. Sparkes to Mrs. Foster Rockwell (Margaret), Vice Chairman, Arizona Commission, Coronado Cuarto Centennial Exposition, Prescott, April 11, 1940, Sparkes Collection, AHS, Box 23, Folder 956.

36. Grace M. Sparkes to Burdett Moody, April 7, 1942, Sparkes Collection, AHS, Box 7, Folder 297.

37. Mining Deed, Burdett and Sarah C. Moody sell and quitclaim to Grace Sparkes, June 9, 1942, Sparkes Collection, AHS, Box 12, Folder 470; also see Folder 468.

38. Mining Deed, Thomas J. Sparkes Jr. and wife Maybelle; Charity S. and Perry L. Bones; and Genevieve Sparkes, widow of John G. Sparkes; all of Yavapai County, sell and quitclaim all of the mine claims to Grace Sparkes, September 21, 1942, Sparkes Collection, AHS, Box 12, Folder 470.

39. "History of Coronado Activity," Coronado National Monument Files, WACC, Folder H 14.

40. Peter M. Van Cleve, "History of Mining in the Coronado National Memorial" (1997), Coronado National Memorial Files, p. 8.

41. "History of Coronado Activity," Coronado National Monument Files, WACC, Folder H 14.

42. Ibid.

43. Sarah Moody to Grace Sparkes, Los Angeles, 1946, Sparkes Collection, AHS, Box 7, Folder 299.

44. Gray Metals Co., Huachuca Mts. Abstracted from *Arizona Mining Journal,* Vol. 3, No. 12, (1920) : 21, by C. F. Willis in "Copy letter American Smelting & Refinding [*sic*] Company, Tucson, August 8, 1951 (appended notes dated May 26, 1959)."

45. See appendix 4A for the text of Willis's note.

46. Mineral Claim, State of Texas Mine, Bisbee, Arizona, October 2, 1936, Arizona State Department of Mines and Minerals, Phoenix, AZ.

47. The report, "Mineral Claim, State of Texas Mine," read as follows: *"Gold = .05 oz; Silver = 9.41 oz; Copper = .67%; Lead = 5.15%; and, Zinc 20.24%."* Mineral Claim, State of Texas Mine, Bisbee, AZ, October 2,1936, Arizona State Department of Mines and Minerals, Phoenix, AZ.

48. Ibid.

49. Diamond Drilling Report of Radar Geophysical Service survey Made by Harold Ferrin, geologist and geophycist [*sic*]. No date 1940, attached to Sparkes to Coupal, Prescott, September 27, 1940, Arizona State Department of Mines and Minerals, Phoenix, AZ.

50. Diamond Drilling Report of Radar Geophysical Service survey Made by Harold Ferrin, geologist and geophycist [*sic*]. No date 1940, attached to Sparkes to Coupal, Prescott, September 27, 1940, Arizona State Department of Mines and Minerals, Phoenix, AZ.

51. Ibid. The assay report was based on two samples: Sample No. 1: Taken at five feet six inches "below where ore was pierced. The extent of the core sample was 8 feet of ore. Gold = .02 oz; Silver = .28 oz; Copper = .09%; Lead + .2%; Zinc + 27.6%. Sample No. 2: Taken 25 and one half inches from Sample No. 1. The extent of the core sample was 2 feet of ore. Gold = .06 oz; Silver + 9.0 oz; Copper 4.16%; Lead + .3%; Zinc = 45.2%."

52. Ibid. The assay report indicated "Gold = .02 oz; Silver + 2.2 oz; Copper .05%; Lead + .1%; Zinc = 25.1%." The report went on to say that another test was made and reported the findings as follows: Sample No. 3 was taken at 64 feet. The assay showed "Gold = .02 oz; Silver = 2.2 oz; Copper = .05%; Lead = .1%; and Zinc =25.1%. Six feet of ore had been cored. The geology of the cored area indicated beddings of garnets, garnetized lime (at a depth of 64 feet), sulphides (at a depth of 64–70 feet); highly mineralized lime and garnets 75 to 89 feet; and porphyry granite at 89 to 97 feet."

53. "Synoptic Report of State of Texas Mine," Engineer J. S. Coupal, May 1, 1941, Arizona State Department of Mines and Minerals, Phoenix, AZ.

54. Supplemental Report, State of Texas Mine, Engineer J. S. Coupal, May 1, 1941, Arizona State Department of Mines and Minerals, Phoenix, AZ.

55. Blueprint could not be located in file.

56. Supplemental Report, State of Texas Mine, Engineer J.S. Coupal, May 1, 1941, Arizona State Department of Mines and Minerals, Phoenix, AZ.

57. Ibid. The assay analyses were made from the samples as shown in the report. Please see appendix 4B.

58. Shattuck Denn Corporation Ore Settlement report of May 14, 1943 on State of Texas ores received on May 3, 1943, Arizona State Department of Mines and Minerals, Phoenix, AZ. In the report, the gross assay, based on 54.682 tons, indicated the following minerals: "Gold = .02 oz.; Silver = 8.50 oz; Copper =.28%; Lead = 4.05%; Zinc =10.70%."

59. Shattuck Denn Corporation Ore Settlement report on State of Texas ores received on May 25, 1943, Arizona State Department of Mines and Minerals, Phoenix, AZ. In the report, the gross assay," based on 49.687 tons, indicated the following minerals: "Gold = .01 oz.; Silver = 2.75 oz; Copper =.34%; Lead = 1.42%; Zinc =14.5%."

60. Shattuck Denn Corporation Ore Settlement report on State of Texas ores received on June 2 and 5, 1943, Arizona State Department of Mines and Minerals, Phoenix, AZ. In the report, the gross assay, based on 106.357 tons, indicated the following minerals: "Gold = .020 oz.; Silver = 10.95 oz; Copper =.52%; Lead = 4.05%; Zinc =16.40%."

61. Shattuck Denn Corporation Ore Settlement report on State of Texas ores received on June 11, 1943, Arizona State Department of Mines and Minerals, Phoenix, AZ. In the report, the gross assay, based on 55.279 tons, indicated the following minerals: Gold = .015 oz.; Silver = 10.70 oz; Copper =.71%; Lead = 3.57%; Zinc =19.40%.

62. Diamond Drilling Report—Radar Geophysical Service Survey made by Harold Ferrin, geologist and geophycist [*sic*], July 4, 1948, Arizona State Department of Mines and Minerals, Phoenix, AZ.

63. "Copy letter American Smelting & Refinding [*sic*] Company, Tucson, August 8, 1951 (appended notes dated May 26, 1959)", Arizona State Department of Mines and Minerals, Phoenix, AZ.

64. "Copy letter American Smelting & Refinding [*sic*] Company, Tucson, August 8, 1951 (appended notes dated May 26, 1959)." The assay sample report indicated the following minerals: "Gold = .016 oz; Silver = 10.82 oz; Lead = 5.99%; Copper = 0.42%; and Zinc = 22.5%. Non-sulphide minerals = .5%."

65. The following discussion is based on Axel L. Johnson, "State of Texas Mines, Field Engineers Report," September 11, 1951, Arizona State Department of Mines and Minerals, Phoenix, AZ, 1.

66. Ibid.

67. Ibid.

68. Ibid. D.H. = drill hole.

69. Ibid.

70. Ibid.

71. Ibid.

72. "Copy letter American Smelting & Refinding [*sic*] Company, Tucson, August 8, 1951 (appended notes dated May 26, 1959)." Arizona State Department of Mines and Minerals, Phoenix, AZ.

73. Ibid.

74. Ibid.

75. Because there are no existing patented or valid unpatented mining claims at Coronado National Memorial, mining within its boundaries is illegal. See 36 Code of Federal

Regulations (CFR) Part 2.1 (a) and part 2.5 (a) and CFR, Part 9, Subpart A. Mining is prohibited in all units of the National Park System. Also the Mining Act of 1872 prohibited mining in all parks. However, in 1933 mining was allowed in Death Valley National Park. The Mining in the Parks Act (1976) closed Death Valley National Monument to mining and the filing of new mining claims, banned open-pit mining in parks, and required the NPS to investigate and monitor all mining claims.

76. C. F. Willis, Abstracted from *Arizona Mining Journal*, Vol. 3, No. 12, 1920, Gray Metals Co., Huachuca Mountains, p. 21.

CHAPTER 5

Prospectors, Speculators, and Miners

The Origins, Decline, and Fateful End of the Doredor Mines Group

Property gives a fine showing of rich surface ores. . . . Company is composed of experienced mining men with strong financial backing, and the property is to be developed vigorously.

— *Copper Handbook*, 1903[1]

Although authorized in 1941, Coronado National Memorial was not established until 1952. In 1978 the boundary was expanded to the north side of Montezuma Canyon, which included the Doredor and other mines. In 1980 the NPS acquired the Doredor Mines as part of the memorial.[2] The history of the Doredor Mines is old, probably reaching back to Spanish colonial and Mexican period times when Hispanic miners ventured into Montezuma Canyon. Traces of their work have been noted over time. Certainly, by the late-nineteenth-century Anglo-American prospectors had wandered into Montezuma Canyon following rumors of Spanish mining in the area. Since that time, and into the early twentieth century, prospectors, speculators, and miners, hoping for untold wealth, created what would be known as the Doredor Group, a collection of low-producing mining sites in Montezuma Canyon. Their story began as speculators planned their marketing schemes around the hopes of others.

Looking to buy a few claims near the rich Copper Queen mine at Bisbee, Arizona, in 1899 a group of mining men met in Calumet, Michigan, to organize a company that would suit their needs. They decided to take a chance on a questionable mining operation called the Irish Mag claim, twenty-five miles east of Bisbee. By February 1901 they had sunk a shaft and hit an ore body that eventually netted for the backers of the Calumet & Arizona Mining Company $245 million worth of copper. Their discovery set off speculators on a frenzied search for similar ore bodies throughout the region.[3]

Meanwhile, in 1902 two other speculators, Samuel Mitchell, a Michigan banker and mining man, and James Chenowith, an investor in the Michigan copper mines, decided to take a chance on claims in the Huachucas. With their Michigan partners, they formed the Mitchell Development Company. Mitchell served as president and Chenowith as vice president. By the end of the year, the Mitchell Development Company had created option claims to a total of sixty-four potential mines, including the State of Texas and what would become the Doredor Group. Before long, the company stock shot up as reports were made of favorable findings of copper ore in the Montezuma canyon claims.[4]

In June 1878 one of the first stakings of a part of the Doredor Group occurred when John L. Harris and George A. Roskruge, both surveyors, staked several claims. One of the claims, the Augusta Extension, was on what would later be part of the Doredor. It appears that Harris and Roskruge did little more than the annual assessment work before abandoning the claim in 1884.

Meanwhile, Peter Conner, Charles Mansur, and Ambroise Chedal each restaked or worked other claims in the canyon as well another part of later known Doredor.[5] The Panic of 1893 caused many of the claims to be abandoned in the area. In the wake of the Panic, particularly after January 1, 1901, Chedal restaked several claims as his and renamed them the Enterprise #1 to #4 claims, which later became part of the Doredor Group. On January 11, 1901, Gus Baron helped him file and record the claims.[6] These mining activities were generally small scale or nonexistent. Merely moving around claim stakes was sufficient to hold the ground without any actual mining. That way the prospector could sell the claim without having to mine it. For marketability purposes, shallow, primitive pits, called prospects, exposed or displayed the potential for finding a major ore body. Prospects commonly predominated in the region. Thus, many nineteenth-century operations in Montezuma Canyon were prospects, and were not mines aimed at luring investors.

Investors were needed to open the claims, and the Mitchell Development Company would entice them. In 1902 lawyer William Bateman of Calumet, Michigan, for Mitchell and Chenowith, began bonding for purchase claims in Montezuma Canyon. He acquired thirty-three claims in the canyon, nearly all of the claims in the area, inclusive of Chedal's Enterprise numbers 1 through 4. Chedal received from Bateman $2,000 up front with a promissory note for the remaining $10,000 after two years. On January 31, 1903, as the front man for the Mitchell Development

Company of Ishpeming, Michigan, Bateman exchanged his interests in the claims for 1,250 shares of stock in the company worth $10 per share.[7]

In the first reports to the *Copper Handbook,* the industry investment bible, Bateman, who had become the company secretary, touted the prospects. The *Handbook* reported that the mines included an "old mine operated under Spanish dominion." Furthermore, indicated the *Handbook,* the mines were managed by "experienced mining men with strong financial backing." The publicity statement promised that the "property is to be developed vigorously."[8] As an example of that promise, a stockholder who had visited the mines reported to the Calumet, Michigan, newspaper, "He[the stockholder] is very enthusiastic over what he saw."[9] Portraying the company's spirit of optimism, the *Copper Handbook* added, "The management is honest and conservative. The prospects of the property. . . were decidedly promising."[10]

The Mitchell Development Company constructed a camp near the mine site. Just below the future Doredor Mines site and a little southeast of the State of Texas Mines, the compound consisted of a wood frame camp with office/assay shop, residences, and mess hall. A fifteen-mile wagon road connected the mines to the railroad siding at Hereford. Travel during winter, however, was hampered because of the lack of a bridge across the San Pedro River. Although the presently existing shaft and adit of the Enterprise (Doredor) were initiated, the Mitchell Development Company focused its work on the adjacent State of Texas Mines.

Plans were initiated for a mill in the canyon. Steam and gasoline hoist engines were brought in for excavating a shaft in the main outcrop. The hoist house and head frame operated a steam hoist at the Enterprise (Doredor). Remnants of this machinery can still be seen at the mine site. On a terrace near the adit, a compressor and blacksmith shop were situated. Similar operations were commenced at the State of Texas Mines. Crude wagon roads up the hillside connected both mines to the compound.

Unfortunately, as the two-year time allowed under the options-to-purchase neared its deadline, the management and claim owners could not agree on an extension of time. Greed had intervened. The mine owners now thought their properties worth more, double the initial price offering. The Michigan mining men balked. According to the *Engineering & Mining Journal,* "It is supposed the company is through."[11] The *Copper Handbook* for 1905, the industry watchdog publication, noted that the company was reorganized and a year extension given on the bonds, but no major ore body had been found by the end of the year.

In 1906 the Mitchell Development Company had collapsed, and the claims reverted to their original owners. Sadly, many of the owners, including those of the future Doredor Mines, had failed to demonstrate that they had developed their claims as was required to hold onto them. In the end, the most important contribution made by the Mitchell Development Company was the opening of the Doredor.[12]

The failure of the Mitchell Development Company led to the rise of H. Bruce Doredor in Montezuma Canyon. Two years earlier in about 1904, 43-year-old Doredor had traveled from Ohio and arrived at Lowell, a suburb of Bisbee, to work as a miner. Then, Doredor had invested in Bisbee lots and rental housing, including the Copper Queen Boarding House on Chihuahua Hill.[13] By 1905 he was making loans to claim holders. Interestingly, the aging Charles Mansur, a mining stakeholder in Montezuma Canyon, was one of Doredor's clients. When the Mitchell Development Company failed in 1906, Mansur transferred his Montezuma Canyon claims to Bruce Doredor as payment on his loan.[14]

Doredor's holdings began to grow. In 1907–8 he acquired Chedal's numbers 1 through 4 through Bisbee saloon man Charles Gerdes (who had temporarily restaked them as the Paris numbers 1 through 4). Doredor restaked them again as the Paring numbers 1 through 4. On April 14, 1908, he staked the Doredor claim consisting of old claims that lay partially over the old adjacent to the State of Texas group. Moving swiftly to grab other old claims, most of them abandoned by prospectors who had hoped to sell to the Mitchell Development Company, Doredor staked and claimed other mining sites in the canyon. Doredor formed a partnership with Joseph McCabe, another Ohioan, age forty-three in 1910, to acquire other claims. McCabe moved to the canyon with his wife Belle and nephew Earl. Hoping to acquire the State of Texas, they learned that Gus Baron had leased the property to his Tombstone mining friend, Douglas Grey. With McCabe on site, Doredor had, by 1910, acquired three blocks of claims over a two-mile stretch along Montezuma Canyon. By far, the Doredor Group (Doredor, Paring number 1 through 4) was the most promising.[15]

During the 1910s and 1920s, Doredor worked as a real estate agent and mine broker in Bisbee. The Bisbee business directory listed him as living at 11 Naco Road, and later at 45 Naco Road, the main highway into Bisbee from the south. Tax lists indicated that he owned a dozen small rental houses of either adobe or wood frame. Indeed, the 1920 and 1930 census enumeration sheets showed he owned his home (worth $500 in

1930 Depression-era dollars) and rented rooms. Doredor was a bachelor all his life, but an odd affidavit by McCabe in the Cochise County Records states that in 1920 Bruce Doredor did not have a wife. Doredor died on December 21, 1932. He was buried in Bisbee's Evergreen Cemetery.[16]

There is little doubt that Bruce Doredor acquired the Doredor claims as a speculator. Like others in the area, he probably hoped that he could sell his claims to an exploration company like the Mitchell Development Company. During the 1910s and 1920s, when the Bisbee copper mining district was at its peak, Doredor and others hoped new investors would be willing to speculate on prospects in Montezuma Canyon. Meanwhile, Doredor needed to complete the $100 assessment work required each year on each claim in order to hold it.

During the World War I era, 1913–18, Doredor, McCabe, and their Bisbee backers informally organized an operating company based in Bisbee. The works, of course, would be at the Doredor Group in Montezuma Canyon. The group hired a manager and crew to continue blasting the adit, which eventually reached a depth of 450 feet. As a marketing ploy, a cut along the outcrop was opened only to show the bright copper stain at its bottom. The old camp built by the Mitchell Development Company at the base of the hill was reused. Too, the houses and mess hall, office and assay shop, as well as the equipment at the mine workings were still standing.

During the high mineral market prices of World War I, the Doredor Mines appeared productive. Its ore was sent downhill to a custom mill near Hereford for processing by a steam traction engine, remnants of which remain at the mine site. Custom mills bought ore from miners, processed the batch, and then charged a set fee for milling. Often the transportation and milling costs were higher than the cash given miners for ore sales. Production at the Doredor was low and costs high. The Doredor soon shut down.[17] In the end, with the collapse of the mineral market after World War I, the Doredor, like many other operations in the West, shut down. The Doredor Mines, never a consistent producer, proved to be a poor choice as an investment.[18]

To protect his property, Bruce Doredor continued to keep a small workforce or watchman at the site. The 1920 census lists Juan Flores as the only miner in Montezuma Canyon. With his wife Jesús María and their two children, Flores lived among the ruins and rubble stone structures. It is possible that he worked for Doredor doing annual assessment work on his many claims. Meanwhile, he and his family guarded Doredor's interests in Montezuma Canyon.

In the interim, Doredor pressed forward to assert his ownership over his mining claims in Montezuma Canyon. On June 10, 1922, the federal government granted him the mineral patent to the Doredor Group of five claims (Doredor, number 1 through 4). On the same day he also received a patent to the little-worked eight claim group up the canyon from the Doredor Group—the Z. T. Parker, Chief, Fraction, Rubio, Tunnelsite, Miss Stake, Grub Stake number 2, Grub Stake number 3.[19] If nothing else, Doredor had become the undisputed owner of what became known as the Doredor Group.

After Doredor died in 1932, several speculators attempted short-lived ventures. They attempted to reopen the mine, but none of them were able to find any additional metal. In 1938–39 the last serious effort to open the mines was made by Bill Clark and Bill Smith, a couple of out-of-work Bisbee miners. This final attempt was typical of the Great Depression era small-scale miners in the mountains. They refurbished the camp and built a garage, but soon gave up without producing any ore. Especially with the closing of the major mines in the 1930s, most miners like Clark and Smith turned to operating old claims. Upon finding a lead or stringer of ore, they extracted what they could and moved on. Clark and Smith hung on to their claims until the 1950s. Aside from the Doredor they also worked the Parker group of mining prospects up the canyon during the 1930s, making enough to keep them going toward better days.[20]

Other speculators included rancher Joe Zaleski, who funded the opening of a prospect at the mouth of the canyon. That claim was reworked for tungsten, a metal that was prized during World War I. The Zaleski claims had an eighty-foot adit but were closed by 1941 and the claims reverted to the public domain.[21]

The identification of the Doredor Group claims can be traced to include a number of sites within Montezuma Canyon. To begin, most of the Doredor claims were ultimately controlled by the Victorio Company, which had once been owned by Bruce Doredor.[22] The claims were in two groups separated by the State of Texas mine properties. East from there were Doredor, Paring No. One, Paring No. Two, Paring No. Three, and Paring No. Four. To the west were Z. T. Parker, Chief, Fraction, Rubio, Tunnelsite, Miss Stake, Grub Stake No. Two, and Grub Stake No. Three.

According to a summary of mine claims compiled at Coronado National Memorial, the Miss Stake, Grub Stake No. Two, and Grub Stake

No. Three mine claims, along with three others in their immediate vicinity, were claimed by Felix Livercio in March 1899. Bruce Doredor claimed the Doredor, Paring No. One, Paring No. Two, Paring No. Three, Paring No. Four, Z. T. Parker, Chief, Fraction, Rubio, and Tunnelsite. The four Paring mines were claimed in 1901 and the Doredor claimed in 1920. The western group is said to have been claimed in 1909.[23] On April 10, 1920, Bruce Doredor patented all thirteen claims.[24] One source placed Doredor in the canyon on those claimed areas much earlier, probably before 1900.[25]

The same summary of mine claims cited above lists the purchase of Z. T. Parker, Chief, Fraction, Rubio, Tunnelsite, Grub Stake No. Two, and Miss Stake by "Clark and Smith" in 1938.[26] Bill Clark was on the board of supervisors and was said to have purchased the property for back taxes.[27] Clark and Smith owned the claims through the 1950s but did little or nothing to exploit them.

As Coronado International Memorial was being designed during the 1940s, mining property within its eventual boundaries was largely limited to two owners. The State of Texas claims were owned, or at least managed, by Grace Sparkes, while Clark and Smith owned two groups of claims surrounding Sparkes's lands. The same was true of the lands formerly contained in four homesteads at the mouth of Montezuma Canyon on the east side of the Huachuca Mountains. The Zaleski family still owned three and had just sold the fourth. The Montezuma Ranch was still being run as a camp and tourist ranch.[28]

The seemingly never-ending story of the memorial's land took on a history of its own. Although the NPS had pursued a joint memorial with Mexico for nearly ten years, in the end, hopes for a Coronado International Memorial were dashed. Finally, in 1952, Congress created the present Coronado National Memorial. In the next decades, as the memorial expanded its protective boundary, other adjacent lands came into play.

The physical design of the memorial was explicitly shaped by a desire to avoid the extraction of mineral deposits and protect the grazing rights of a few local ranchers outside the memorial area. The outcome was the creation of Coronado National Memorial that was proclaimed by the president on November 5, 1952.[29]

The eastern properties, the Doredor, Paring No. One, Paring No. Two, Paring No. Three, and Paring No. Four claims, made up Tract 101-09, 84.31 acres in size. Tract 101-09 was further divided by sale in 1979. The western half of that property was sold to James J. and Jacqueline S.

Wardle.[30] The eastern half of Tract 101-09, which continued to be owned by the Victorio Company, was designated Tract 101-21. That tract contained 42.16 acres and made up of portions of the Doredor, Paring No. One, Paring No. Two, Paring No. Three, and Paring No. Four lode mining claims. On March 26, 1980, the Victorio Company sold 196.73 acres to NPS for $340,000.[31]

After the Wardles, and their Wardle Realty business of Sierra Vista, obtained Tract 101-22, they quickly moved to develop and market it. Evidently, negotiations with the NPS began almost immediately. Near the end of December 1979, an appraisal of $101, 200 was approved as a base for negotiations with the government. The owners countered with a figure of $160,000. In March the Wardles lowered their asking price to $125,000, "provided the transaction could be promptly consummated." Unfortunately, it could not be consummated for quite some time due to budgetary constraints so the Wardles set about dividing and developing the property.[32]

In January 1980 Jacques and Audrey C. O'Keefe bought the western portion of Tract 101-22 in a deal financed by the Wardles under an all-inclusive agreement that scheduled payments from the O'Keefes. This property, including just over twelve acres, was split into three tracts.[33] The memorial petitioned for condemnation to head off further development of the Wardle property and continued to do so for the next few years. In May 1980 the major concern of the superintendent was that one or more roads would be built into the lands owned by Wardle and O'Keefe.[34]

In early 1981 it was reported that Wardle was cutting trees to clear access for a road into a portion of the property that he had recently sold. Wardle told Bob Cousins, an NPS official, that the new owner intended to build a single-family residence. Cousins reported that, due to the site's high visibility from the main road, "Superintendent Dale feels it is of highest priority to acquire this parcel by a Declaration of Taking." Therefore, Cousins continued, it would be monitored closely for evidence of building activity so that such action could be taken.[35] In April a road was bulldozed into the Wardle property.[36]

As the NPS worried about development of the Wardle and O'Keefe properties, Wardle expressed equal concern about the actions of the NPS staff at the memorial. An exchange of letters in 1982 resulted from Wardle's complaint to his political representatives that federal officials had interfered with his attempts to sell his land. Wardle asserted that potential buyers had been told, "The Forest Service [*sic*] is in the process of buying up [taking over] all of that property," and "There isn't any water up there."[37] NPS officials, the actual targets of Wardle's complaint, replied that their only mention of water was a statement that there was no surface water on the land. They admitted, "Superintendent Dale mistakenly informed one individual that a Declaration of Taking had been filed against the Wardle property." In the future, promised NPS acting director Ira Hutchison, interested parties would be referred directly to the owner.[38]

In March 1983 rock was blasted on the road that had been bulldozed in 1981. Wardle Realty said that more roadwork was planned, and the memorial staff braced for residential development.[39] In 1983 the O'Keefe's subdivided and sold their land. With the Wardles also selling some of their holdings in the same year, most of the property bought from the Victorio Company by Wardle was transferred during that year. The first parcel to go was Tract 101-35, the southwest section of Tract 101-22, which included portions of the Paring No. Two and Paring No. Three mining claims.[40] It was sold by the O'Keefes to Paul E. and Laurel A. Froelich in April 1983. A joint tenancy deed was signed naming the Froelichs as tenants and the O'Keefes as *"Grantor, Mortgagor or Trustor."*[41] On the same day, a warranty deed transferring the property from the Wardles to the O'Keefes was also signed, showing that the O'Keefes still owed money to the Wardles as part of the 1980 all-inclusive agreement.[42]

On August 29, 1983, the O'Keefes sold Tract 101-36, the western section of Tract 101-22, and made up of portions of the Doredor, Paring No. Two, and Paring No. Three mining claims.[43] Valentin Castro III and Deborah Castro purchased it in August 1983.[44] On the same day, the Wardles sold Tract 101-33 to Richard D. and Judy L. Compton.[45] Tract 101-33 was made up of the southeast section of Tract 101-22, portions of the Paring No. Two and Paring No. Three mining claims.[46] The Comptons also bought a tract, called Tract 101-34, from the O'Keefes.[47] Tract 101-34 was made up of a portion of the Doredor claim, in the northwest section of Tract 101-22.[48]

As the year 1983 came toward an end, Superintendent Dale summarized what was occurring to the land that had formerly made up Tract 101-22: "Instead of having one owner as we did in early 1980, we now have five owners and potential private homes—a small subdivision in the heart of the Memorial. This parcel of land is highly visible and any building of private homes and roads would be very noticeable and obtrusive—especially from the Montezuma Pass area. The beauty, purpose, and setting of the Memorial should not be destroyed by an urban development within the scenic heart of this Park." Dale closed with yet another plea for acquisition: "In view of the high visibility of this land, the imminent threat of construction and the adverse impact this construction would have on the natural features of the Park, the acquisition of this parcel should be given immediate emergency attention."[49]

Soon thereafter, in early 1984, the Huachuca Audubon Society weighed in on the side of NPS acquisition of the Wardle property. A letter from its president to Senator Barry Goldwater, however, criticized NPS inaction on the issue, suggesting that the slow-moving NPS did not fully grasp "the true ecological and historical significance of this unique bit of real estate." In fact, it went on, "key personnel . . . may not be well acquainted with the fact that Coronado National Memorial was established as both a natural and historical site."[50] A February 1984 summary of inholdings in the memorial concluded by making one exception to its opposition to acquisition by condemnation. The property was still identified with Wardle, despite the fact that it had been held by multiple owners; it was deemed a "new and blatant intrusion and disregard of the natural resources of the area," which should be condemned before further damage could be done.[51]

Thus, the battle lines seemed to have been drawn and interests lined up for and against acquisition. The Wardles had been willing to sell the property that then made up Tract 101-22 to the memorial and, in early 1980, had compromised on price, offering it for $125,000. Aware that the money for purchase was unlikely to be made available any time soon, they had moved to subdivide and develop the property. NPS officials, at the memorial and elsewhere, continued to petition for acquisition, by sale or by condemnation. As the process dragged on, state and federal representatives responded to Wardle's concerns that his private property rights were being infringed upon, while environmentalists and park supporters sought to expedite the acquisition. At one point in 1981 it was explained that acquisition funds were limited "to assist President Reagan in his efforts to reduce the Federal budget."[52]

Eventually, funding was made available. In 1985 the memorial finally acquired the remainder of the lands that had once made up the Doredor/Victorio mining claims. On February 6, 1985, James J. and Jacqueline S. Wardle sold Tract 101-37, 16.75 acres, to NPS for $120,600.[53] On February 12, the Comptons sold Tract 101-33, 13.05 acres, in three parcels, to the NPS for $118,750. On the same day, the Comptons also sold the

4.02 acre 101-34 to NPS for $33,400.[54] On February 25, Valentin Castro III and his wife, Deborah, sold Tract 101-36, 4.04 acres, to NPS for $33,400.[55] To complete the series of sales, on July 5 Paul E. and Laurel A. Froelich sold the 4.03 acre Tract 101-35 to NPS for $32,250.[56] In the four years that elapsed since 1980, when the Wardles offered Tract 101-22 for $125,000, and 1985, when the sales were completed, the price of the property had jumped to $338,400.

As a result of the 1978 boundary adjustment and the 1976 "Act to Provide for the Regulation of Mining Activity," one other set of properties came into dispute, though they were not purchased or condemned by the NPS. The dispute itself is somewhat confused, but concerned several unpatented claims worked by W. P. Witkopp of Sierra Vista and his partner, John T. Porter. Witkopp was involved in thirty-two claims north of Montezuma Pass, in Coronado National Forest, with his company, Tako Mining.[57] Porter was a partner in some of his operations, including five claims, all or part of which were brought within the boundaries of the memorial as a result of the 1978 adjustment.[58]

Exactly what happened to Witkopp's claims is unclear from the various accounts of his story to be found in surviving documents. In February 1982 the Bureau of Land Management (BLM) ruled that a total of nine claims, including those that extended into the memorial, were abandoned and void due to failure to file appropriate paperwork before a deadline in late 1980. Samuel Riley, who leased the claims and acted as Witkopp's agent at the time of the missed filing, appealed the ruling unsuccessfully in April 1982. He offered, according to the decision, no new evidence, but stated that he was still working the claims.[59] Witkopp, himself, appealed in October 1983. He testified that Riley had been dealing with family illness at the time of the original problem and had only missed the deadline by days that they had since lost contact and that he, Witkopp, had not been informed of subsequent decisions.[60]

In a letter that he wrote to President Reagan in 1984, Witkopp added that Riley "had taken the liberty to assume authorization to file the affidavits" that had not been filed. He added that even before the deadline for filing had arrived, the NPS had confiscated the disputed claims. He recalled that he had heard rumors of the land exchange in 1978 and approached memorial staff. They responded, according to Witkopp, "that as far as NPS was concerned that I had no mineral rights within the area whatsoever and that the NPS and USFS were Federal agencies, and as such could do whatever they wished at any time they wished."[61]

Elsewhere, he wrote that he first heard about the exchange from an NPS employee in July 1979. He was, according to this telling, told that as soon as the legislation was read into the Federal Register the claims would become NPS property and he could no longer work on them.[62]

Immediately after the exchange, the NPS agreed that Witkopp would be owed compensation for his claims provided that they proved valid and after their value was appraised.[63] A preliminary examination of the claims was conducted, and Witkopp was notified that a survey would follow. He was soon told, however, that there would be no survey or settlement because the claims were void, based on the BLM ruling.[64] The NPS informed Mr. Witkopp that it had no basis for acquiring his claims unless they were properly filed. Since he had failed to file in a timely fashion in 1980, the claims were null and void as ruled by BLM and on subsequent appeals. In addition, it was pointed out that BLM was responsible for making the ruling regardless of what federal agency actually controlled the land on which the claims were located.[65]

Although the whole tale of W. P. Witkopp's claims is not entirely comprehensible from the documents, it seems that he might have been caught in a confusing tangle of agency overlaps and bureaucratic rulings as well as by his own incompetence. Through it all, though, he continued to profit from his claims up to the last possible minute. Well after the 1978 or 1979 date, when he later said that he understood that he had been dispossessed of his claims by the NPS, he continued to lease them, first to Samuel Riley and later to Wayne Jeppson. In 1983 he asserted that he was facing fraud charges for the latter lease because BLM had ruled against him but failed to notify him that he no longer owned, and could not lease, the claims.[66] As noted, however, he later claimed that his responsibility for the claims ended four to five years earlier. Most probably, Witkopp, like most people would in his position, changed tactics and stories based on what seemed most likely to work. It also seems that NPS officials were not totally clear about what was occurring on every front while they were trying to sort out the extent of Witkopp's rights and their responsibilities. In that, the Witkopp case was far from unique in the annals of Coronado National Memorial.

In July 1970 Ruth M. Clark, a widow, and Charles A. and Paquita C. Smith, sold several mining properties, including the thirteen Doredor claims in the Hartford Mining District of the Huachuca Mountains that fell within the eventual boundaries of Coronado National Memorial. Evidently, the sellers were Bill Clark's widow and his partner. The buyer was the Coronado Investment Company, a partnership comprising Peter G. Wray and H. Wayne Pruett.[67] In 1973 the properties were transferred to the Pruett-Wray Cattle Company, made up of the same partners.[68] By 1979 Pruett-Wray had changed its name to the Victorio Land and Cattle Company and then to the Victorio Company.[69]

The history of the Doredor Group spanned the twentieth century. Today, the mines are dormant; but, the memory of what happened in Montezuma Canyon lives on in the annals of Coronado National Memorial.

Notes

1. Horace J. Stevens, *The Copper Handbook*, vol. V (Houghton, MI 1903), 390.

2. See Sánchez, Erickson, and Gurulé, *Between Two Countries*, for a history of mining properties at Coronado National Memorial.

3. Robert Spude, "A Speculative Gamble: The Doredor Mine" (unpublished manuscript), National Park Service, Santa Fe, New Mexico, 2006; and H. Mason Coggin, "Roots of the Calumet: a Short History of the Calumet and Arizona Mining Company," in J. Michael Canty, *History of Arizona Mining*, vol. 3 (Tucson: Arizona Mining Foundation, 1999), 155–176.

4. Spude, "A Speculative Gamble" (unpublished manuscript). Also see biography and photograph of Mitchell in *Memorial Record of the Northern Peninsula of Michigan* (Chicago: Lewis Publishing, 1895), 595–97; on Chenowith see Erik Nordberg, "The Arizona & Michigan Mining Company of Globe District, Arizona Territory," *Mining History Journal* (1999): 77–88; Stevens, *The Copper Handbook*, 3, 390; *Copper Country Evening News*, Calumet, MI, May 22, 28, 1903.

5. Spude, "A Speculative Gamble" (unpublished manuscript); Location Notices, book 1,255–58, Cochise County Recorder's Office.

6. Spude, "A Speculative Gamble" (unpublished manuscript); Location Notices and Books of Deeds, and Great Register for 1886; U.S. censuses for 1880 and 1900, Cochise County Recorder's Office.

7. Spude, "A Speculative Gamble" (unpublished manuscript); Miscellaneous Agreements Book 7, 4–9, 193–97, Cochise County Recorder's Office.

8. Miscellaneous Agreements Book 7, 4–9, 193–97, Cochise County Recorder's Office.

9. *Copper Country Evening News*, Mitchell Development Company entries in Copper Handbook for 1903, March 24, 1903, p. 390.

10. *Copper Country Evening News,* Mitchell Development Company entries in *Copper Handbook* for 1903, 390, and 1904, March 24, 1903, p. 504–5.

11. *Engineering and Mining Journal,* October 6, 1904.

12. Spude, "A Speculative Gamble" (unpublished manuscript); Horace J. Stevens, *The Copper Handbook*, vol. V (Houghton, MI 1905, 1907), Cochise County Recorder's Office.

13. Spude, "A Speculative Gamble" (unpublished manuscript); Great Register, Cochise County Recorder's Office, 1904, 1922.

14. Spude, "A Speculative Gamble" (unpublished manuscript); Doredor entries, tax record books, 1906, 1912, 1922, Cochise County Archives.

15. Spude, "A Speculative Gamble" (unpublished manuscript); Book of Deeds 23, 265; Book of Deeds 29, 424; Book of Deeds 29, 425; Book of Deeds 30, 326, 332; Location Notices, Book 60, 60–75, Cochise County Recorder's Office.

16. Spude, "A Speculative Gamble" (unpublished manuscript).

17. Spude, "A Speculative Gamble" (unpublished manuscript); Huachuca Mountains mines file, Bisbee Mining and Historical Museum, Bisbee, AZ.

18. Spude, "A Speculative Gamble" (unpublished manuscript); information in manuscript courtesy Keith Long, U.S. Geological Survey, Tucson.

19. See Sánchez, Erickson, and Gurulé, *Between Two Countries,* for a history of mining properties at Coronado National Memorial.

20. Spude, "A Speculative Gamble" (unpublished manuscript), mining files, Coronado National Memorial. A reminiscence of a typical small-scale operation on the Huachucas in the 1930s is Robert Lenon, *It Seems Like Yesterday: Mining and Mapping in Arizona's First Century,* vol. 2, *Bisbee and Patagania* (New York: Universe, 2005), 35–38.

21. Spude, "A Speculative Gamble" (unpublished manuscript); Eldred D. Wilson, Tungsten Deposits of Arizona, Arizona Bureau of Mines Bulletin 148 (Tucson: University of Arizona, 1941), 49.

22. George Brown. "Dude Ranches at Coronado National Memorial: A Brief History." Interview, 1998. See draft prepared by Bart Barbour for the National Park Service, Santa Fe. See Joseph P. Sánchez, Bruce A. Erickson, and Jerry L. Gurulé, *Between Two Countries: A History of Coronado National Memorial 1939-1990* (Albuquerque: Río Grande Books, 2007), for a history of mining properties at Coronado National Memorial.

23. "A Summary of the Abandoned Mineral Lands"; "Abandoned Mineral Lands (AML) and Related List of Classified Structure (LCS)," n.d., CORO Files.

24. "A Summary of the Abandoned Mineral Lands," National Register of Historic Places eligibility report, Doredor Mine, copy at Technical Information Center, National Park Service, Denver.

25. Dale to Mulhern, "A Summary of the Abandoned Mineral Lands." Hereford, February 23, 1976, Coronado National Memorial, CORO Files.

26. Ibid.

27. Ibid.

28. See "Dude Ranches at Coronado National Memorial: A Brief History," draft prepared by Bart Barbour for the NPS, Santa Fe. See Sánchez, Erickson, and Gurulé, *Between Two Countries,* for a history of mining properties at Coronado National Memorial.

29. Presidential Proclamation was supported by *An Act to Provide for the Establishment of the Coronado International Memorial,* in the State of Arizona, Approved August 18, 1941 (55 Stat 630), CORO Files, as amended by Public Law 478, 82nd Congress, approved July 9, 1952.

30. That property became known as Tract 101-22. Joint Tenancy Deed, The Victorio Company, an Arizona Corporation; formerly Victorio Land and Cattle Company, an Arizona Corporation; formerly Pruett-Wray Cattle Company, an Arizona Corporation, to James J. Wardle and Jacqueline S. Wardle, husband and wife, signed December 18, 1979, CCR, Deeds of Real Estate, Docket 1388, 333–34.

31. That sale comprised Tracts 101-05 and 101-21. CCR, Deeds of Real Estate, Docket

1388, 333–34. Grant Deed, The Victorio Company, to NPS, Executed March 26, 1980, CCR, Deeds of Real Estate, Docket 1388, 333-334.

32. Howard Chapman, Regional Director, Western Region, to Associate Director, Management and Operations, NPS, July 10, 1980, WACC, Folder L 1425: Land Holdings—Wardle & Acquisition F14. That sale comprised Tracts 101-05 and 101-21. CCR, Deeds of Real Estate, Docket 1388, 333–34. Grant Deed, The Victorio Company, to NPS, Executed March 26, 1980, CCR, Deeds of Real Estate, Docket 1388, 333-334.

33. The tracts were numbered 101-34, 101-35, and 101-36. All-inclusive agreement, James J. Wardle and Jacqueline S. Wardle, husband and wife, to Jacques O'Keefe and Audrey C. O'Keefe, husband and wife, Signed January 5, 1980, CCR, Deeds of Real Estate, Docket 1395, 484–487.

34. Dale to Regional Director, Western Region, Hereford, May 27, 1980, WACC, Folder L 1425: Land Holdings—Wardle & Acquisition F14.

35. Bob Cousins, Realty Specialist, Division of Land Acquisition, Western Region, to Acting Chief, Division of Land Acquisition, Western Region, March 10, 1981, ILRPC Files.

36. Dale to Regional Director, Western Region, Hereford, March 22, 1983, WACC, Folder L 1425: Land Holdings—Wardle & Acquisition F14.

37. Bill English, State Representative, to U.S. Senator Barry Goldwater, June 29, 1982, in Folder L 1425: Land Holdings—Wardle & Acquisition F14.

38. Ira J. Hutchison, Director, Acting, NPS, to Barry Goldwater, Washington, DC, November 4, 1982; Folder L 1425: Land Holdings—Wardle & Acquisition F14.

39. Dale to Regional Director, Western Region, Hereford, March 22, 1983, WACC, Folder L 1425: Land Holdings—Wardle & Acquisition F14.

40. Dale to Chief, Energy, Mining and Minerals Division, Minerals Overview Report and Map, Hereford, March 20, 1986; Grant Deed, Paul E. Froelich and Laurel A. Froelich, his wife, to NPS, Signed July 5, 1985, ILRPC Files.

41. Joint Tenancy Deed, Jacques O'Keefe and Audrey C. O'Keefe, husband and wife, to Paul E. Froelich and Laurel A. Froelich, husband and wife, Signed April 8, 1983, CCR, Deeds of Real Estate, Docket 1671, 164–66.

42. Warranty Deed, James J. Wardle and Jacqueline S. Wardle, husband and wife, to Jacques O'Keefe and Audrey C. O'Keefe, husband and wife, Signed April 8, 1983, and recorded April 29, 1983, CCR, Deeds of Real Estate, Docket 1671, 162.

43. Dale to Chief, Energy, Mining and Minerals Division, Hereford, March 20, 1986; Grant Deed, Valentin Castro III and Deborah Castro, husband and wife, to NPS, Signed February 25, 1985, ILRPC Files.

44. Joint Tenancy Deed, Jacques O'Keefe and Audrey C. O'Keefe, husband and wife, to Valentin Castro III and Deborah Castro, husband and wife, Signed August 29, 1983, CCR, Deeds of Real Estate, Docket 1708, 40–43.

45. Joint Tenancy Deed, James J. Wardle and Jacqueline Wardle (aka Jacqueline S. Wardle), husband and wife, to Richard D. Compton and Judy L. Compton, husband and wife, Signed August 29, 1983, CCR, Deeds of Real Estate, Docket 1700, 285–86.

46. Dale to Chief, Energy, Mining and Minerals Division, Hereford, March 20, 1986; Grant Deed, Richard D. Compton and Judy L. Compton, husband and wife, to NPS, February 12, 1985, ILRPC Files.

47. Joint Tenancy Deed, Jacques O'Keefe and Audrey O'Keefe, husband and wife, to Richard D. Compton and Judy L. Compton, husband and wife, Signed December 28, 1983, CCR, Deeds of Real Estate, Docket 1730, 579–80.

48. Dale to Chief, Energy, Mining and Minerals Division, Hereford, March 20, 1986; Grant Deed, Richard D. Compton and Judy L. Compton, husband and wife, to NPS, Signed February 12, 1985, ILRPC Files.

49. Dale to Regional Director, Western Region, November 9, 1983, WACC, Folder L 1425: Land Holdings—Wardle & Acquisition F14.

50. Anna Hirst, President, Huachuca Audubon Society, to Barry Goldwater, January 10, 1984; WACC, Folder L 1425: Land Holdings—Wardle & Acquisition F14.

51. Clay to Regional Director, Western Region, February 2, 1984, ILRPC Files.

52. Chapman to Gordon Douglas, Coronado Resource Conservation and Development, November 19, 1981, WACC, Folder L 1425: Land Holdings—Wardle & Acquisition F14.

53. Grant Deed, James J. Wardle and Jacqueline S. Wardle, his wife, to NPS, Signed February 6, 1985, ILRPC Files.

54. Grant Deed, Richard D. and Judy L. Compton, to NPS, Signed February 12, 1985.

55. Grant Deed, Valentin Castro III and Deborah Castro, to NPS, Signed February 25, 1985.

56. Grant Deed, Paul E. and Laurel A. Froelich, to NPS, Signed July 5, 1985.

57. Wilbert P. Witkopp to Unknown, July 26, 1979, ILRPC Files.

58. Witkopp to Unknown, November 7, 1983, ILRPC Files.

59. U.S. Department of the Interior, Office of Hearings and Appeals, Interior Board of Land Appeals, Ruling, Tako Mining, Arlington, April 9, 1982, ILRPC Files.

60. U.S. Department of the Interior, Office of Hearings and Appeals, Interior Board of Land Appeals, Ruling, Tako Mining, Arlington, October 31, 1983, ILRPC Files.

61. Witkopp to President Reagan, Sierra Vista, July 13, 1984, ILRPC Files.

62. Witkopp to Unknown, July 26, 1979 ILRPC Files.

63. Chapman to Congressman Morris K. Udall, San Francisco, September 25, 1979, ILRPC Files.

64. Witkopp to Reagan, Sierra Vista, July 13, 1984, ILRPC Files.

65. Chapman to Witkopp, Draft, September 17, 1984, ILRPC Files.

66. Witkopp to Unknown, November 7, 1983, ILRPC Files.

67. Warranty Deed, Ruth M. Clark, a widow, and Charles A. Smith and Paquita C. Smith, his wife, to Coronado Investment Company, a partnership comprised of Peter G. Wray and H. Wayne Pruett, co-partners, Recorded July 2, 1970, CCR, Deeds of Real Estate, Docket 645, 543–545.

68. Warranty Deed, Coronado Investment Company to Pruett-Wray Cattle Company, Signed May 1, 1973, CCR, Deeds of Real Estate, Docket 871, 481–483.

69. Deed (Joint Tenancy), The Victorio Company, an Arizona Corporation; formerly Victorio Land and Cattle Company, an Arizona Corporation; formerly Pruett-Wray Cattle Company, an Arizona Corporation, to James J. Wardle and Jacqueline S. Wardle, husband and wife, Signed December 18, 1979, CCR, Deeds of Real Estate, Docket 1388, pages 333–34.

CHAPTER 6

Mexican Rancheros, Homesteaders, and Dude Ranch Operators

Frankly, this section of Arizona needs your earnest action. . . . Ranchers and resorts look to this Park for the stimulant they need to induce travel; Bisbee has organized a Sunshine Club to advertise its marvelous climate.

— GRACE SPARKES, 1946[1]

A new era in the history of settlement in the San Pedro Valley began during the early nineteenth century when land was granted by the Mexican government to private landowners. The legal process of making the first grant in the vicinity of the memorial was under way as Mexico's struggle for independence neared its end in 1821. José Jesus Pérez, a soldier from Arispe, Sonora, requested four leagues of land in the vicinity of the abandoned town of Las Nutrias on which to graze livestock. Local officials negotiated with Pérez and another citizen who was already grazing stock along the river, and a tract was surveyed. At issue was a *ciénaga* (marsh), that both men considered the most significant source of water in the area. Perhaps during a drier time the *ciénaga* described in the documents might have been the same place where Nicolás Lafora had earlier described a *laguna* (a shallow body of water).

The San Pedro grant was measured northward from a house known as San Pedro, evidently within the town of the same name, about seven miles south of the present international border. The line passed "the foot of Huachuca Mountain" just north of the midpoint of the grant. The granting process continued with Pérez paying stipulated fees for the land and papers being forwarded to the proper authorities to be approved. At that point Mexico gained its independence and the procedure was, as far as can be told, never completed. In 1832, the land was transferred to Rafael Elías and a legal title was issued. However, subsequent to the Gadsden Purchase Treaty of 1853 much of the San Pedro Valley belonged to the United States and all land titles had to be confirmed by the new rulers. The San Pedro grant was rejected by the United States, mainly on the basis of government evidence that supported a contention that the grant was wholly within the new boundaries of Mexico.[2]

The disputed boundary of the San Pedro grant, in turn, affected the eventual disposition of two grants directly to its north along the San Pedro River. In 1827 the San Rafael del Valle grant was measured from the north line of the San Pedro grant to the north line of the San Juan de las Boquillas y Nogales grant. During its confirmation, the case of the San Rafael del Valle grant had the distinction of being appealed to the U.S. Supreme Court twice, for different issues, once by the government and once by the petitioners. In the end, both grants were confirmed, though neither ended up being nearly as large as the petitioners anticipated. Though they were all originally surveyed, as noted, with common boundaries, the resulting grants did not come near touching one another.[3] Regarding their involvement in both the San Pedro and the San Juan de las Boquillas y Nogales grants, the Elías family transferred its interests before the confirmation process.

The Elías clan had other interests in the area. They were original claimants to the vast San Ignacio del Babocomari grant, north of the Huachuca Mountains on Babocomari Creek.[4] There, in 1832, the clan claimed nearly "130,000 acres a few miles north of the present-day city of Sierra Vista."[5] To defend their land against Apache warriors, the Elíases said they had constructed defensive structures there. In the spring of 1833 the Elíases built a "fortified hacienda on Babocomari Creek. The hacienda was built of adobe and consisted of 15-foot high walls that formed a square about 100 feet long on each side. There was only one entrance, a gate on the eastside. The interior of the square was lined with rooms, the roofs of which formed a fighting platform behind the wall. The layout was typical of the early fortified haciendas on Mexico's northern frontier."[6] Doubtless, their other landholdings contained defensive structures. Likely a small stone fort found in Montezuma Canyon—if it is a defensive structure—is one such construction.

Although the San Rafael del Valle grant had been one of the family's prized possessions, the Elíases sold it to members of the Camou family of Hermosillo, Sonora, before it was confirmed.[7] In 1905 copper and cattle baron William Cornell Greene added it to his transnational empire. Greene owned the San Rafael de la Zanja grant, directly west of the Huachuca Mountains, at that time. In 1912, after Greene's death, his family sold San Rafael del Valle to the Boquillas Land and Cattle Company along with more than fifty smaller ranches in Arizona and Sonora.[8]

The Boquillas Land and Cattle Company owed its name to the San Juan de las Boquillas y Nogales grant, which it had purchased in 1901 from the famous Hearst newspaper family of California. Senator George Hearst, the father of William Randolph Hearst, had been a partner of George Hill Howard, who had bought up the grant from the original heirs. The Boquillas Land and Cattle Company eventually became a subsidiary of the Kern County Land and Cattle Company, one of the largest landowners in the United States through its ranching and farming interests all over the west. In 1967, Kern merged with Tenneco, Inc., which has developed some of its land in the San Pedro Valley.[9]

The tale of the San Pedro Valley grants, particularly the San Rafael del Valle and the San Pedro grants, with featured roles played by large-scale landowners and prominent families, such as the Elíases, Greenes, and Hearsts, illustrates one aspect of the region in the nineteenth century. Mixed in among the giants, however, were many small operations run by poor families just trying to survive the arid climate on the bounty of their land. When settlement increased in southeastern Arizona after the Gadsden Purchase Treaty, the newcomers, like their predecessors, sought the water necessary to survive in the desert. Much of the land along the San Pedro River was controlled by the Mexican grants and then by their successors. The earliest homesteads in the valley were founded in the early 1880s along the river's tributaries and at nearby springs. Among the existing watercourses that drew early settlers to the area was Montezuma Creek.

Originally from the Big Bend country of Texas, William Ratliff was the first Anglo-American settler in Montezuma Canyon. He moved his family from the Gila River valley in New Mexico to the Huachucas by covered wagon in the 1880s or 1890s.[10] Ratliff chose Montezuma Canyon because it had a permanent stream at that time and he planned to do some farming. To provide immediate income, the Ratliff family began to log in the Huachuca Mountains, delivering the wood to Naco.[11] They brought some horses and a small herd of cattle to the area at the same time.[12] The Ratliff family is thought to have begun building a residence on Montezuma Creek in 1902.[13] At the very least, the residence, later known to locals as Baumkirchner's adobe house, was built prior to 1916.[14]

According to documents filed by the surveyor general's office in 1917, William Ratliff officially applied for his 160-acre claim on October 22, 1911. The survey was executed March 12–13, 1914, and approved August 8, 1917, for 158.23 acres. Ratliff's "Homestead Entry Survey No. 311" consisted of the south half of the northwest quarter and north half of the southwest quarter of Section 17, Township 24 South, Range 21 East, Gila and Salt River Base and Meridian. Montezuma Wash ran through the southwest corner of the property from northwest to southeast.[15]

Ed Ratliff, William's oldest son, made a homestead claim directly west of William's place. Papers filed in 1917 show that Ed Ratliff applied for his 160-acre claim on February 3, 1911. The survey was executed March 11–12, 1915, and approved August 8, 1917, with 157.72 acres. Ed Ratliff's homestead consisted of the south half of the northeast quarter and north half of the southeast quarter of Section 18, Township 24 South, Range 21 East. Montezuma Wash ran through it from northwest to southeast as well.[16]

Another son, named William, came to own claims to the east and southeast of his father's land.[17] The younger William's property was, according to a later family member, sold to George Brown.[18] In addition, a daughter named Inez, but called "Tiny," married John Pyeatt, who owned the claim directly east of the original Ratliff homestead. Pyeatt's claim was later known as the Montezuma Ranch. By the middle of the second decade of the twentieth century, the Ratliff family was settled around the base of the Huachuca Mountains along Montezuma Creek.

William Ratliff died in 1917, leaving the land to be split among his heirs. At the time, he was also grazing cattle on National Forest Service land. Ed Ratliff was the executor of his father's will and representative of the heirs. In 1932 nine Ratliffs by name or marriage transmitted their claims to George Ratliff, another son of the elder William. Ed and his wife, Ira, quitclaimed an unspecified tract, evidently Homestead Entry Survey No. 310, to George in a separate transaction. On September 30, 1933, George and Annie Ratliff conveyed both Homestead Entry Surveys, 310 and 311, to Marko Vucinich. On November 21, 1933, Vucinich, in turn, transferred both homesteads to Joe Zaleski.[19]

Zaleski came to own at least four homestead entry surveys at the mouth of Montezuma Canyon. Another was the Homestead of John Pyeatt. Pyeatt first took up a claim in Cochise County under the Homestead Act of 1909. His first claim was on the east side of the San Pedro River, northeast of Coronado National Memorial. He built a small house and repaired an already existing structure, strung fence, and put in a crop on five or six acres. Later in the same year a flood destroyed or damaged all of the improvements that he had made on the land. Deciding that he could not afford to start over again, Pyeatt abandoned the entry. He was able to sell the vestiges of his improvements on the land to Rufus M. Thompson for $250 before the end of 1909.[20]

In November 1915 Pyeatt settled on the Montezuma Ranch site. He applied for a homestead claim in June 1917.[21] That tract had also been claimed and relinquished previously. Cornelius N. Driscoll had first claimed the Montezuma Ranch land in July 1913.[22] By the middle of 1914, as Pyeatt was migrating west, Driscoll moved east across the San Pedro River and made a new claim under the Homestead Act. Driscoll explained that he had relinquished his first claim because the road to it had washed out. In addition, he had learned from neighbors that water was a problem because the creek was dry and wells needed to be drilled to a depth of two hundred feet.[23]

Pyeatt seemed to have a shady side to him. Sometime during those years, Pyeatt applied for some relief or credit to assist him in developing his second claim. In the fall of 1917 he wrote to Senator Carl Hayden seeking "credit for time in proving up on my claim by reason of my services the same as enlisted regular soldiers." Pyeatt claimed he had enlisted as a packer "during the Spanish [American] war." He said he had served in the Philippines for fifteen months in "H Troop, 3rd Cavalry." Convinced of Pyeatt's service to his country, Hayden forwarded the request to the General Land Office. Officials there made an inquiry to the Quartermaster General of the Army regarding Pyeatt's service. Nothing emerged to suggest that Pyeatt had served in the national army, the regular army, or the National Guard.[24]

Despite such inconsistencies, Pyeatt's claim was approved, along with a deed for the second property in July 1921. Pyeatt's patent was recorded, having "been established and duly consummated, in conformity to law," on December 4, 1925.[25] The 160-acre property was described as the south half of the northeast quarter and north half of the southeast quarter of Section 17, Township 24 South, Range 21 East of the Gila and Salt River Base and Meridian, Arizona.[26] John Pyeatt, as already mentioned, married Inez "Tiny" Ratliff, the daughter of the family that owned the two claims west of his new homestead and probably more. According to local lore, Inez's parents worked for the Ratliffs. One night they suddenly left, leaving their daughter behind with the Ratliffs, who adopted her.[27]

As John and Tiny were filing their homestead claim, around 1917, they built a small house on the property. It was remodeled and added to over the years, but remains as the center of a ranch house that exists today. That house is the farthest west of the two large buildings still standing on the Montezuma Ranch.[28] John Pyeatt died within four years of his receiving final approval for his second homestead. His widow moved to Paso Robles, California, and in March 1929 she sold the lot to Joseph Zaleski.[29] Joe Zaleski's granddaughter, Betty Peterson-Stowe, added that Zaleski was approached by the president of the Miners and Merchants Bank that, evidently, held a loan on the property, about buying it from Tiny Pyeatt. The Zaleski family then lived on a homestead in the Hereford area.[30] According to one source, they owned other land in Cochise County as well, some of it located within what would eventually become the town of Sierra Vista.[31]

A few years after he bought the Pyeatt Homestead, Zaleski also bought the Ratliff properties, to the west, as described above. Filling out Zaleski's small empire was the Kudzmi claim to the south. The Kudzmi Homestead was made up of the south half of the southeast quarter of Section 17 and Lots 1 and 2 of Section 20, Township 24 South, Range 21 East, Gila and Salt River Base and Meridian. It was first claimed within the 160-acre homestead claim of Elmer L. Hertel, as reflected in field notes dated March 3, 1915.[32] Simon Kudzmi, a naturalized immigrant from Russia and veteran of World War I, settled on the same land in October 1928 and built a house in February 1929. Joe Zaleski was one of the witnesses for Kudzmi when he filed the final proofs for his homestead, which was approved at 133.67 acre.[33] Eventually Zaleski bought the claim from Kudzmi.

About 1935 or 1936 Zaleski, with a partner named Rudy Becker, converted his property into a dude, or guest, ranch. They called it the Border Ranch and later Montezuma Ranch. When they opened Border Ranch, Zaleski and Becker built another house, originally one story with a basement, to the east of the original cabin. The house contained common rooms as well as guest rooms. Guests also stayed in small cabins. The Border Ranch was run as a family business and was frequented by locals as well. A 1937 feature article named Rudy Becker's son Wes as one of the "top wranglers" and Frank Zaleski, Joe's son, as a "top cowhand." Neighbor George Brown was described as "one of the most interesting and up-to-date ranchers in the state."[34]

Guests at the ranch enjoyed many activities, including participation in seasonal roundups, watching rodeos in which local cowboys competed, and western dances in Hereford. Most of the pastimes, according to descriptions, centered on horseback riding. Among the destinations were local landmarks such as Smuggler's Pass and the caves. They could also ride into the mountains to fish for trout, pan for gold, visit nearby goldmine shafts, and take in the now-famous views. Across the plains, guests were encouraged to visit neighboring ranches and cross the border into Mexico.

Naco, Arizona, offered a golf course, while the Sonora side featured shopping for souvenirs and the "thrill in visiting a foreign country." Also across the border was the possibility of "a fiesta in one of the neighboring Mexican villages where you can enjoy watching the people from another land." At the border crossing were "dashing, colorful Mexican vaqueros herding the cattle through the disinfectant vats."[35] Dude ranches were marketed to an urban audience as relaxation in a rustic setting, and the Montezuma Ranch was no exception. As an added attraction, the Montezuma Ranch also offered the exotica of ready access to a romanticized vision of Mexico.[36] World War II cut into the tourist business but occasioned the expansion of Fort Huachuca. For a time, the Army used the guest ranch to house officers.[37]

The Zaleski and Becker names both remained associated with the ranch for more than a decade. Neighbor George Brown thought that Becker bought Zaleski out. Becker was sometimes listed as the manager of the dude ranch, as was Frank Zaleski. Frank Zaleski came to own the property and he kept it until the end of 1949. Around 1946 or 1947 Harry H. and Ruth Ethlyn Petersen began to manage the Montezuma Ranch.[38] Citing a source from the Cochise County Assessor's office, one author asserts that the Petersens purchased the ranch from Frank Zaleski on December 13, 1949.[39] However, in a June 1947 letter, Mr. Petersen described his wife and himself as the owners of the Montezuma Ranch.[40] Very likely the Petersens bought the property earlier, but paid off the property in 1949 when they sold it. On the same day that the Petersens completed their purchase in 1949, they transferred title to the property to Nancy Carter Nelms.[41] In October 1950 Joe Zaleski transferred ownership of the rest of his property to his son Frank by way of a gift deed.[42]

Nancy Nelms, along with managers Don Brooks, Jean Faye, and Rex Watts, ran Montezuma as a dude ranch and a summer camp for young girls for a few years. The summer camp taught horseback riding, among other things. During that time a concrete swimming pool was installed near the original ranch house. A 1950 newspaper article described the eighty-thousand-gallon, thirty-foot by sixty-foot pool as a Christmas gift from Nelms's mother. Guests at Montezuma Ranch continued to go on cattle roundups on the adjacent Zaleski ranch. Frank Zaleski still owned more than four hundred acres around the mouth of Montezuma Canyon as Coronado National Memorial prepared to open in 1952.[43]

The business of running dude ranches in southern Arizona had many dimensions inclusive of advertising and promotions to draw tourists to the area. Many guests, for example, came from the Midwest and the East. Some came from Chicago, others from New York, and, at least one visitor in 1937 came from Winnipeg, Canada. According to the article in *Highway Traveler,* guests came from all walks of life. Some were college professors, teachers, or professional men and their families, others were mothers and daughters on tour, vacationing students, wealthy sightseers, and occasionally a "gallant gentleman. . . loafing away an enforced holiday because of shattered nerves."[44]

In its prime, the Border Ranch operated year-round. Generally, winter is southern Arizona's best season, which is always less rigorous than most places in the western United States. In the early days, lodging at the Border Ranch was moderately expensive and not every traveler could afford it. The cost of $60 a week included almost everything a guest needed for a week-long stay: room, meals, horses, and entertainment, which typically meant a night out at a cowboy dance hall in nearby Hereford, or a side trip to nearby Bisbee. Comparatively, prices for a week at a dude ranch in southern Arizona varied from $25 to $125 per week.[45]

Information presented by the Greyhound Bus Lines and several other brochures printed by rail companies promoted dude ranches in southern Arizona. In 1937, the Rock Island–Southern Pacific line's Golden State Route, for example, published a list of "Hotels-Guest Ranches in Arizona, New Mexico, El Paso, Texas." The Border Ranch blurbs advertised twelve rooms costing "$70.00 & up" a week for a single room with private bath. A double room went for "$100.00 & up" per week. Nearby, the Lightning Ranch rented rooms for $45 and $80 "& up" for single and double rooms per week. Prices listed under the American plan meant that all costs covered lodging and meals. Extraordinary expenses, such as specially requested pack trips, could be arranged for additional fees.[46]

A printed railroad guide stated that the "modern and comfortable" Border Ranch featured a "new concrete guest building" and "four 1- and 2-room cottages," and that each room had a private bath. Accommodating up to thirty guests, the ranch also boasted "New Monterey ranch-style furniture in all rooms and club home." John Pyeatt's old residence was the site of the so-called club home, completed by 1937.[47]

In 1938 the Southern Pacific Railroad again listed Border Ranch in its pamphlet titled "Guest Ranches Along Southern Pacific Lines." The pamphlet included the notation that Rudy Becker managed the ranch. A pamphlet published under the same title in 1941 indicates that Rudy Becker continued to manage the ranch. Perhaps some quarters were not then in use, for the maximum number of guests had been reduced to eighteen. Possibly in response to the exigencies of the Depression, room rates had apparently been cut as well. Winter rates, which in sunny Arizona were customarily higher than summer rates, were set at "$35 and up per week," while "Special summer rates" were also available.[48]

By late 1941 or early 1942 the Border Ranch had been renamed Montezuma Ranch. Frank Zaleski still ran the dude ranch. As the Great Depression waned, the growing wartime prosperity provided relief to the economy. Rates at the Border Ranch ranged from $57.00 and $110.00 weekly for single and double occupancy of the ten rooms then available. "Of the three ranches then listed in the Hereford area—Y Lightning Ranch, Carr Canyon Ranch, and Montezuma Ranch—the Montezuma was the most expensive. Guest capacity was set at eighteen persons."[49]

The Border Ranch was in existence for about fifteen years. Over time, the property had several owners. The property is located about two miles from the Coronado National Memorial Visitor Center. In the late 1990s the property still contained six residential structures, one of which was the owner's residence; the other five were for use by dude ranch guests. The property also had two shopping areas, a swimming pool, and a water tank. At that time the remains of an orchard were still evident along with other structures such as fencing and concrete and brick walls.[50]

To put this into perspective, during the 1930s at least sixty-five dude ranches operated in Arizona. Only Montana and Wyoming, where dude ranches originated, had more. Dude ranches initially appeared for several reasons. One common factor resulted when cattle prices fell dramatically during the early 1920s. At the same time, a rising number of tourists entered the West seeking new vacation spots. Ranchers whose spreads were located in picturesque settings began to supplement their incomes by opening their homes to paying guests. Dude ranch associations sprang up in several states, in effect institutionalizing the industry. In time ranch operators constructed lodges that offered a Western flavor, improved their recreational programs to include horseback riding, and made certain that good food was available.[51]

Eventually, a business relationship developed between dude ranchers and the railroads within their regions. In the 1920s the first of several short-lived dude and guest ranchers' associations appeared in Arizona. The railroads, in particular the Southern Pacific Railroad, supported the industry by luring passengers to destinations that had dude ranches.[52] Thus, the 1920s and 1930s were excellent years for many Western dude ranches. Alas, the post–World War II years brought dramatic growth and change to Arizona. The end of the dude ranch era was at hand. The trend shifted toward resorts and away from old-style dude ranches.[53]

The ranching tradition began when rugged cattlemen introduced livestock during the Spanish and Mexican periods. In the middle of the nineteenth century, equally tough Anglo-American stockmen continued the ranching pattern by reintroducing cattle into the area. Climate changes, economic downturns, and other factors changed the lifestyles of the area when miners and other people bought land for homesteading purposes. Bucolic in character, the homesteads and the old ranch houses were easily converted into dude ranches that imitated the ranching traditions of the Southwest. Modernization following World War II once again changed the character of the region. By the late twentieth century the area modernized once again. Today, vestiges of the Old West survive in the rich cultural resources that are preserved in Montezuma Canyon.

Notes

1. Grace Sparkes to Carl Hayden, October 25, 1947.

2. J. J. Bowden, "Private Land Claims in the Southwest," Thesis for degree of Master of Laws in Oil and Gas (Southern Methodist University, Dallas, Texas, 1969), Vol. 2, pp. 1927–1937.

3. Bowden, "Private Land Claims," ibid., 1910–1926.

4. Bowden, "Private Land Claims," ibid., 1881–1898.

5. Anonymous, "Eulalia Elías, 1786–1865," in Arizona Women's Hall of Fame, Arizona Historical Society, Museum Monograph, Central Arizona Division, Phoenix, AZ, 1987, 31.

6. "Eulalia Elías, 1786–1865," in Arizona Women's Hall of Fame, Arizona Historical Society, Museum Monograph, Central Arizona Division, Phoenix, AZ, 1987, 32.

7. See Bowden, "Private Land Claims in the Southwest," ibid., 1917–1926.

8. Wagoner, *Early Arizona*, University of Arizona Press, Tuscon, pp. 192-97; *Charles Leland Sonnichsen, Colonel Greene and the Copper Skyrocket; The Spectacular Rise and Fall of William Cornell Greene: Copper King, Cattle Baron, and Promoter Extra-ordinary in Mexico, the American Southwest, and the New York Financial District.* Tucson: The University of Arizona Press, 1974, 237-39, 290 fn14. The complex saga of the San Rafael de la Zanja grant is worthy of a chapter of its own; for a summary, see Bowden, "Private Land Claims in the Southwest," 1819–1830.

9. Wagoner, *Early Arizona*, University of Arizona Press, Tuscon, pp. 192-97.

10. One local source recalled that Ratliff arrived in the late 1890s (George Brown, interview by Thomas B. Carroll, September 20, 1974). Another thought it was about 1885 (Buck D'Albini, "Presentation," n.d., CORO Files).

11. George Brown, interview by Thomas B. Carroll, September 20, 1974 CORO Files, George Brown, 1974.

12. George Brown, interview by Thomas B. Carroll, September 20, 1974 CORO Files, Buck D'Albini, "Presentation," CORO Files.

13. "The Ratliff Ranch: A Chronology," Cochise chapter of the Arizona Archeological Society, n.d., CORO Files.

14. Laurel Dale, Superintendent, Coronado National Memorial, to Thomas Mulhern, Historic Preservation, Western Regional Office, Hereford, February 23, 1976, Re: Historic Structures at Coronado National Memorial, CORO Files ibid. George Brown is given as the main source of information for this report.

15. Approval of field notes of "Homestead Entry Survey No. 311," Office of the U.S. Surveyor General, Phoenix, AZ, August 8, 1917, CORO Files, ibid.

16. Approval of field notes of Homestead Entry Survey No. 310, CORO Files, ibid.

17. Sketch map of homestead claims, n.d., in Approval of field notes of Homestead Entry Survey No. 310, CORO Files.

18. Jack Ratliff, interview by Sandra Tate and Ellen Bolduc, n.d., in Approval of field notes of Homestead Entry Survey No. 310, CORO Files.

19. Cochise Chapter of The Arizona Archeological Society, "The Ratliff Ranch," n.d., CORO Files

20. Application for Second Entry, John Pyeatt, U.S. Land Office, Phoenix, AZ, June 4, 1917, WACC, Folder L 1425: Land Holdings—Pyeatt F6; Bart Barbour, "Dude Ranches at Coronado National Memorial: A Brief History," n.d., CORO Files.

21. Testimonies of Witnesses Zeno Aston and Robert Fourr, Homestead Entry, Final Proof, April 14, 1921, WACC, Folder L 1425: Land Holdings—Pyeatt F6; Homestead Entry Application, John Pyeatt, Received U.S. Land Office, Phoenix, AZ, WACC, Folder L 1425: Land Holdings—Pyeatt F6.

22. Office of the Acting Secretary of Agriculture to Office of the Secretary of the Interior, Washington, DC, December 27, 1913, U.S. Land Office, Phoenix, AZ, WACC, Folder L 1425: Land Holdings—Pyeatt F6.

23. Application for Amendment, Cornelius N. Driscoll, September 23, 1914, WACC, Folder L 1425: Land Holdings—Driscoll F7.

24. Barbour, "Dude Ranches," 2. CORO Files. Also see Final Certificate, Homestead, June 29, 1921; Affidavits of Witnesses, June 4, 1917; letter from Carl Hayden, Washington, DC, to Clay Tallman, General Land Office, November 13, 1917; letter from D. K. Parrott, General Land Office, to Adjutant General, United States Army, November 23, 1917, all in files at WACC.

25. Barbour, "Dude Ranches," 3, CORO Files. Deed of Real Estate Book, no. 95, page 411, Cochise County Recorder's Office, Bisbee, AZ.

26. Final Certificate, Homestead, John Pyeatt, Approved June 29, 1921, WACC, Folder L 1425: Land Holdings—Pyeatt F6; Barbour, "Dude Ranches."

27. Jack Ratliff, interview by Sandra Tate and Ellen Bolduc, n.d., CORO Files.

28. Rufus D'Albini, interview by Peter Van Cleve, December 3, 1997; Buck D'Albini,

"Presentation;" Jack Ratliff, n.d.; Barbour, "Dude Ranches," ibid; George Brown, interview by Barbara Alberti, August 18, 1998, CORO Files.

29. Barbour, "Dude Ranches," ibid; George Brown 1998, CORO Files, ibid.

30. Betty Peterson-Stowe and Frank Peterson, interview by Donna B. Bertolini and Scott Sticha, July 16, 1999, CORO Files.

31. Barbour, "Dude Ranches," ibid.

32. Field Notes, Coronado National Forest, Elmer L. Hertel, March 3, 1915, WACC, Folder L 1425: Land Holdings—Kudzmi F8.

33. Notice of Publication, Simon Kudzmi, August 29, 1929; Testimony of Claimant, Simon Kudzmi, Final Proof, December 28, 1929; Testimonies of Witnesses William Norick and Joseph Zaleski, Homestead Entry, Final Proof, December 28, 1929, WACC, Folder L 1425: Land Holdings – Kudzmi F8.

34. Barbour, "Dude Ranches" ibid; George Brown 1998, CORO Files, ibid; Also see, Betty Peterson-Stowe and Frank Peterson 1999; Tyne Turrie, "Riding the Range at Border Ranch," *Highway Traveler* (June/July 1937), 12–13, 40–44, CORO Files.

35. Barbour, "Dude Ranches," ibid; George Brown 1998, CORO Files, ibid.

36. Turrie, "Riding the Range at Border Ranch."

37. George Brown 1998, CORO Files, ibid.

38. Barbour, "Dude Ranches," CORO Files, ibid. Also see Tracking Book, Cochise County Assessor's Office, Bisbee, AZ.

39. Barbour, "Dude Ranches," CORO Files, ibid. Also see Tracking Book, Cochise County Assessor's Office, Bisbee, AZ.

40. H. H. Petersen to Sidney P. Osborn, Governor of Arizona, June 28, 1947, WACC, Folder H 14: Area and Service History 41-52 F3.

41. George Brown 1998, CORO Files, ibid; Barbour, "Dude Ranches" ibid.

42. Barbour, "Dude Ranches," CORO Files ibid. Also see Tracking Book, Cochise County Assessor's Office, Bisbee, AZ.

43. Barbour, "Dude Ranches," ibid; George Brown 1998, CORO Files, ibid; Grace Sparkes, "Huachuca Area," Bisbee Daily Review, June 18, 1950, n.p.; Peter Van Cleve, "List of Classified Structures, CCC/WPA, Coronado Establishment and Land Acquisitions," 1996, CORO Files. The names Jean Faye and Rex Watts were supplied by CORO staff, personal communication, July 2001.

44. Barbour, "Dude Ranches," ibid, 4.

45. Details on prices and employees' names are from Tyne Turrie, "Riding the Range at Border Ranch," *Highway Traveler* (June/July 1937), 12–13, 40–44, CORO Files.

46. Barbour, "Dude Ranches," ibid, 6.

47. Ibid.; "Hotels-Guest Arizona, New Mexico-El Paso, Texas," published in Chicago by Rock Island-Southern Pacific Railroad, 1937 (copy courtesy University of Arizona Special Collections).

48. "Guest Ranches along Southern Pacific Lines," published by Southern Pacific Railroad, 1938, 1941, University of Arizona Special Collections.

49. Barbour, "Dude Ranches," ibid, 6; "Hotels, Guest Ranches, Schools in Arizona, New Mexico, El Paso, Texas Most Comfortable Reached via the Low Altitude Golden State Route," published by the Rock Island-Southern Pacific Railroad, 1941, University of Arizona Special Collections.

50. Barbour, "Dude Ranches," ibid, 1.

51. Barbour, "Dude Ranches," ibid, 9. Also see Lawrence Borne, *A History of Dude Ranching* (Albuquerque: University of New Mexico Press, 1983), 119, 216, and chapters 3 and 4.

52. Lawrence Borne, *A History of Dude Ranching.* (Albuquerque: University of New Mexico Press, 1983), 185 and chapter 9.

53. Barbour, "Dude Ranches," ibid, 12.

CHAPTER 7

Mexico, the United States, and the Establishment of Coronado National Memorial

1939 to 1952

It is believed that the creation of an international monument... in which can be established an international museum to commemorate the explorations of Coronado... is desirable and feasible, provided the Governments of Mexico and the United States cooperate fully to bring about the establishment and maintenance of such an area.

—Dr. Aubry Neasham, NPS Historian, 1940[1]

In 1941 the Coronado International Memorial (the predecessor of the present Coronado National Memorial) was authorized. The opportunity to create an international monument had presented itself in the 400th anniversary of the Francisco Vázquez de Coronado Expedition. The impetus for the international monument grew from the work of the Coronado Cuarto Centennial Commission that had been created by the U.S. Congress in 1935. Soon after, the New Mexico Commission was created as part of the National Advisory Committee. Four years later, the Arizona Coronado Commission was created by the Gubernatorial Proclamation of July 27, 1939.[2] Working together, the Arizona supporters of the international monument on local, regional, national, and international levels worked to establish a monument on the border with the anticipated cooperation of Mexico.

On August 30, 1939, the Coronado Cuarto Centennial Commission of Arizona adopted a resolution proposing that an international monument and a museum be established on the United States–Mexico border, specifically between Arizona and Sonora, Mexico. The monument's purpose would be to commemorate the four hundredth anniversary of the Coronado Expedition that had explored from western Mexico, through

Arizona, New Mexico, western Texas, Oklahoma, and central Kansas. The Arizona Coronado Commission had been empowered to work with the necessary departments and agencies of the U.S. government, in conjunction and cooperation with the president of Mexico and the necessary departments and agencies of the Mexican government. Their goal was to set aside and create an international monument, at the place of their choosing.[3]

Because 1940, the commemorative year of Coronado's *entrada* of 1540, was approaching, the Arizona Coronado Commission members felt a sense of urgency. Charles M. Morgan, executive secretary of the Coronado Cuarto Centennial Commission, wrote to powerful friends and pushed their commitment. He sought the support of Governor R. T. Jones of Arizona and his old friend, Senator Carl Hayden (D-Arizona), and implored them to use their influence on the matter.

Their response encouraged Morgan. Governor Jones wrote, "I trust, that you will write the President, the secretaries of State and Interior, and any others, who, in your judgment, will be able to help expedite action on this proposal. It is important that it be pushed through as rapidly as possible, since 1940 is just around the corner."[4] Throughout September 1939 Senator Carl Hayden took his lead from the resolution, and worked to establish the proper channels to communicate, diplomatically, with Mexican officials as well as with members of the U.S. president's cabinet regarding the proposed international monument and museum.

Seeking ways and means to create an international monument, Hayden wrote to Cordell Hull, secretary of state, saying, "I presume that such an international monument could only be established by joint proclamation of the Presidents of the United States of America and of the United Mexican States."[5] Hayden requested that the secretary of state contact the U.S. ambassador to Mexico so that he could present the proposal to the proper Mexican officials.

Next, Hayden, in early October, wrote to the secretary of the interior asking for the involvement of the NPS in this effort. Pending a response from the Mexican government, Hayden requested that the NPS investigate the feasibility of a land cession and the creation of a monument "along the lines proposed by the Coronado Cuarto Centennial Commission of Arizona." Hayden, however, reminded the secretary of existing legislation aimed at establishing a monument to commemorate the historical event. "You will recall," he recounted, "that Public Law No. 186 of the 76th Congress, approved July 17, 1939, authorizes the sum of $10,000 to be spent for the erection of a monument of this type, but does not, of course, specify that such a monument shall be of an international character."[6]

Meanwhile, on October 10, 1939, Secretary of State Cordell Hull replied to Hayden's missive. Hull advised him that he had communicated with the U.S. Embassy in Mexico advising the ambassador to ascertain the general attitude of the Mexican government on the matter. As yet he had not heard back. To that end Hull assured Hayden, "I shall be glad to give every possible consideration to the international aspects of the Cuarto Centennial celebrations and render all appropriate assistance in that connection."[7] Hull, nevertheless, quickly pointed out that the proposed domestic activities would be the responsibility of the secretary of the Department of the Interior.

Meanwhile, John W. Finch, acting assistant secretary, the Department of the Interior, replied to Hayden, informing him, "I am asking the National Park Service to consider the feasibility of the plan. Finch proposed that the National Park Service determine, if possible, the point where Coronado crossed into what is now Arizona, and, "if this point can be located to recommend appropriate boundaries."[8]

On October 21, 1939, Hayden wrote to his friend R. T. Jones about the NPS's involvement and advised him that "that no final action can be taken by the Interior Department until the attitude of the Mexican Government is ascertained."[9] However, the Coronado Cuarto Centennial Commission and Governor Jones' office had already been in contact with Mexican officials in Mexico City. Jones also informed Hayden that the U.S. Coronado Exposition Commission member states of Arizona, New Mexico, and Texas had adopted a resolution to send a delegation to Mexico City to discuss the details of the Mexican government's involvement. In his communication with Hayden, Jones justified his actions by citing a dispatch from the Associated Press in Mexico City dated September 29. The dispatch communicated that the Mexican government "will send a delegation to take part in the Coronado Cuarto Centennial Celebration." Jones truly believed that Mexican officials would cooperate in the establishment of a monument to Coronado on the border. The Arizona Coronado Commission was abuzz about the possibility of the establishment of the Coronado International Monument and a Coronado Memorial Museum.[10] Hayden soon learned that the U.S. Embassy in Mexico City could not confirm the Associated Press story.

The issue of Mexican participation remained unresolved for months.

Months later, in February 1940, the Mexican government responded to the U.S. Embassy in Mexico City. Clinton P. Anderson, managing director of the United States Coronado Exposition Commission in New Mexico, learned of the response from a copy of a letter from the U.S. Embassy. The letter read, in part, "The American Ambassador to Mexico informs the United States Coronado Exposition Commission that the Mexican Government will accept the invitation to cooperate in the Exposition, and will later discuss the plans of participation."[11] Still, the Mexican government's response fell short of a commitment. Nonetheless, it stirred in Anderson a need to do something to draw Mexican interest.

As Mexican participation floundered, so too, did the commission's hope for international cooperation. In response to questions raised by Anderson about proceeding with the proposal for a monument, Hayden advised him to wait until Mexico's position could be clarified.[12] On another matter, Hayden was hard put to answer Anderson's query. Anderson wanted to know if the NPS or the Department of the Interior could indicate by February 20 whether a favorable recommendation could be submitted to Congress regarding the creation of an international monument at or near the point where Coronado first entered what is now the United States. Second, he asked if an international museum within such an international park would be looked on with favor by the United States.[13] At that point, the questions were rhetorical. No one had a clear answer to either question.

Meanwhile, the NPS's investigation of the feasibility of the proposed international monument had been made at the NPS's Region III Office in Santa Fe. The report, when completed, was communicated to Hayden.[14] The field investigation team, led by Dr. Aubry Neasham, the regional historian for the NPS in Santa Fe, and a committee, had visited Arizona in mid-December. Among his consultants was Dr. Emil Haury, head of the Department of Anthropology at the University of Arizona, Tucson. Haury supported the idea of the Coronado International Monument. Optimistically, he advised Neasham, "Soliciting the cooperation of the Mexican government should, it seems to me, be accomplished without too much difficulty."[15] Haury obviously did not know about the difficulty Hull and Hayden had already experienced in their attempts to get a response from the Mexican government.

By February 1940 Neasham had generated a series of reports dealing with the prospect of an international monument commemorating the Coronado Expedition of 1540. The consultants to these reports included

Jerome C. Miller, associate landscape architect; and W. Ward Yeager, associate forester of the NPS Region III, as well as Dr. Haury and Dr. Russell Ewing of the University of Arizona. By mid-December 1939 they had met with a team to survey the international border between Nogales and Naco to determine the location of an international monument "at or near the point where Coronado crossed from Mexico into what is now Arizona."[16]

Meanwhile, Neasham, accompanied by Herbert E. Bolton and George P. Hammond, both distinguished historians, headed a survey team along the border. Their report had been delayed because of the need to identify Coronado's route. The team had spent several weeks tracing the route of the Coronado Expedition, and by February 1940 the survey was nearly completed.[17]

Their reports made some observations and recommendations regarding the establishment of the international monument. They stressed, moreover, the importance of Mexico's cooperation in the establishment of an appropriate commemorative site. Neasham's report, nonetheless, reflected the hopes of those on the United States side who worked to establish the Coronado International Monument. Of its significance, he wrote, "It is believed that the creation of an international monument . . . in which can be established an international museum to commemorate the explorations of Coronado . . . is desirable and feasible, provided the Governments of Mexico and the United States cooperate fully to bring about the establishment and maintenance of such an area."[18] Throughout his report, Neasham stressed that "cultural understanding" was the pillar on which the international monument would be built.

Neasham hoped that the desired cooperation between the two nations in regard to scientific endeavors would eventually take place. On that point, he reported, "It is believed that an international monument established in the area indicated will be of great value in advancing the relationships of the United States and Mexico upon a friendly basis of cultural understanding. Furthermore, such an area with its international museum would serve as a common clearing ground for scientific endeavor between Mexico and the United States."[19] The museum was, indeed, an integral feature of the international monument because in it could be displayed important artifacts and documents illustrating the history and culture of that area.

Next, Neasham added another enthusiastic point for the justification for the international monument. In his conversations with a certain

Señor Gonzales who was the Mexican consulate in Phoenix, Neasham explored significance of a proposed international highway that would be completed in two years. The highway, running from Guadalajara, Mexico, would straddle the Pacific Coast before turning inland, and would terminate in Nogales, Arizona, thus stimulating increased tourism in all of those areas. Neasham pointed out that the international parkway or freeway would eventually connect the proposed international monument and Nogales on the U.S. side. Neasham saw many possibilities growing out of the international freeway that would pass along "a scenic border country."[20]

Unabated in his enthusiasm, Neasham wrote, "The area of Bisbee and Douglas, Arizona, could tie in with that parkway without difficulty. The War Department, too, may be interested in developing such a parkway, because of its close proximity to the Mexican border and Fort Huachuca. It is believed that the people of Arizona would enter wholeheartedly into the development of an international monument, museum, and parkway along the international border." To that end, he recommended that an international survey party comprising representatives from the United States and Mexico investigate the possibilities for the creation of an international monument, museum, and parkway. "Mexico," he wrote, "has indicated that she will cooperate fully with this government in celebrating this year's Coronado Cuarto-Centennial, of which the establishment of an international monument is an important phase."[21]

Neasham's report also recommended that an international advisory board be formed to further such interests on both sides of the border. Three citizens from each country would make up the board, hopefully headed by Dr. Herbert E. Bolton of the Advisory Board on National Parks, Historical Sites, Buildings, and Monuments. That committee, read the report, would "do much to insure[*sic*] the success of the international monument, in view of the sympathy, contacts, and cultural understanding of such an individual."[22]

In context, it would be unfair to characterize Neasham's enthusiastic report as a product of naivete, for a genuine feeling on the part of the United States—through the Coronado Cuarto Centennial Commission and the NPS—was based on the hope that all could ride on the coattails of interest engendered by the opportunity presented by the four hundredth anniversary of the Coronado Expedition. Neasham's report expressed the hope that "international travel, advancement of good will, and cultural relationships with Latin America" could be spurred by this effort.[23] Indeed, it was an interesting time in the history of the United States, as war clouds burst into the violence of World War II.

In his transmittal of Neasham's report to Hayden, Harold L. Ickes, secretary of the interior, clarified the position of the Department of the Interior. The department, he wrote could not approve "a proposal for an international project of this character prior to receiving an expression of the views of the State Department."[24] Ickes, moreover, stated that Interior policy prohibited the creation of an international park, but would permit an international monument or memorial.

In preparation for his proposed legislation, Hayden considered the question regarding the size of the monument and suggested "Eleven sections of land are vastly more than is needed for a monument of this type. I should assume that an acre or two would be ample."[25] The eleven sections were to be taken from the Coronado National Forest for the monument. Given that grazing privileges existed on that land, they too would be taken into consideration. Hayden recommended that the secretary of the interior deliver a copy of the proposal for the monument to the secretary of agriculture so that the U.S. Forest Service could study and reach an agreement regarding the boundaries. Evidently, some discussions between Hayden and his constituents had taken place over the size of the proposed monument, grazing privileges, and any subsurface minerals that could exist within the projected boundaries.

To Hayden's concerns, Arno B. Cammerer, director, NPS, responded that once the State Department informed the Department of the Interior of the possibility of an international monument, the NPS would make "further studies . . . to insure[*sic*] the exclusion of mineral lands from the proposed area."[26] The issue of the size of the monument would resurface several times in the next few weeks.

The pressure to propose legislation for the monument grew in Hayden's mind. On March 18 he received a letter from E. K. Burlew, first assistant secretary of the interior, repeating that the Department of the Interior could not approve a proposal for an international monument unless it received a favorable expression from the Department of State. "Until such an expression has been received," wrote Burlew, "the Department of the Interior cannot submit a proposal to establish an international monument to the Department of Agriculture. It is understood, however, that the Coronado Cuarto Centennial Commission is presenting the above-mentioned proposition to the Department of State for its consideration. If that Department favors the proposal, the Department of the

Interior will submit it to the Department of Agriculture for study."[27] About the same time, Ickes formally requested an opinion from the Department of State concerning the feasibility of an international monument.[28]

The Department of State moved slowly. In a telegraph to Stuart M. Bailey, chairman of the Arizona Coronado Cuarto Centennial Commission, Hayden advised him that the Department of State would not be able to present the proposal to Mexico by April 15. Meanwhile, he suggested that the NPS make an additional study regarding the boundary and mineral possibilities on the proposed land. In his telegram Hayden explained that the Department of Agriculture had to be included in the discussions because the land in question was located within the Coronado National Forest and managed by the U.S. Forest Service.[29]

By consensus, Hayden and Baily agreed to reduce the amount of land originally requested by 50 percent equaling 2,750 acres. They justified the request by explaining the need for an international monument that would represent the desired relationships between the two countries. U.S. Forest Service officials understood that the purpose of the monument on the international boundary would include a sufficient area that, with the area to be provided by the Mexican government, would give the monument the desired international aspect.[30] They, too, believed that the Mexican government would support the monument.

Based on their findings, U.S. Forest Service officials thought that forest values—that is, its minerals and other natural resources—were negligible in the small area under consideration and that grazing use would not be disturbed except for the small plots immediately around the structures. They believed that a compromise could be reached between the U.S. government and the stock raisers. They believed that the NPS would recommend the establishment of the national monument by leaving intact all valid existing rights that would include pertinent mining claims already of record and outstanding grazing permits for the remainder of the contract terms. Arguing that time was of the essence, because "the dedication ceremonies are desired at the earliest possible date," U.S. Forest Service officials acquiesced to the compromise in a joint proposal. Regarding the 2,750 acres, they prepared a report.[31]

The resulting report, dated April 4, was signed by John A. Adams, regional forest inspector, Division of Recreation and Lands, in Albuquerque. The proposed Coronado International Monument, wrote Adams, "is located in the Huachuca Division of the Coronado National Forest, approximately thirty miles west of Bisbee, Arizona. The area contains

2,745 acres in T. 24 S., Rs. 20 and 21 E., adjoining and north of the International boundary."[32] A survey of the area had been made by U.S. Forest Service personnel on March 12 and 13 to determine the location, land status, range use, range improvements, and forest products, beyond which there were other amenities. Perhaps the panoramic vistas afforded from the high point offered the best vantage point from which to commemorate the Coronado Expedition. The writers of the report aptly observed, "The lookout or observation point is located half a mile south where the road crosses the saddle in the southern part of Sec. 11. From this point an unexcelled view is had of the country north of the Sonora Valley, as well as the Cananea Mountains in Mexico. To the west is seen the Patagonia Range across the San Rafael Valley. From the Sonora divide following north viz. The San Pedro Valley is the probable route of Francisco Coronado during the year 1540."[33] The land offered the best vantage point for interpreting the historical event and the geography of the area.

Meanwhile, Hayden had second thoughts about the size of the land to be taken for the monument and argued that the size be reduced. At that historical moment, tall, lanky, charming, Clinton P. Anderson prepared a response. Sitting at his desk, he looked over a copy of Hayden's letter that called for limiting the acreage of the proposed international monument. With a twinkle in his eye, Anderson began his response. Diplomatically, Anderson waxed eloquent, expressing to Hayden how he appreciated his thoughts on the proposed size of the international monument. "I wish I could discuss this with you intelligently," he wrote, "but I do feel that the National Park people are so much more capable of a decision than I am that I have followed their proposals and given them my general support."[34] Anderson reminded him that private lands were not involved. Applying logic to the situation, Anderson posited

> I wish that before they reach a final decision you could take a look at it. I think that would help you to appreciate the suggestion made by the Park Service. Their lookout is back a short distance from the border. It is at a very excellent location and I really feel that it would be very much worthwhile to connect the lookout point with the museum site. If you do that you stretch the area quite a little distance along the border I admit, but the land is not of great value for any purpose other than a park area. It is rather sandy at the bottom and rather steep on the grades which go up toward the lookout. It would be one thing to transfer this much acreage from private ownership to Federal ownership, but it is quite another thing to transfer it from Forest Service land to Park Service land.[35]

The last sentence surely caused Hayden to raise his eyebrows and tilt his head in approbation. Clearly, he grasped Anderson's meaning: the land in question was largely, if not entirely, being transferred from one government agency to another. Using salesmanship skills, Anderson wrote, "I believe it will be a splendid national attraction." He described the historical landscape and ended by saying, "All the rest is wilderness looking just as it did when Coronado crossed it 400 years ago. There are very few areas in the United States of which that can be said. . . . I know of no place along the border which serves as well as the lookout point selected by the Park Service."[36]

Returning to the lack of response from Mexico, Hayden transmitted a copy of Anderson's letter to Cordell Hull. "I assume," he wrote, "that if legislation establishing the proposed international monument is to be sought, there will be no great point in your presenting any proposals along these lines to the Republic of Mexico, at least until the legislation has been formulated and introduced."[37] Hull quickly responded. He mentioned that State Department officers working on the Coronado matter would be able to meet with Hillory A. Tolson in Washington. Beyond that, Hull astutely reiterated the desire of his office to assist in the Coronado matter in any way. He instructed the U.S. Embassy in Mexico City to act "as soon as the [Coronado] Commission presents to the Department [of State] a definite proposal with regard to the international monument. . .in honor of Coronado."[38] Still, Mexican officials, apparently cool to the idea, had not responded.

Whatever transpired to change Hayden's mind on presenting a bill to Congress establishing the Coronado International Monument is not clear in the record. On Monday, April 17, 1940, Hull wrote to Hayden saying that Tolson informed him that "he was now in a position to make recommendations to the United States Coronado Commission on the basis of which the Commission could present a definite plan to the Department of State."[39] Possibly after a few telephone calls, he decided to move forward with his proposal. On Monday, April 22, 1940, Hayden informed W. E. Clark, clerk of the Cochise County Board of Supervisors, as well as a selected group of people, mostly leaders of associations in Arizona, that he would present a bill providing for the creation of the Coronado International Monument in Arizona to the Committee on Public Lands and Surveys. In his correspondence he provided a print of a bill dated April 20, 1940, to set aside an area for "a Coronado international monument."[40]

The bill called for the establishment of the international monument with the prerogative to grant grazing privileges as well as prospecting and mining privileges within the monument area as consistent and appropriate with public uses. Despite his earlier objections to the contrary, Hayden's bill called for 2,960 acres. It was the first legislative step in the creation of the monument. The bill remained in committee until May 28, when a new draft was presented. Section 2 of the new bill read, "The National Park Service, under the direction of the Secretary of the Interior, shall promote and regulate the use of the Coronado International Monument for the benefit and enjoyment of the people of the United States."[41] Slowly, legislation that would establish the Coronado International Monument under the administration of the NPS emerged.

By late summer 1940 the Committee on Public Lands and Surveys submitted its report recommending that the bill pass and attached supporting letters from the acting secretary of agriculture and the acting secretary of the interior. Additionally, the report included a printed invitation to Mexico from the United States Coronado Exposition Commission. The invitation, addressed to Mexico's minister for foreign relations, expressed the hope that Mexico would join the United States in developing Coronado International Monument as a binational effort.[42]

Word spread quickly that Hayden had introduced the legislation. On September 30, an elated Hayden announced the passage of his bill by the Senate. With subdued enthusiasm, he sent a telegram to Charles F. Willis, state secretary of the Arizona Small Mine Operators Association in Phoenix, and copied eighteen other supporters of the bill. In it he expressed the following: "Very glad to advise Senate today passed my Bill S4130 providing for the establishment of the Coronado International Monument in Cochise County Stop Bill now goes to House of Representatives where I hope early action can be had."[43]

The House did not take up the bill until mid-November 1940. Congressman Church, from Illinois, announced, "I ask unanimous consent that the bill be passed over without prejudice."[44] Another hurdle had been surmounted as the bill progressed through the legislative processes. One more stop, the Oval Office, and the bill, with the president's signature, would become law. Finally, the Coronado International Memorial received official confirmation with the Act of August 18, 1941.[45]

Meanwhile, the Arizona Coronado International Memorial Commission scrambled to move their planning forward. There was still time to commemorate the four hundredth year of Coronado's famed expedition into the heart of North America. Since October, members of the Arizona Coronado International Memorial Commission had preliminary sketches of the memorial drawn by the NPS.[46] The commissioners quickly reviewed the plans in anticipation that the Coronado International Memorial would soon be developed on both sides of the border. Time was of the essence. Despite the congressional action of 1940–41, the Arizona Commission moved slowly and very little toward the establishment of the Coronado International Memorial occurred.

In 1940 Mexican support for an international monument was, at best, lukewarm, even though the proposal to establish a suitable monument received a "hearty approval of both President Manuel Avila Camacho and President Franklin D. Roosevelt."[47] On June 1, 3, 5, and 10, 1942, U.S. representatives met with the Mexican International Park Commission in Mexico City to discuss plans for the proposed Coronado International Memorial.[48] The U.S. representatives included Hillory Tolson, chairman; Miner E. Tillotson, Dr. Aubrey Neasham, Mrs. Foster Rockwell, Odd S. Halseth, and Dr. Herbert E. Bolton.[49] The members of the Mexican Coronado International Commission, named by Secretary of Agriculture Marte R. Gómez, were Fernando Romero Quintana, chairman, Carlos Villas Pérez, Rafael Fernández McGregor, Juan Manuel Corona, José Garcia Martínez, and Agustín Gómez y Gutierrez.[50] The joint recommendations submitted to Secretary Gómez called for a survey of the proposed site in Sonora that was occupied by the Cananea Cattle Company.

For a brief moment it appeared that Mexico would concur and support the idea of an international monument. The United States–Mexico representatives that had met in Mexico City recommended that the president of Mexico issue "a decree establishing the Coronado International Memorial in Sonora." In accordance with the recommendations, the surveyor, Villas Pérez, a trained engineer, traveled to the border to "survey and fence the proposed area in Sonora, and to negotiate with the Cananea Cattle Company."[51]

Astutely, the Mexican Coronado International Commission members had noted that the Cananea Cattle Company's land abutted the international boundary facing the proposed Coronado International Memorial on the U.S. side. To them, taking private land from a wealthy American entrepreneur to establish the Mexican counterpart to the memorial would be much more favorable to nationalists. At the same time, in June 1942 the over-enthused U.S. participants optimistically reported "that they [the Mexicans] would like to see an area of approximately the same acreage [2,800 acres]" on the Mexican side.[52] Unfortunately, World War II intervened and the project lay inactive until 1947.

World War II took up much of the country's energies, and, during the war years the Arizona Coronado Commission had been deactivated. In effect, the Act of August 18, 1941 put the proposed Coronado International Memorial on hold until Mexico reciprocated with a memorial mirroring the U.S. effort on the border. By all means, the word *international* required the agreement of both Mexico and the United States to erect the proposed memorial on the border. Given the wartime concerns, Hayden did not return to establishing an international memorial near Bisbee until the late 1940s after the war had ended.

Supporters of the Arizona Coronado International Memorial kept their plans alive during the war years through correspondence and meetings between the Arizona Commission and the NPS. In August 1943 Emilio Gutierrez Roldán, Mexico's director general of forests and game, wrote to the NPS director advising him that an agreement had been reached with the Cananea Cattle Company regarding land for the monument in Mexico. In correspondence to Hayden, Tolson said that Gutierrez Roldán said that the company "had offered to place the land at the disposal of the Director of General of Forests and Game for an indefinite period, subject only to the condition that the Company be allowed to graze cattle on it and to terminate the grant at such time as the land is no longer used as an international park." For a while it looked auspicious. On October 11, 1943, the NPS responded affirmatively, but soon after communications from Mexico stopped. On April 1, 1944, Tolson asked George Messersmith, U.S. ambassador to Mexico, to inquire of Gutierrez Roldán the status of the letter and their plans for the Coronado International Memorial. On May 3, L. D. Mallory, the agricultural attaché of the U.S. Embassy in Mexico City, met with Villas Pérez, "who located our letter of October 11, 1943, and found that a reply had not been made to it."[53] He promised a reply, but as of May 27, 1944, none was forthcoming.

Mexico City remained silent on the issue of the Coronado International Memorial. On August 19, 1944, Tolson wrote to Halseth, saying, "We feel sure that Ing. [Engineer] Villas Pérez is still interested in the international memorial project, and has not been in position to get his Department to reply to our communications due to circumstances beyond his control."[54]

Finally, as a last resort, Tolson was willing to forego an international monument. Given the Mexican government's inexplicable silence regarding the recommendations of the Mexico–United States commission that had met in Mexico City in June 1942, Tolson began to rethink the idea of an international memorial. The Act of August 18, 1941, he wrote, "should be amended to eliminate the requirement for an international memorial and instead move for a national memorial within the state of Arizona."[55] Hopeful of Mexican cooperation, Tolson suggested that the NPS proceed with plans to establish the U.S. version of the memorial. In anticipation of the end of the war and a need for a public works program, he wrote,

> It may be held by some that this is a matter that need not be pressed at this time. However, it is probable that the wars against Hitler's Germany and Japan will be terminated within the next year. If so, active plans, presumably, will be made to handle the resulting unemployment; and funds will probably be made available for some type of public works program. The establishment of the memorial. . .will involve. . .reaching agreements with the proper Mexican officials with respect to the developments to be placed in the companion areas of. . .this splendid international memorial area (which is important because of its great possibilities in the promotion of a friendly relationship between Mexico and the United States in addition to providing a fitting memorial for the Coronado expedition).[56]

Optimistically, Tolson hoped for Mexican support for the memorial in the postwar years. Communications with Mexico in 1945 were minimal to nonexistent, as they had been in previous years. As 1945 rolled into 1946, little had been accomplished toward establishing Coronado International Memorial. By February 1946, Tolson could see the handwriting on the wall in regard to the notion that Mexican participation would not be forthcoming.[57]

As the postwar years set in, a new optimism grew alongside it that things would change for the better. From that parallax view, the Mexican presidential election of 1946 appeared to bode well. In late November Tolson learned that he and Dr. Jesse L. Nusbaum, an NPS archeologist in Santa Fe, had been appointed to the U.S. International Park and Forest Commission by the secretary of the interior.[58] Tolson hoped that his appointment would put him in better position to deal with his Mexican counterparts as a peer.

Meanwhile, the NPS's efforts were thwarted by the actions of the Cananea Cattle Company. Not long after the promising July 18 meeting in Mexico City, Tolson, much chagrinned, received some upsetting news. The most recent information he had "regarding the Coronado Memorial was that Mr. C. E. Wiswall of the Cananea Cattle Company had gotten in touch with the representatives of the State Department of this Country and of the Mexican Government to protest the creation of the memorial."[59] That protest, in large part, led to the decision of the Department of State to demur on the matter.

The following year, on December 21, 1948, Senator Hayden contacted Villas Pérez advising him that the U.S. Department of State had informed the Mexican government that it could not insist that Mexico cooperate in the Coronado Memorial project because of "its policy of not pressing the Mexican Government too strongly for action in matters where American interests are involved."[60] The "American interests" revolving around the Coronado International Memorial in Sonora were those of the Cananea Cattle Company. Having no response from Villas Pérez for a year, Hayden seemed at a loss to find ways to encourage Mexican interest in the Coronado International Memorial.

The prospect that the government might, as it eventually would, expropriate the land, was the Cananea Cattle Company's greatest fear. The company reasoned that if it agreed to release any property for the park it could lead the government to seize more. If the company willfully relinquished land, the Mexican government would conclude that the company didn't need it all and undermine the company's claim.

The Cananea Cattle Company operated in Mexico under Mexican laws. The citizens and government of Mexico, as well as the Cananea Cattle Company, were far more concerned with the expropriation issue than with the construction of a memorial to Coronado. Thus, statements by Colonel William Cornel Greene, Wiswall, and the company as a whole regarding the memorial must be considered in the context of the expropriation struggle in Mexico.

It was clear that the Cananea Cattle Company was not interested in the creation of the Coronado Memorial. At the same time that Wiswall and Greene discussed the project in reasonable terms with the NPS and the Bisbee Chamber of Commerce, they expressed their opposition to the highest levels of government in Mexico City and Washington, DC. Yet, for almost a decade, Arizona boosters had taken the side of the Cattle Company and blamed the Mexican government for not collaborating with them to develop the international memorial. In early 1952 Senator Hayden realized the futility of the effort. He opined, "So long as

[Wiswall] has anything to say about it, there will be no Cananea Cattle Company land made available for a Mexican area as a part of a Coronado National Monument."[61]

For its part, the Mexican government had much larger concerns in the area. It considered the Ranchos de Cananea where the Cananea Cattle Company was located to be illegal, contrary in both the letter and spirit to the national constitution. Expropriation was coming, whether or not the government wanted it, and taking land from foreign citizens only to dedicate it to a joint project with a foreign government was not politically correct.

The early movers and shakers to establish the memorial on the U.S. side simply did not understand Mexico. Few of them understood that the historical processes in Mexico could not support the celebration of a colonial hero if for no other reason than the Revolution of 1910 was a struggle against neo-colonialism and its close cousin, imperialism. Others in the United States who were involved in the creation of the memorial did not care to learn about events south of the border. They were more than willing to involve themselves in Mexican affairs than was appropriate. One who understood the situation was Odd S. Halseth of the old Arizona Coronado Commission. In July 1951 Halseth commented to Grace Sparkes, "From the beginning I have had the feeling that we neither had any business to negotiate with a Mexican company, nor that our good intentions necessarily would be considered so by the Mexican government. Reverse the situation and consider the possible reaction by our State Department."[62]

For nearly a decade Mexican officials did not respond to the concept of a reciprocal international monument. Finally, as 1951 came to an end with no action from the Mexican government, Senator Carl Hayden suggested to Grace Sparkes, one of his constituents leading the proposal for an international monument, that the United States ought to "ignore the Mexican angle and see if our Congress can be persuaded to set aside the generally agreed upon public lands located in the United States as a National Monument to the Coronado Expedition."[63] Even though Hayden had sought a response from President Miguel Alemán regarding a proposed meeting about the international monument proposal, none was forthcoming.[64]

Seeing no other recourse, on March 24, 1952, Hayden introduced Senate Bill 2909, requesting that "the words 'Coronado National Memorial' are hereby substituted in lieu of the words 'Coronado International

Memorial' wherever such words occur in the Act of August 18, 1941." Section 1 of the Act of August 18, 1941 "is hereby amended by striking out" the portion requiring Mexican participation in the establishment of the Coronado International Memorial. A month later, on April 23, H.R. 7553, a companion bill in the House of Representatives, was introduced. The language was the same.[65] The long wait was over. Hayden and the Arizona Coronado International Memorial Commission were now committed to a course that would establish the Coronado National Memorial. Sensing an end to the long struggle to establish the memorial, Sparkes asked Hayden "if you would have your file on our Coronado Project bound and sent to us—or present it to the U.S. Park Service." She also asked other supporters to do the same saying that they would be kept in the museum at Bisbee.[66]

By the end of June 1952, S. 2909 had passed the Senate and the House bill was pending on the calendar of the House.[67] On July 2, 1952, Hayden wired Sparkes the following message: "House today passed S. 2909 clearing it for the president."[68] The next step toward creating the Coronado National Memorial would be a presidential proclamation, which was being prepared for President Harry Truman.[69] The proclamation worked its way slowly to the president after it first cleared the Bureau of the Budget and the attorney general.

Reading a Western Union telegram he received from his aide in Washington, DC, U.S. Senator Carl Hayden, now in his Phoenix office, must have allowed himself a smile as he uttered the words, "Just been advised President Truman on November 5 [1952], signed *Coronado National Memorial* Proclamation, Executive Order 2995."[70]

It was a fitting end to a process that would commemorate a historical moment and heritage as a part of the national story of the United States. Earlier, when Sparkes led a tour to the site on July 25, 1952, she believed that the place, the historical moment, and the panoramic view were right. In that tour were Conrad L. Wirth, director of the NPS; R. L. Lee, assistant director of the NPS; and M. R. Tillotson, regional director of the NPS. As they wound their way down from Coronado Peak, Sparkes recollected later, "It was way beyond my expectations, for it goes beyond the thought of a place for an historical marker—there lies the route before you of Coronado—you actually feel it and see it."[71] Still, in her heart, she wished that one day Mexico would come around to make Coronado National Memorial an international area. In the 1960s another serious attempt at an international memorial began to make headway in Arizona, but it, too, died a quick death in Mexico.

As a postscript, in 1980 Cuauhtémoc Cárdenas, the son of Mexican president Lázaro Cárdenas and a government official in his own right, visited Coronado National Memorial. He told officials of the NPS and the Coronado International Memorial Commission that Mexico was not interested in building a monument to Coronado or to any other Spanish conquistador.[72] In 1810, after all, Mexico's independence originated in a peasant and Indian revolt against Spanish colonialism. Through its history as an independent nation, Mexico has suffered interventions and invasions by Spain, France, England, and the United States. The Revolution of 1910 was a reaction to the Mexican experience of the nineteenth century. Modern Mexico celebrates, at least symbolically, its Indian heritage rather than the arrival of European colonizers. The Spanish conquest of Mexico is seen as the beginning of a process of colonial exploitation of Mexico.

In another instance, decades after Mexico refused to participate in an international monument to a colonial figure and event, Mexican officials, in contrast to its efforts in the 1940s, did cooperate in establishing a commemorative border park celebrating the signing of the Chamizal Treaty of 1963. The establishment of the United States' Chamizal National Memorial and Mexico's Parque Público Federal El Chamizal along the El Paso–Juárez portion of the international boundary between the two countries served a far different purpose, for it aimed to commemorate the harmonious relationships between the two countries. Indeed, Chamizal National Memorial and the Parque Público Federal El Chamizal celebrate the peaceful resolution to a hundred-year border dispute to a border issue caused by the meandering Rio Grande during flood times.[73] At times when the river flooded it created a new riverbed that often moved the boundary line southward, leaving land belonging to Mexico on the U.S. side of the boundary. By international law the middle of the river determined the boundary line. Finally, the river bed was concreted and the boundary once again fixed by the Chamizal Treaty of 1963.

With time, the strong negative feelings and attitudes about colonialism among Mexicans had, at least, been alleviated. In 2001 the United States commemorated 404 miles of the 1,600-mile historic colonial road known as the Camino Real de Tierra Adentro National Historic Trail. That small stretch of the Camino Real de Tierra Adentro (Royal Road of the Interior) ran from the United States–Mexico border through a small part of southwestern Texas at El Paso and north from there through a long corridor of New Mexico to Santa Fe. The other 1,200 miles lay in Mexico. Between 1540 and 1821, the Camino Real ran from Mexico City to Santa Fe, New Mexico, and became a corridor in the regional development of both countries.

In efforts by both countries to commemorate a common heritage and patrimony, Mexico reciprocated with a series of symposia sponsored by the NPS's Spanish Colonial Research Center and the NPS Mexico Affairs Office in cooperation with the Instituto Nacional de Antropología e Historia (National Institute of Anthropology and History) (INAH). The symposia were held alternately in both countries every year for eight years in cities associated with the Camino Real de Tierra Adentro. In 2011 Mexico's interest and efforts resulted in UNESCO designating the Camino Real de Tierra Adentro World Heritage Site within the Mexican portion of the trail. Thus, while the Coronado International Monument failed for lack of cooperation between the two countries, the lessons learned have become part of the legacy of our shared patrimony and heritage, which includes Spain and regional Native American tribes along the route and corridor of the Camino Real de Tierra Adentro.

In the 1940s, however, the efforts to include Mexico in the deliberations to establish an international monument commemorating the four hundredth anniversary of the Coronado Expedition failed. Still, the U.S. proponents of an international monument continued to communicate with their Mexican counterparts in the hope of reviving the proposal.

To Mexicans the proposal to honor Francisco Vásquez de Coronado and 'Colonel' William Cornell Greene, a 'big business' copper mining entrepreneur in Mexico, did not bode well. That newly hatched proposal, in the same monument, ignored the trauma of historical topics related to the European conquest of Mexico, the U.S. invasion of 1846, and the foreign exploitation and ownership of the lands and mines of Sonora in the twentieth century. At the very time that the United States sought to erect a monument to a man who had pioneered the region, the Mexican public, which had undergone two long revolutions for that independence (in 1810 against Spanish colonial rule, and in 1910 against a dictator who had violated the liberties of Mexico's people in favor of foreign enterprises) demanded the exclusion of such topics from their history books. Mexicans had little interest in celebrating a history of foreign domination. In the end, the U.S. efforts in 1940 to commemorate a common history with Mexico instead emphasized the ideological difference in the perception of history between the two countries.

The creation of the memorial left in its wake many lessons about the process in establishing an international park. On its face, the proposal for establishing a park on the United States–Mexico border between two friendly countries appears to be a simple matter of getting both parties to agree to the proposition. Yet, the historical complexity on which the relationship is based is profound. In the first place, the historical experiences of the two nations resulted in disparate political practices and institutions, disparate cultural or world views, and disparate historical traditions resulting in how each would define its public policies. In the political and cultural contexts of relationships between Mexico and the United States during the last half of the twentieth century, the concept of an international memorial was, at least, improbable, as it turned out. Still, hope springs eternal in certain circles today as it did for the NPS representatives in the 1940s who wished that Mexico would respond to their proposal for a Coronado International Memorial. In the end, the NPS settled for a national memorial that would commemorate the eventful Coronado Expedition of 1540 and the harmonious relationship between Mexico and the United States.

Notes

1. Report of Vernon A. Neasham in Special Report covering the Proposed Coronado International Monument submitted by Region III Headquarters, National Park Service, Department of the Interior, Santa Fe, New Mexico, February, 1940, Carl Hayden Papers, Arizona Collection, Arizona State University, Tempe (hereafter cited as Hayden Papers), AC, ASU, Box 591, folder 2.

2. Resume of the Coronado Project, probably authored by Odd S. Halseth in 1951, Hayden Papers, AC, ASU, Box 201, folder 3. The entry for 1939 reads: "United States Congress passed a bill creating the United States Coronado Exposition Commission, with an appropriation of $200,000 for a program of Folk Festivals, publication of historical material and pageants to celebrate the Coronado Entrada in the various states supposed to have been visited by his expedition, namely Arizona, New Mexico, Colorado, Oklahoma, Texas and Kansas. These states set up 'Coronado Commissions' to plan for participation in this program, but received no share of the federal appropriation, except for the sum of 'not more than $10,000 for the establishment of a suitable monument' at or near the place where Coronado crossed the present border between Mexico and the United States."

3. Charles M. Morgan to the President of the United States, September 1, 1939, Hayden Papers, AC, ASU, Box 591, folder 2.

4. R. T. Jones to Carl Hayden, Phoenix, AZ, September 13, 1939, Hayden Papers, AC, ASU Box 591, folder 2.

5. Carl Hayden to the Secretary of State, Washington, DC, September 21, 1939, Hayden Papers, AC, ASU Box 591, folder 2.

6. Both quotes this paragraph, Hayden to the Secretary of the Interior, Washington, DC, October 12, Hayden Papers, AC, ASU Box 591, folder 2.

7. Cordell Hull to Carl Hayden, October 10, 1939, Hayden Papers, AC, ASU Box 591, folder 2.

8. John W. Finch to Carl Hayden, Washington, DC, October 20, 1939, Hayden Papers, AC, ASU Box 591, folder 2.

9. Hayden to Jones, October 21, 1939, Hayden Papers, AC, ASU Box 591, folder 2.

10. Jones to Hayden, Phoenix, AZ, October 19, 1939, Hayden Papers, AC, ASU Box 591, folder 2.

11. Clinton P. Anderson to G. C. Dickens, Albuquerque, New Mexico, February 2, 1940, Hayden Papers, AC, ASU Box 591, folder 2.

12. Hayden to Anderson (Telegram), February 12, 1940, Hayden Papers, AC, ASU Box 591, folder 2.

13. Hayden to the Secretary of the Interior, February 8, 1940, Hayden Papers, AC, ASU Box 591, folder 2.

14. Oscar L. Chapman to Hayden, Washington, DC, January 4, 1940, Hayden Papers, AC, ASU Box 591, folder 2.

15. Emil W. Haury to Aubrey Neasham, Tucson, December 19, 1939, AC, ASU Box 591, folder 2.

16. Report of Vernon A. Neasham in Special Report covering the Proposed Coronado International Monument submitted by Region III Headquarters, National Park Service, Department of the Interior, Santa Fe, New Mexico, February, 1940, Hayden Papers, AC, ASU, Box 591, folder 2.

17. A. J. Wirtz to Carl Hayden, Washington, DC, February 14, 1940, Hayden Papers, AC, ASU, Box 591, folder 2.

18. Ibid., 1.

19. Ibid., 3.

20. Report of Vernon A. Neasham in Special Report covering the Proposed Coronado International Monument submitted by Region III Headquarters, National Park Service, Department of the Interior, Santa Fe, New Mexico, February, 1940, Hayden Papers, AC, ASU, Box 591, folder 2, p. 3.

21. Both quotes, ibid., pp. 4–5.

22. Ibid., p. 6.

23. Ibid.

24. Harold L. Ickes, Secretary of the Interior to Hon. Carl Hayden, Washington, DC, February 27, 1940, Hayden Papers, AC, ASU, Box 591, folder 2.

25. Hayden to Ickes, Washington, DC, March 8, 1940, Hayden Papers, AC, ASU, Box 591, folder 2.

26. Arno B. Cammerer to Hayden, Washington, DC, March 14, 1940, Hayden Papers, AC, ASU, Box 591, folder 2.

27. E. K. Burlew, First Assistant Secretary, to Hayden, Washington, DC, March 18, 1940, Hayden Papers, AC, ASU, Box 591, folder 2.

28. Hayden to Anderson, March 18, 1940, Hayden Papers, AC, ASU, Box 591, folder 2.

29. Hayden to Stuart M. Bailey, Postal Telegraph, March 22, 1940, Hayden Papers, AC, ASU, Box 591, folder 2.

30. Ibid.

31. Discussion this paragraph, ibid.

32. Report signed by John A. Adams, Albuquerque, New Mexico, April 4, 1940, Hayden Papers, AC, ASU Box 591, folder 2.

33. Ibid., 2.

34. Anderson to Hayden, Albuquerque, New Mexico, April 11, 1940, Hayden Papers, AC, ASU, Box 591, folder 2.

35. Ibid.

36. Ibid.

37. Hayden to Hull, Washington, DC, April 16, 1940, Hayden Papers, AC, ASU, Box 591, folder 2.

38. Hull to Hayden, Washington, DC, April 16, 1940, Hayden Papers, AC, ASU, Box 591, folder 2.

39. Hull to Hayden, Washington, DC, April 17, 1940, Hayden Papers, AC, ASU, Box 591, folder 2.

40. Hayden to Hull, Washington, DC, April 22, 1940, Hayden Papers, AC, ASU, Box 591, folder 2. Copies with the same date were sent to Fred Winn, Mrs. J. M. Keith, Secretary of the Arizona Cattle Growers Association in Phoenix, Charles F. Willis, State Secretary of the Arizona Small Mine Operators Association, Phoenix, Arizona, and William Alberts, State Land Commissioner, Phoenix, Arizona, Hayden Papers, AC, ASU, Box 591, folder 2.

41. This paragraph, including quote, from a bill to provide for the establishment of the Coronado International Monument in the State of Arizona, Revised Committee Print, May 28, 1940, Hayden Papers, AC, ASU, Box 591, folder 2.

42. Report, Committee on Public Lands and Surveys, Calendar No. 2220, September 10 (legislative day, August 5), 1940, Hayden Papers, AC, ASU, Box 591, folder 3.

43. Hayden to Willis, September 30, 1940, Western Union Telegram, Hayden Papers, AC, ASU, Box 591.

44. Congressional Record—House, November 18, 1940, Hayden Papers, AC, ASU, Box 591, folder 3.

45. An Act to Provide for the Establishment of Coronado International Memorial in the State of Arizona, Approval, August 18, 1941 (55 Stat. 630), United States Statutes at Large, Volume 66, 82nd Congress, 2nd Session, CORO Files.

46. G. E. Michaels to Pete Riley, October 25, 1941, WACC, Folder H 14: Area and Service History (41-52) F3.

47. Resume of the Coronado Project, probably written by Odd S. Halseth in 1951, Hayden Papers, AC, ASU, Box 201, folder 3.

48. Tolson to Sparkes, Washington, July 18, 1951, Hayden Papers, AC, ASU, Box 201, folder 3. In this correspondence, Tolson gives these dates and place of the 1942 meeting.

49. Ibid. Also see Tolson to G. R. Michaels, Chicago, January 29, 1944, WACC, Folder H 14: Area & Service, History (41–42) F3.

50. Tolson to Sparkes, Washington, July 18, 1951, Hayden Papers, AC, ASU, Box 201, folder 3.

51. Tolson to G. R. Michaels, Chicago, January 29, 1944, WACC, Folder H 14: Area & Service, History 41–42 F3.

52. Tolson to Sparkes, Washington, DC, December 6, 1950, Hayden Papers, AC, ASU, Box 201, folder 3.

53. Tolson to Hayden, Chicago, May 27, 1944, WACC, Folder H 14: Area and Service History (41-52) F3.

54. Tolson to Sparkes, Washington, DC, July 18, 1951, Hayden Papers, AC, ASU, Box 201, folder 3. Here, Tolson quotes from his letter to Halseth dated August 19, 1944.

55. Ibid.

56. Ibid.

57. Tolson to Michaels, Chicago, February 8, 1946, WACC, Folder H 14: Area and Service History (41-52) F3.

58. Tolson to Tillotson, Chicago, November 20, 1946, WACC, Folder H 14: Area and Service History (41-52) F3. Also see Dean Acheson, Acting Secretary, Department of State, to Julius A. Krug, Secretary of the Interior, November 8, 1946, WACC, Folder H 14: Area and Service History (41-52) F3. Other members were P. V. Woodhead, U.S. Forest Service, Albuquerque; William H. Zeh, Office of Indian Affairs, Phoenix; and John C. Gatlin, regional director, U.S. Fish and Wildlife Service, Albuquerque.

59. Tolson to Sparkes, Washington, DC, July 18, 1951, Hayden Papers, AC, ASU, Box 201, folder 3.

60. Ibid. Toldon informed Davidson of Department of State "Assistant Secretary Peurifoy's reply of December 3, 1948, stating that, because of the American interests involved in these proposed park areas, the Department of State hesitates to make further inquiry of the Mexican Government, at this time, concerning the status of the two decrees. Mr. Peurifoy also stated that the state Department would be glad to have its representatives discuss this matter further with representatives of the Interior Department, and, if this was desired, to get in touch with Mr. Paul J. Reveley, Chief, Division of Mexican Affairs, to arrange for a time and place for the meeting." Hayden to Halseth, Washington, DC, February 14, 1949, Hayden Papers, AC, ASU, Box 201, folder 3.

61. Hayden to Sparkes, January 2, 1952, WACC, Folder H 18: Biographical Data F11.

62. Odd S. Halseth to Sparkes, Phoenix, July 21, 1951, WACC, Folder H 18: Biographical Data F11.

63. Hayden to Sparkes, Washington, DC, January 2, 1952, Hayden Papers, AC, ASU, Box 201, folder 3.

64. Sparkes to Tolson, Hereford, January 12, 1952, Hayden Papers, AC, ASU, Box 201, folder 3.

65. H.R. 7553 in the House of Representatives, April 23, 1952, introduced by Congressman Patten, Hayden Papers, AC, ASU, Box 201, folder 3.

66. Sparkes to Hayden, Hereford, April 2, 1952, Hayden Papers, AC, ASU, Box 201, folder 3.

67. Hayden to Sparkes, June 23, 1952, and Hayden to Father Bonaventure Oblasser, O.F.M. June 28, 1952, Hayden Papers, AC, ASU, Box 201, folder 3.

68. Hayden to Sparkes, telegram, July 2, 1952, Hayden Papers, AC, ASU, Box 201, folder 3.

69. Hayden to Sparkes, August 26, 1952, Hayden Papers, AC, ASU, Box 201, folder 3.

70. George A. Brubaker, Assistant Secretary to Senator Hayden, to Senator Carl Hayden, Western Union Telegraph, November 7 1952, Hayden Papers, AC, ASU, Box 252, folder 38.

71. Sparkes to Hayden, July 28, 1952, Hayden Papers, AC, ASU, Box 201, folder 3.

72. Larry Dale, "The Coronado International Memorial Project," n.d., WACC, Folder H 14: Area and Service History, General F6.

73. See the following three publications regarding the establishment and purpose of Chamizal National Memorial and the Parque Público Federal El Chamizal: Joseph P. Sánchez, *Comparative Colonialism, the Spanish Black Legend, and Spain's Legacy in the United States: Perspectives on American Latino Heritage and Our National Story* (Denver, CO: National Park Service, U.S. Department of the Interior, 2013), 48–49; Carlos J. Sierra, compilador y editor, *El Chamizal, monumento a la justicia internacional* (Mexico City: Secretaría de Hacienda y Crédito Público, 1964); Antonio Gómez Robledo, *México y el arbitraje internacional* (Mexico City: Editorial Porrúa, 1965).

CHAPTER 8

Land Acquisition, Mining Interests, and Montezuma Canyon

Under no *circumstances should any additional potentially mineral bearing lands be withdrawn.*

—TED H. EYDE, 1975[1]

Back in the early 1950s, Grace M. Sparkes was working to set up a park called Coronado National Memorial. . . . Now, some 25 years later, the National Park Service is working to run the late Mrs. Sparkes's nephew, Will, out of the park and house in which she raised him—a house that has been owned by his family since 1903.

—HOWARD FISCHER, 1979[2]

The Huachuca Mountains and Montezuma Canyon were full of mining claims during the early decades of the twentieth century. Collections containing their descriptions and histories in Arizona's many documentary depositories are voluminous. By 1978, when the memorial expanded to the north side of Montezuma Canyon, the Victorio Company, once owned by Bruce Doredor, who some said was an Italian immigrant, already owned thirteen claims.[3] Separated by the State of Texas Mines properties, the claims were in two groups. East from there were Doredor, Paring No. One, Paring No. Two, Paring No. Three, and Paring No. Four. To the west were Z. T. Parker, Chief, Fraction, Rubio, Tunnelsite, Miss Stake, Grub Stake No. Two, and Grub Stake No. Three.

According to a summary of mine claims compiled at Coronado National Memorial, the Miss Stake, Grub Stake No. Two, and Grub Stake No. Three mine claims, along with three others in their immediate vicinity, were claimed by Felix Livercio in March 1899. Bruce Doredor claimed the Doredor, Paring No. One, Paring No. Two, Paring No. Three, Paring No. Four, Z. T. Parker, Chief, Fraction, Rubio, and Tunnelsite. The four Paring mines were claimed in 1901 and the Doredor was claimed in 1920. The western group are said to have been claimed in 1909. All thirteen claims were patented by Bruce Doredor on April 10, 1920.[4] One source placed Doredor in the canyon and on those claims much earlier, probably before 1900.[5]

The same summary of mine claims cited above lists purchase of Z. T. Parker, Chief, Fraction, Rubio, Tunnelsite, Grub Stake No. Two, and Miss Stake by Ruth M. Clark and Charles A. Smith in 1938.[6] Bill Clark was on the board of supervisors and was said to have purchased the property for back taxes.[7] Clark and Smith owned the claims through the 1950s but did little or nothing to exploit them.

As Coronado International Memorial was being designed during the 1940s, mining property within its eventual boundaries was largely limited to two owners. The State of Texas claims were owned—or at least managed—by Grace Sparkes, while two groups of claims surrounding Sparkes lands were owned by Clark and Smith. The same was true of lands formerly contained in four homesteads at the mouth of Montezuma Canyon on the east side of the Huachuca Mountains. The Zaleski family still owned three and had just sold the fourth. The Montezuma Ranch was still being run as a camp and tourist ranch.

The seemingly neverending story of the memorial's land had taken on a history of its own. Although the NPS had pursued a joint memorial with Mexico for nearly ten years, in the end hopes for a Coronado International Memorial were dashed. Finally, in 1952, Congress created the present Coronado National Memorial. In the next decades, as the memorial expanded its protective boundary, other adjacent lands came into play.

The physical design of the memorial was explicitly shaped by a desire to avoid mineral deposits and protect the grazing rights of a few local ranchers within the area. The outcome was the memorial that was proclaimed by the president on November 5, 1952; its specifications were based on "section 1 of the act of August 18, 1941, 55 Stat. 630 (16 U.S.C. 450y) as amended by Public Law 478, 82nd Congress, approved July 9, 1952."

The memorial was originally located in Township 24 South, Range 20 East: Section 10, Section 11, Section 13, Section 14, Section 15, Section 22, Section 23, and Section 24; and Township 24 South, Range 21 East: Section 17, Section 18, Section 19, and Section 20.[8] Those sections are along the international boundary, in the south end of the Huachuca Mountains, both east and west of Montezuma Pass, and generally south of an unpaved road that became the main road through the memorial.

When Coronado National Memorial was founded in 1952, the NPS hoped to begin planning its development. However, the 1952 bill specified that no money would be appropriated for the memorial.[9] It was not until July of 1954 that funding was finally approved for the memorial.[10] Shortly thereafter the memorial still had no money, no master plan, and no permanently assigned personnel. Nor was it known where personnel would stay once they were assigned to the memorial.[11] Upon hearing that funds had been appropriated, Grace Sparkes, owner and resident of the State of Texas Mines, immediately contacted NPS. She offered to provide housing for the newly appointed superintendent to Coronado National Memorial.[12] Sparkes, a member of the Arizona Coronado Commission, had already proven herself a supporter when she signed a right-of-way agreement in June 1951, before the memorial was actually established.[13] The *"camp,"* as Sparkes called it, had four cottages, one thoroughly modern with REA (Rural Electrification Administration) electricity and potable water.[14] They were probably the ones described in 1946 by J. Bryant Kasey of the Prescott Engineering Company. Kasey wrote, "Living quarters consist of four well-built and vermin-tight cabins bordering the graded road which switchbacks to the west to the divide and continues westward to Lochiel."[15]

In the meantime, immediate plans were formulated for two residences for memorial staff and a building containing a visitor center and administrative facilities. In February 1960 the memorial took possession of the two residences and the new administration and visitor center.[16] Memorial staff moved into the new, permanent facilities during the same month.[17] The last lease agreement between Grace Sparkes and NPS ran out in June 1960.[18] That ended the use of the State of Texas Mine lands for memorial administration and housing. The land on which these new buildings were placed did not yet belong to the memorial. Meanwhile, the NPS had already reached an agreement with the U.S. Forest Service to make an exchange that would bring them into the memorial.[19] Furthermore, legislation was in the works to make the agreement a reality. Southwestern Monuments Association would play a role in the acquisition of those lands.

Given the historic identification of the Huachuca Mountains and Montezuma Canyon with mining, it is not surprising that mining interests mounted a concerted opposition to adding land to the park. Some groups and individuals were against any action that would remove mineral lands from potential exploitation. The Southwestern Minerals

Exploration Association opposed any land transfers or change to mining lands whatsoever. On October 29, 1975, Ted H. Eyde, secretary of the Southwestern Minerals Explorations Association in Tucson, stressed, "Under no circumstances should any additional potentially mineral bearing lands be withdrawn." He emphasized that withdrawals had diminished Arizona's resource base.[20]

John E. Kinnison, a mining consultant and geologist, opposed the withdrawal of any land until a thorough study of its mineral potential could be undertaken; oddly, he also opposed spending the money to conduct such a study. In fact, he was generally averse to any enlargement of the NPS or the expansion of its personnel base.[21] Similarly, D. A. Heatwole, a geologist for the Anaconda Mining Company, weighed in, on company letterhead, with the certainty that it was only a matter of time before large lodes, probably of copper, would be found in the area under consideration.[22] Charles Morgan, who had been deeply involved in the creation of the memorial, commented more specifically on the mineral issue. Identifying himself as "the person responsible for the very existence of the Coronado Memorial," Morgan expressed the opinion that the State of Texas Mines had the potential to be developed into "another big copper mine." He thought that possibility should not be "foreclosed by its inclusion in the Memorial."[23] The National Parks and Conservation Association disagreed, specifying that such a possibility anyplace within view of Coronado Peak should be averted through legislation.[24]

The issue of including more mining lands within the memorial took on additional importance, and dissension, especially after an act was passed by Congress late in 1976 while the adjustment process was being debated. The law bore the title "An Act to Provide for the Regulation of Mining Activity Within, and to Repeal the Application of Mining Laws to Areas of the National Park System, and for Other Purposes." A section of this act applied directly and solely to Coronado National Memorial. It repealed the section of the original act of 1941 that permitted mining within the memorial. More generally, the 1976 act gave the secretary of the interior the right to regulate mining within the National Park System "in order to preserve for the benefit of present and future generations the pristine beauty of" parks.[25] By the 1976 act, the protection previously guaranteed to miners took a backseat to protection of the memorial's resources.

The only other patented claims beside the State of Texas known to be directly affected were those owned by the Victorio Company. At the time the land adjustment was under consideration, the Victorio Company was negotiating a land swap, which would never be consummated, with the U.S. Forest Service.[26] Although as yet unable to actually purchase the land, in 1978 the NPS entered into discussions with the landowners regarding the Victorio property. The two parties disagreed over the value of the land and it was listed with several local brokers.[27] Before the end of 1979 NPS was informed that the Victorio property had been divided and the sale of a portion of it was imminent. A. W. Gray of the NPS Division of Land Acquisition requested that the sale be delayed to allow the NPS, which by then had the necessary funds appropriated, to approve an appraisal and bid on the land.[28] However, the sale was consummated, leaving NPS to negotiate with other owners, including the Victorio Company.

Some opposed any expansion of NPS lands even if it came at the expense of the U.S. Forest Service. Their concerns were with big government in general. Others generally shared the same feelings, but phrased their opposition in terms of concern for property rights, sometimes mentioning the loss of tax base that would occur if the private inholdings (i.e., privately owned lands within the memorial) were later acquired by the memorial. One representative commented, "We need private property."[29] Another commented, "We do not have the right to impose anything on private property owners . . . This is a free country yet."[30]

Others, including environmental groups and varied citizens and scientists who had visited the memorial and enjoyed its resources, supported the adjustment. The Baumkirchner brothers, Fred E. and Everett M., who had owned a lot of land in the Montezuma Canyon area and still retained a sizeable tract, were in favor of the swap. They pointed out that land in the area was being bought up quickly. If public entities did not act quickly it would be too late to set aside much-needed space for recreation, public use, and sanctuary for wildlife.[31] The transfer was approved in 1978. The land acquired by the memorial encompassed private land within Homestead Entry Surveys 310 and 311 along with the State of Texas and the Victorio mining properties. They would have to be added through purchase, which would excite more opposition to the memorial as it grew to its present size and shape.

Some people were already hostile to the NPS and the memorial's plans. The State of Texas Mine had been a specific concern of the "Radical Proposal."[32] It became the immediate target of the same forces opposed to the 1978 boundary adjustment. In September 1979, well after the NPS had entered into negotiations with William Sparkes, Grace's nephew, an article appeared in a Tucson newspaper, entitled "His Aunt Helped Build Park That Could Dispossess Him." It reported Sparkes's determination to retain ownership of the land and his rejection of a compromise that would have allowed him to stay on the land after acquisition by the memorial. Sparkes recounted the promise made a few years earlier, probably by John Clay and Coronado Memorial Superintendent Laurel W. Dale, that private landowners would not be forced to sell and threatened to launch a petition campaign.[33]

Several months later, in the spring of 1980, NPS received a petition against acquisition of the State of Texas Mine bearing 448 signatures.[34] It was accompanied by a letter from William P. Ullrich, of Hereford, that summarized the feelings of the signers: "We feel you have abundant land to serve your purpose and that this is just another land grab."[35] Just a few weeks earlier, the Huachuca Conservation Council had forwarded a resolution urging acquisition. It singled out the State of Texas Mine as "an unattractive inholding," and the only exception to the "exquisite scenic setting" of the memorial.[36] A letter from the same organization also favored "quick acquisition of all other inholdings."[37]

The superintendent of the memorial at that time, Laurel W. Dale, commented that the Sparkes property presented "a cluttered appearance." He explained that the owner was a general contractor who, lacking other storage facilities, kept his equipment parked along the main road through the memorial. However, Dale also recalled the key role of Sparkes's aunt, Grace, in the establishment of the memorial. He concluded by urging "that the Service refrain from any actions that would seriously undermine the very good relationship that we now have with the Sparkes family."[38] There was also a professional relationship between William Sparkes and the memorial. Sparkes and his contracting company, Payne & Sparkes, used the equipment to provide maintenance services for the Montezuma Pass Road under contract with Coronado National Memorial.[39]

Sparkes was a supportive neighbor in emergency situations as well. In December 1974 the memorial thanked him for his help in a recent rescue effort.[40] Superintendent Dale also supported him when Sparkes planned to remodel his house on the State of Texas Mine property. Dale thought that the remodeling might improve the appearance of the property, adding, "They have been really good neighbors and have always lent a helping hand when needed. If we do all that can be done legally and in the process help our neighbors and keep their friendship, then we have half the battle won already."[41] Apparently, the relationship between Sparkes and the memorial was more cordial in person than it was in local politics and newspapers.

By 1979 Will Sparkes was publicly telling a different story. Somehow, Grace Sparkes's involvement in working toward the establishment of Coronado National Memorial in order to protect the State of Texas Mine had long been forgotten. Howard Fischer, a reporter for the *Arizona Daily Star,* began his story with these words: "Back in the early 1950s, Grace M. Sparks [*sic*] was working to set up a park called Coronado National Memorial. . . . Now, some 25 years later, the National Park Service is working to run the late Mrs. Sparkes' [*sic*] nephew, Will, out of the park and house in which she raised him—a house that has been owned by his family since 1903. The newspaper story went on to explain that when the memorial was created, the Sparkes property was surrounded by U.S. Forest Service lands. "But," wrote Fischer, "about three years ago, in an effort to maintain better control of the park, the two agencies worked out a swap." That meant that the NPS received lands that contained Sparkes's property, which were annexed into the memorial. The western portion of the original memorial went to the U.S. Forest Service. Sparkes's property now lay within the memorial boundary. "This made the Sparks [*sic*] property 'in-holdings'"; wrote Fischer, "and the Park Service began procedures to acquire it." Arguing that federal officials said that private landowners would not be forced to sell, Will Sparkes and his wife, Dean, proclaimed, "The family doesn't intend to move without a fight."[42] For now, the Sparkes family refused to compromise and threatened to reopen the State of Texas Mine.

Between 1980 and 1986 Will Sparkes and his wife continued to own the State of Texas Mine. During that period inspectors found that there had been no activity at the mine since 1971. Finally, in September 1986 Keith Miller, an NPS employee, visited the site and spoke to Will Sparkes. Miller reported that after some years of refusal, Sparkes was "now willing to sell the property." Clemmer and Miller spent two days on the property reviewing documents held by Sparkes. The mineral appraisal consisted of "two patented claims and two patented mill sites." That appraisal was carried out by Robert E. Dietrich of Burke, Hansen, Homan and Klafter, real estate appraisers and consultants from Tucson, Arizona. They also took samplings from the underground and surface of the mine. They proclaimed, "The underground workings are in bad shape and filled with bats and guano."[43]

The recent history of the State of Texas Mine, dating from 1971, indicated that little if any development of the mine had occurred despite claims by Sparkes that the mine had been worked. For example, the entry of notes for April 1, 1971, by "GWI" and "QR" reads "State of Texas mine is reported to be doing a little work." Two months later, on June 30, 1971, GWI noted that the "owners of the State of Texas mine in Montezuma canyon are planning on doing some work." Three years later, on December 19, 1974, GWI and WR note, "There appears to be some sort of activity at the State of Texas mine; the mine inspector says no." Then six years later, MG and WR visited the State of Texas Mine on March 14, 1980, and noted, "There is no obvious activity at this property." Three years later, MG and WR, on March 11, 1983, visited the mine and spoke with Will Sparkes, reporting that "there is no mine activity." Two years later, on August 16, 1985, MG and WR visited the mine and reported: "There is no activity at this mine." They noted that it was believed that "Mr. & Mrs. William Sparkes [*sic*] still live on the patented property."[44] On the contrary, although Will Sparkes always hoped to begin a mining operations at the State of Texas Mine, his plans were never brought to fruition. In 1979 he argued, "Although there is still 'plenty of good ore' in the mine, the cost of shipping it has made mining out of the question."[45]

Turning the State of Texas Mines into a productive enterprise had always been Grace Sparkes's dream. Throughout the early 1940s she spoke to anyone and everyone who would listen about inspecting her mine to determine its mineral wealth and any possibility for a return on her investment. If she was not in contact with local authorities and politicians, she was in Washington, DC, walking through halls of federal agencies and knocking on doors of bureaucrats who could help her. On one occasion, after a trip to Washington, she contacted Sam Coupal, director of the Arizona Mineral Resource Board. She wrote

> Dear Sam,
> During some of the work which I did in Washington, I had occasion, quite unexpectedly, to discuss with Mr. John Norton, the mining property on the border. He told me if we would prepare an up to the minute engineering report of this property, with an outline as to what we desired to do, and have a clear cut statement of the property made with a recheck of the assaying and the trenching of the ground, with the favorable showing in other reports, in his opinion this would be passed for a silver property and a loan.
>
> In the face of this I feel the need of your help. It seems to me logical

> now that you have been over the property, you should return as soon as possible to make this recheck. Will you please advise me when you feel you can make the trip, and I will arrange to have Perry accompany you.
>
> I told Mr. Norton the ground was trenched, but I did not know the values, and was under the impression the ore was exposed in the trenches.
>
> This is the biggest concession I have been able to get, and it seems to me with the property hanging fire, the price of metals and the need for zinc, the matter warrants your best help and attention.[46]

In response, Coupal wrote Sparkes that he would be in Prescott the following week of March 23 and 24, and that he would meet and discuss the matter with her. He added that he hoped to "arrange my time so as to get to the property again at an early date and see what can be done toward supplying the needed information."[47] The outcome of that meeting is not revealed in the documentation, but Sparkes continued her correspondence with Coupal over the next year.

Meanwhile, Sparkes submitted an application to the Reconstruction Finance Corporation (RFC) in Washington for a development loan for the State of Texas Mine. On August 19, 1942, Sparkes received a letter from C. A. Rockwood, supervising engineer at RFC. Rockwood wrote, "Our Washington office has encountered a difficulty in connection with the consideration of your application for a Development Mining Loan." He added, "In studying over your application and the engineer's report after his examination, they cannot find that you are actively engaged in any type of mining work on this property as no work has been done for some time and in order to qualify it will be necessary for you to submit some evidence of current work on the property." Rockwood further explained that the RFC made loans to "corporations, individuals, and partnerships engaged in the development of ore bodies."[48]

Rockwood's letter triggered a firestorm of letters generated by Sparkes and her supporters. Sparkes had worked hard to attract consultants to her mine in order to push her application for a loan forward. To that end, Coupal wrote her saying that he had asked Bill Broadgate "to see if any steps could be taken to speed it up."[49] Two days later, on August 20, 1942, Grace Sparkes telephoned Coupal, who noted that she had received a letter from Washington indicating that her application "did not show that she was in the mining business or that any work was being done on the property."[50] Coupal contacted Broadgate and explained that the object of the loan application was "to get a property into production or into development for production . . . I hope you will take the letter to the proper sources and get this matter straightened out."[51]

Sparkes pushed hard against the RFC to get her loan. Writing to Coupal on August 20, 1942, she expressed her frustration with the process and her enthusiasm to get the loan while the nation clamored for zinc. She wrote, "The thing that bothers me most is the delay caused by such back and forth stuff. . . With your reports, that of their own engineer, the government clamoring [*sic*] for this type of ore—and for the first time in our lives being able to have the ore handled at the Shuttuck Denn—I cannot understand why they delay. Anything you can do to expedite this will be greatly appreciated."[52]

Sparkes was relentless in pushing her contacts in Arizona to deal with the RFC regarding her loan. She still wanted answers to the letter the RFC had written to her. Frustrated at the situation and pressured by Sparkes, Broadgate wrote a quick note to Coupal, as indicated by the stamped receipt: "Received Aug 24 1942, Dept. Mining Resources, Phoenix Arizona." He wrote, "I will wait until I get a copy of the letter the RFC wrote Grace before I do anything on this. . . . If the letter is what Grace indicates, I am going over and raise Hell with someone. I am getting tired of the RFC fiddling while Rome burns and when I get some more data I want, am going to get a shakeup of the Class B Procedure or bust a gut, to be vulgar."[53] Broadgate fired off another letter to Sparkes via Coupal's office on August 23, 1942, expressing his empathy and support of her. Mincing no words, he wrote,

> This sort of nonsense makes me furious, and a storm is building up about the RFC due to such silly technicalities and delays. They are being brought to the attention of Senators and Congressmen by constituents every day and a little start will roll up a great snowball of protest which may result in a purge. I happen to know that there is even a bill partly drawn which would transfer the whole mine loan division authority to the WPB where it really belongs, as they are actually responsible for production. There is even a possibility of a Congressional investigation. However, if the announced intent to streamline these loans is accomplished, the storm will die down. What can be done is shown by the rational handling of C loans, which do not suffer from a decade of Jone's red tape.[54]

Broadgate ended his letter by telling Sparkes that he would take up the issue with the chief counsel on the following Monday. He advised

Sparkes to point out that she, her brother, and her brother-in-law had continuously been working at the State of Texas Mine. It seems Coupal telephoned Sparkes and read her Broadgate's letter.

Meanwhile, Sparkes, sensing victory, wrote to Coupal as if she had been seriously injured. She wrote, "Please send me a copy of Bill's letter re: the Texas application. Seems to me the statement from Washington represents pure asinity [*sic*]. What did they think I wanted the loan for—'to play ping pong?' Why did they think I went to the trouble to seek your help that of the RFC engineer, etc. etc. Is this an excuse to turn it down?" Evidently, Sparkes intended to air the letter over the radio. She asked Coupal to send her the letter and press releases and all other data related to the issue. In uppercase letters, she added, "NEED THIS FOR OUR ACTIVITIES. WISH YOU WOULD TRY TO SEND US SOME DATA TO REACH HERE TUESDAY (NOT LATER THAN AFTERNOON) FOR OUR REGULAR BROADCASTS THAT EVENING."[55] Coupal sent Sparkes the materials under the guise that he was, as a matter of course, forwarding them to her on his own account without ever having received a solicitation from her.

Coupal knew full well, as a bureaucrat, that he could not afford to present even a perception that he was in cahoots with Sparkes. He politely communicated, "I am enclosing the last two press releases which may be of interest to you and am sending under separate cover some of the recent circulars from Washington which are distributed from this office. I will make note to have all of the press releases and circulars sent to you when, and as, they come out. With best wishes and kindest regards, I am yours very truly, J. S. Coupal, Director."[56]

Another round of correspondence followed with similar vitriolic tones about how the RFC mishandled Sparkes's loan application. By the end of August 1942 the stage was set for the capitulation by the beleaguered RFC. On September 2, 1942, Broadgate wrote, "I have good (unofficial) reason to believe that the Board of Directors acted favorably on this application today and that Grace will be notified by wire, perhaps tomorrow."[57] Two days later, Sparkes sent Broadgate a telegram saying, "Deeply appreciate your cooperation loan approved subject resolution apparently under way."[58]

Fresh from her victory over the RFC, Sparkes prepared plans to move forward with the development of her mine. By then she knew that the mine potentially held ores related to zinc, lead, copper, willemite, and silver. She held out hope that the mine would be rich in those minerals, but, in the end she was disappointed.

By March 1943 it appeared that work at the State of Texas Mine was under way. Sparkes communicated with Coupal, saying that willemite had been found in the mine, but she did not have a mineral light to test its illumination factor. Perry Bones, she said, ran a weaker light and the entire mine glowed with a green light along a vein. "What further information can you give me on willemite and franklinite?"[59] she asked. Coupal responded,

> Regarding willemite, I will say that it is a silicate of zinc and that it has a specific gravity of 3.89 to 4.18. It is commonly found with zinc minerals and in the Mine Hill, Franklin Furnace, New Jersey, occurs in such quantity as to make an import ore of zinc. From its specific gravity no difficulty should be found in table concentration. I do not know what could be done with the ore on flotation. If the occurrence is widely spread, I do believe some good samples should be taken and sent to the Arizona Bureau of Mines for testing. As to the best flow sheet, we can best determine that after further developments and after we have a look at it. . .If it goes to the Shattuck Denn plant, I would be very much interested in the settlement sheet to find out whether or not they will pay for or recover the zinc which occurs as willemite. This occurrence may be of real value.[60]

In May 1943 George A. Ballam sent a memorandum to Coupal describing a visit to the mine. "Spent a few hours with Perry Bones and Tom Sparkes on the property. They are doing a good job in the face of difficulties, and have shipped three cars of ore running about 17% Zn and up to 5% Pb with about 8 ounces. Ag. They have a bad water situation, the well having failed, and they are obliged to haul water from the Border ranch, some four or five barrels a day for all purposes." Ballam noted that copper was not yet a factor, but the zinc was of high quality. Ballam felt that Sparkes should apply "for additional premiums on Pb & Zn." He also said, "They are working only one shift. Believe another shift is advisable if morale can be raised."[61] Ballam's report appeared highly encouraging.

Meanwhile, Perry Bones wrote to Coupal telling him that he was sending him some specimens to evaluate. "P.S.," he added, "specimens are in box with light."[62] In his response to Bones, Coupal reported that he had checked the specimens from the mine, and they did show a presence of willemite. Although he doubted that the willemite was massive, he did say, "One of your specimens is a prize: it not only shows up under the lamp but continues to glow after the light is turned off. When I do come down I will bring the light with me."[63]

At the moment, Grace Sparkes was hopeful of making the enterprise work. By summer 1943 the situation appeared dire. The cost of developing the mine was adding up, and the revenues were reduced to a paltry sum. Sparkes's report, "Tentative Financial Statement—State of Texas Mine—July 15, 1943," indicated that the work was proceeding very slowly and the debt was rising. For example, setting up camp, equipping the mine, and producing 323.358 tons of ore had grossed $15, 541.22. By July 14, 1943, the bank balance showed $2,806.06. The bills were mounting. They included miscellaneous costs of $690.98. Additionally, commissions, payroll for July, truckage, and contingencies totaled $4,499.63. Payments to the RFC loan amounted to $8,000.00. All bills as of July 1943 were past due and Sparkes needed $12,499.63 to pay them.[64]

In a letter to Landon F. Strobel, executive secretary of the Quota Committee in Washington, DC, she explained her situation. She wrote, "After the severe penalties and deductions made by the monitors and the costs which we must take care of beyond the mill returns, we are actually in worse shape than when we started our first correspondence with you." She made a patriotic appeal: "We have done at this in good faith, because we believed our government needed this zinc ore for our war effort." Sparkes asked for time to get the production of the mine up and reconsideration from the committee to revise the quota or "we will eventually shut down."[65] Sparkes was able to hang on for nearly three more years, but by 1946 all work at the mine ceased.

Sparkes's interest in establishing Coronado International Memorial might have had a hidden purpose. In her attempt to convince Moody to invest in the State of Texas, she explained to him how she was defending their property. "I have done a good deal of work," Sparkes wrote in April 1940, "to protect the claims against the Coronado Exposition idea." She continued that this "has meant work with the Arizona Commission, The Forestry, U.S., Park and other officials."[66] During the same month, Sparkes wrote to Margaret Rockwell of the Arizona Commission, who served on the Coronado Cuarto Centennial Exposition. Although she assured Mrs. Rockwell of her support for the memorial, her primary concern was that it not threaten her mine holdings.[67] Apparently, Sparkes thought she had good reason to fear federal projects on her land. She later informed Moody that the "entire camp was stolen when the CCC [Civilian Conservation Corps] constructed the road through the canyon."[68]

Meanwhile, as president of the Arizona Chamber of Commerce Secretaries Association, Sparkes continued to correspond with Senator Hayden about the status of the Coronado Project. During the next two years, Hayden kept her informed regarding the status of the memorial. In her position with Yavapai Associates in Prescott, Sparkes coordinated community groups with which she worked. When lack of funding at Yavapai Associates left her unemployed, she moved to the State of Texas Mines in Montezuma Canyon.[69] By 1946 mineral production at the mine had ceased.[70] Seeking a way to earn some income from her mines, Sparkes attempted to turn the mine into a tourist attraction, calling it Montezuma Canyon Mineral Village.[71]

After her move to Montezuma Canyon, Sparkes continued to support the Coronado Memorial project and continued making contact with both Senator Hayden and the NPS.[72] In late 1947, Sparkes wrote to Hayden, urging him to take action to make the memorial a reality. She reminded Hayden that even though Fort Huachuca had been a big loss, small miners, ranchers, and resort owners look to this park for the stimulant they need to attract tourists. Bisbee organized a Sunshine Club to advertise its marvelous climate.[73]

In her communications with Hayden, Sparkes had assumed, at least in her letter, that everyone in the area supported the memorial. She even mentioned certain ranchers whose interests were contrary to a memorial. She reiterated the economic benefits that the memorial would provide for all of southeastern Arizona, except for the miners like herself. Sparkes maintained a hope that the memorial could be established.[74] In 1947 she expressed to Hayden that the resources of Montezuma Canyon merited such a status. Ever self-serving, she told him that she hoped to get some benefits from the project, such as utilities and a good road.[75]

Once Coronado National Memorial was established in 1952, Sparkes became deeply involved in its development and operation. The 1952 bill that created the memorial appropriated no money and its congressional supporters assured their colleagues that no funds were then needed.[76] Funding was, in fact, not approved until July 1954.[77] In the interim, periodic patrols were carried out from other parks in the region. Even after the memorial was funded, it still lacked a master plan, structures, and personnel.[78] As soon as she heard of the 1954 appropriation, Sparkes came to the rescue with an offer of shelter. She wrote to Superintendent Ray

Ringenbach at Tumacacori National Monument: "I want to cooperate and would like to have your Park official quartered at our camp," meaning the State of Texas Mine.[79]

Meantime, the NPS rented her cabin for use as an office and placed a house trailer, with the necessary electric and plumbing hookups, on the property. [80,81] By 1955 a temporary agreement was worked out and a series of more permanent leases commenced that year.[82] The leases covered an expanded area as the memorial's needs increased.[83] The State of Texas Mine area served as the memorial facilities and personnel until early in 1960, with the last lease running until June of that year.[84] Still, Grace Sparkes never lost sight of the fact that, to her, the State of Texas Mine remained a good deal. In 1959 she had hopes of selling her mining property. She responded to query #17 in the Mine Owner's Report of May 26, 1959, which asked, "If Property for Sale, List Approximate Price and Terms." She wrote, "Would prefer to talk with interested individual or parties who should visit property if interested. Tentative suggestion—owing to illness of owners and inability to go further with property will sell—tentative figure $125,000 Terms to reliable part or parties. Letter should be directed to owner Star Rt—Hereford, Arizona making appointment for mine visit—no telephone rural mail best service."[85]

In a letter to Frank P. Knight, director of the State of Arizona Department of Mineral Resources, Sparkes reiterated her message to sell at first opportunity. "With the assistance of my associate, Perry L. Bones, I have kept my property in tact [*sic*], with the expectation that somedaythe right party or parties would take it over." She described the property in glowing terms. "Our Camp," she said, "is modern and can easily be expanded, is in excellent shape—four cottages, one thoroughly modern, REA electric power, adequate water—assurance that Montezuma Canyon road is to be improved and paved to and beyond our property in 1960. . . . Above all, here is a mighty attractive mining property, which we cannot stress too strongly has copper possibilities and other minerals, which should be re-checked carefully, merits additional diamond drilling and thorough checking of old workings." Just as she had in 1940, when she invited Coupal to visit the mine, Sparkes added,"May I suggest that you pay this property a personal visit and let us hear from you in advance so we will be certain to be here to meet you."[86] Meanwhile, Sparkes readied all reports, maps, assay returns, shipment returns, etc. so that they would be ready for any prospective buyer to see.

The die had been cast: Grace Sparkes had, in effect, given up. She had played both ends against the middle, developing her mine while encouraging the establishment of Coronado National Memorial. Although she was unable to sell her mine to a private operator, in the end she was instrumental in the establishment of Coronado National Memorial. In 1986 the NPS acquired the State of Texas Mines from her nephew, Will Sparkes.

Notes

1. Comments by Ted H. Eyde, secretary, Southwestern Minerals Explorations Association, Tucson, October 29, 1975, WACC, Folder L 1417: Boundary Adjustments—Surveys & Reports F1.

2. Howard Fischer, "Heir Prefers a Fight to Leaving Park Home," *Arizona Daily Star,* September 13, 1979, Arizona Historical Society, Tucson.

3. George Brown, interview by Barbara Alberti, August 18, 1998, in Bart Barbour, "Dude Ranches," CORO Files.

4. "A Summary of the Abandoned Mineral Lands" in "Abandoned Mineral Lands (AML) and Related List of Classified Structure (LCS)," n.d., CORO Files.

5. Dale to Mulhern, "A Summary of the Abandoned Mineral Lands." Hereford, February 23, 1976, Coronado National Memorial, CORO Files.

6. "A Summary of the Abandoned Mineral Lands, AML, CORO Files." Also see, Warranty Deed, Ruth M. Clark, a widow, and Charles A. Smith and Paquita C. Smith, his wife, to Coronado Investment Company, a partnership comprised of Peter G. Wray and H. Wayne Pruett, co-partners, Recorded July 2, 1970, CCR, Deeds of Real Estate, Docket 645, pages 543-545, AML, CORO Files.

7. Dale to Mulhern, "A Summary of the Abandoned Mineral Lands." Hereford, February 23, 1976, Coronado National Memorial, CORO Files.

8. Establishment of the Coronado National Memorial (Name change from International Memorial), Arizona, By the President of the United States, A Proclamation (No. 2995), November 5, 1952, ILRPC Files.

9. Untitled, undated copy of Congressional debate on bill, H.R. 7553, WACC, Folder H 18: Biographical Data, General F11.

10. Senator Carl Hayden to Grace Sparkes, Washington, DC, July 2, 1954, ILRPC Files.

11. Ray B. Ringenbach, Superintendent, Tumacacori National Monument, to Grace Sparkes, Tumacacori, August 10, 1954, ILRPC Files.

12. Sparkes to Ringenbach, Prescott, July 7, 1954, ILRPC Files.

13. Recognition of Right of Way, Signed by Grace M. Sparkes, June 15, 1951, WACC, Folder L 1425: Land Holdings—Sparkes & Acquisition F17.

14. Sparkes to Frank P. Knight, Hereford, May 27, 1959, Arizona State Department of Mines and Minerals, Phoenix, AZ.

15. Report on Geologic and Mine Examination of the State of Texas Mine, October 17, 1946, by J. Bryant Kasey, Arizona State Department of Mines and Minerals, Phoenix, AZ.

16. Completion Report of Construction Project, Contract 14-10-333-509, Signed by Philip Welles, Superintendent, Coronado National Memorial, n.d., WACC, Folder D 3415: Buildings Construction and Maintenance 1960 F25.

17. Memoranda to Acting Superintendent Don Jackson, Coronado National Memorial, February 13 to March 6, 1960, WACC, Folder A 26: Reports, daily logs 1960 F3.

18. Welles to Sparkes, Hereford, May 15, 1959, WACC, Folder H 18: Biographical Data, General F11.

19. William H. Woods Jr., forest supervisor, National Forest Service, to Director, National Park Service, Tucson, July 26, 1956, WACC, Folder L 1417: Boundary Adjustments—Surveys & Reports F1.

20. Comments by Mr. Ted H. Eyde, secretary, Southwestern Minerals Explorations Association, Tucson, October 29, 1975, WACC, Folder L 1417: Boundary Adjustments—Surveys & Reports F1.

21. John E. Kinnison to superintendent, Coronado National Monument, Tucson, December 8, 1975, WACC, Folder L 1417: Boundary Adjustments—Surveys & Reports F1.

22. D. A. Heatwole, regional project geologist, Anaconda Company, to superintendent, Coronado National Monument, Tucson, December 9, 1975, WACC, Folder L 1417: Boundary Adjustments—Surveys & Reports F1.

23. Charles M. Morgan to superintendent, Coronado National Monument, Tucson, December 11, 1975, WACC, Folder L 1417: Boundary Adjustments—Surveys & Reports F1.

24. Robert L. Coshland, southwest representative, National Parks and Conservation Association, to superintendent, Coronado National Memorial, Tucson, December 3, 1975, WACC, Folder L 76: Environmental Impact/Assessment—Public Response 1976 F54.

25. "An Act to Provide for the Regulation of Mining Activity Within, and to Repeal the Application of Mining Laws to Areas of the National Park System, and for Other Purposes, approved September 28, 1976; copy located in CORO Files.

26. Laurel Dale to Regional Director, Western Regional Office, NPS, Hereford, June 13, 1977, WACC, Folder L 1425: Land Holdings—Pruett-Wray/Victorio (LaFevre) F13.

27. A. P. LeFevre, vice president, Land Resources, Victorio Company, to A. W. Gray, Phoenix, September 27, 1978, WACC, Folder L 1425: Land Holdings—Pruett-Wray/Victorio (LaFevre) F13.

28. Gray to Wayne Pruett, Victorio Company, December 19, 1979, WACC, Folder L 1425: Land Holdings—Pruett-Wray/Victorio (LaFevre) F13.

29. Constance M. Dochas to Coronado Memorial, Bisbee, December 20, 1975, WACC, Folder L 76: Environmental Impact/Assessment—Public Response 1975 F53.

30. Bessie J. Payne to Coronado National Memorial, Hereford, December 15, 1975, Folder L 76: Environmental Impact/Assessment—Public Response 1975 F53.

31. Comments by Fred E. and Everett M. Baumkirchner, November 24, 1975, Folder L 76: Environmental Impact/Assessment—Public Response 1975 F53.

32. "Boundary Adjustment—A Radical Proposal."

33. Howard Fischer, "His Aunt Helped Build Park That Could Dispossess Him," *Arizona Daily Star*, September 13, 1979, See WACC, Folder L 1425: Land Holdings—Sparkes & Acquisition F17.

34. "We, the undersigned, do hereby protest the acquisition by the National Park Service of that property owned by William J. Sparkes, which property is situated in Montezuma Canyon, Coronado National Memorial, Cochise County, Arizona, and which property is commonly referred to as the State of Texas Mine," received, Coronado

National Memorial, April 1, 1980, *Daily Star,* September 13, 1979, See WACC, Folder L 1425: Land Holdings—Sparkes & Acquisition F17.

35. Ullrich to Dale, Coronado National Memorial, WACC, Folder L 1425, March 27, 1980.

36. Huachuca Conservation Council, Resolution, Coronado National Memorial, Adopted March 5, 1980, ILRPC Files.

37. Jerome J. Pratt, secretary-treasurer, Huachuca Conservation Council, to Cecil D. Andrus, secretary of the interior, Sierra Vista, March 10, 1980, ILRPC Files.

38. Dale to regional director, Western Region, Hereford, March 17, 1980, ILRPC Files.

39. Paul R. Thompson, Supervisory Park Technician, Maintenance Supervisor, to Registrar of Contractors, Hereford, October 5, 1976, WACC, Folder K 14: Information Requests F1.

40. Dale to Will Sparkes, Hereford, December 27, 1974, WACC, Folder A 34: Commendations F13.

41. Dale to regional director, Western Region, Hereford, February 5, 1980, WACC, Folder L 1425: Land Holdings—Sparkes & Acquisition F17.

42. Quotes this paragraph from Fischer, "Heir prefers a fight to leaving park home," *The Arizona Daily Star,* September 13, 1979. Section E, p. 2, Arizona Historical Society, Tucson.

43. State of Texas Mine, Cochise County file dated September 5, 1986, Arizona State Department of Mines and Minerals, Phoenix, AZ.

44. State of Texas Mine, Cochise County, notes dated April 1, 1971 to August 16, 1985, Arizona State Department of Mines and Minerals, Phoenix, AZ.

45. Fischer, "Heir Prefers a Fight," *Arizona Daily Star,* Section E, p. 2, September 13, 1979. Arizona Historical Society.

46. Grace M. Sparkes to Sam Coupal, Prescott, March 17, 1941, Arizona State Department of Mines and Minerals, Phoenix, AZ.

47. Coupal to Sparkes, Phoenix, March 19, 1941, Arizona State Department of Mines and Minerals, Phoenix, AZ.

48. C. A. Rockwood to Grace M. Sparkes, Washington, DC, August 19, 1942, Arizona State Department of Mines and Minerals, Phoenix, AZ.

49. Coupal to Sparkes, Phoenix, August 18, 1942, Arizona State Department of Mines and Minerals, Phoenix, AZ.

50. Memorandum, J. S. Coupal to W. C. Broadgate, August 20, 1942, Arizona State Department of Mines and Minerals, Phoenix, AZ.

51. Two preceding quotes from Memorandum, J. S. Coupal to W. C. Broadgate, August 20, 1942, Arizona State Department of Mines and Minerals, Phoenix, AZ.

52. Grace Sparkes to Sam Coupal, Prescott, August 20, 1942, Arizona State Department of Mines and Minerals, Phoenix, AZ.

53. Bill Broadgate to RFC, Washington, DC, August 22, 1942, Arizona State Department of Mines and Minerals, Phoenix, AZ.

54. Broadgate to Sparkes, Washington, DC, August 23, 1942, Arizona State Department of Mines and Minerals, Phoenix, AZ.

55. Both quotes this paragraph from Sparkes to Coupal, Prescott, August 22, 1942, Arizona State Department of Mines and Minerals, Phoenix, AZ.

56. Coupal to Sparkes, Phoenix, August 24, 1942, Arizona State Department of Mines and Minerals, Phoenix, AZ.

57. Broadgate to Coupal, Washington, DC, September 2, 1942, Arizona State Department of Mines and Minerals, Phoenix, AZ.

58. Telegram, Sparkes to Broadgate, Prescott, September 4, 1942, Arizona State Department of Mines and Minerals, Phoenix, AZ.

59. Sparkes to Coupal, Prescott, March 6, 1943, Arizona State Department of Mines and Minerals, Phoenix, AZ.

60. Coupal to Sparkes, Phoenix, March 8, 1943, Arizona State Department of Mines and Minerals, Phoenix, AZ.

61. All quotes this paragraph from George A. Ballam to director, Department of Mineral Resources, State of Texas Mine, May 24, 1943, Arizona State Department of Mines and Minerals, Phoenix, AZ.

62. Perry L. Bones to Coupal, State of Texas Mine, March 12, 1943, Arizona State Department of Mines and Minerals, Phoenix, AZ.

63. Coupal to Perry Bones, Phoenix, March 13, 1943, Arizona State Department of Mines and Minerals, Phoenix, AZ.

64. "Tentative Financial Statement—State of Texas Mine—July 15, 1943," Arizona State Department of Mines and Minerals, Phoenix, AZ.

65. Quotes this paragraph from Sparkes to Landon F. Strobel, Prescott, July 16, 1943, Arizona State Department of Mines and Minerals, Phoenix, AZ.

66. Sparkes to Moody, April 22, 1940, Sparkes Collection AHS, Box 7, Folder 295, and others in the same folder.

67. Sparkes to Rockwell, Prescott, April 11, 1940, Sparkes Collection, AHS, Box 23, Folder 956.

68. Sparkes to Moody, April 7, 1942, Sparkes Collection, AHS, Box 7, Folder 297. The Montezuma Canyon Road was built between 1933 to 1935, Laurel Dale, Superintendent, Coronado National Memorial, to Thomas Mulhern, Historic Preservation, Western Regional Office, Hereford, February 23, 1976, Re: Historic Structures at Coronado National Memorial, CORO Files.

69. Tolson to Hayden, Chicago, May 27, 1944, WACC, Folder H 14: Area and Service History (41-52) F3.

70. Peter M. Van Cleve, "History of Mining in the Coronado National Memorial" (1997), 2–8, Coronado National Memorial Files.

71. Mona Lang McCroskey, *Grace Marion Sparkes*, MA thesis, Arizona State University, Tuscon, 1987, 140.

72. Hayden to Sparkes, January 3, 1946; Tolson to Sparkes, Chicago, October 25, 1946, WACC, Folder H 18: Biographical Data F11.

73. Sparkes to Hayden, October 25, 1947 WACC, Folder H 18: Biographical Data F11.

74. Ibid.

75. Sparkes to Hayden, State of Texas Mine, June 28, 1947, WACC, Folder H 18: Biographical Data F11.

76. Untitled, n.d., copy of Congressional debate on bill, H.R. 7553, WACC, Folder H 18: Biographical Data, General F11.

77. Senator Carl Hayden to Grace Sparkes, Washington, DC, July 2, 1954, WACC, Folder H 18: Biographical Data F11.

78. Ray B. Ringenbach, Superintendent, Tumacacori National Monument, to Grace Sparkes, Tumacacori, August 10, 1954, WACC, Folder H 18: Biographical Data F11.

79. Sparkes to Ringenbach, Prescott, July 7, 1954, WACC, Folder H 18: Biographical Data F11.

80.Tolson to Sparkes, November 17, 1954, WACC, Archives, CD Box 3.

81. John M. Davis, general superintendent, Southwestern National Monuments, NPS, to Sparkes, Globe, November 17, 1954; and, Davis to Sparkes, Globe, November 23, 1954, WACC, Folder H 18: Biographical Data F11.

82. D. D. Crumley, chief clerk, Southwestern National Monuments, NPS, to Sparkes, Globe, December 7, 1954; lease between Grace M. Sparkes and the United States of America, January 1, 1955, WACC, Folder H 18: Biographical Data F11.

83. Purchase Order, July 12, 1957, WACC, Folder H 18: Biographical Data F11.

84. Memoranda to Acting Superintendent Don Jackson, Coronado National Memorial, February 13 to March 6, 1960, WACC, Folder A 26: Reports, daily logs 1960 F3; Philip Welles, Superintendent, Coronado National Memorial, to Sparkes, Hereford, May 15, 1959, WACC, Folder H 18: Biographical Data, General F11.

85. Mine Owner's Report, Department of Mineral Resources, May 26, 1959, signed by Grace Sparkes, Arizona State Department of Mines and Minerals, Phoenix, AZ.

86. All quotes in this paragraph from Grace M. Sparkes to Frank P. Knight, Hereford, May 27, 1959, Arizona State Department of Mines and Minerals, Phoenix, AZ.

CHAPTER 9

Mines, Boundary Adjustments, Land Acquisition, and the Sixty Foot-Wide Strip

Certainly the entire historic scene of the San Pedro Valley cannot all be protected but the segment of 270 acres pointing at the heart of the memorial must be acquired to prevent obnoxious developments which would detract from the visitors' park experience.

—Frederick J. Brower, 1974[1]

In 1959 a non-governmental organization, the Southwestern Monuments Association (SMA), having been approached by NPS for their assistance, purchased land along the southern boundary line of Homestead Entry Survey 310. At that time, NPS could not acquire any land for the memorial until after legislation providing funding had been passed. In 1959, the SMA bought the land from John A. and Inez Z. Jones and sold it to NPS in 1962. The action by the SMA paved the way for a boundary adjustment.[2] It altered the memorial boundary in four ways, adding three tracts and withdrawing one. The 49.856-acre triangular tract bought by SMA from the Joneses was purchased by the NPS for the memorial. Just to the northwest of the triangle, 75.33 acres were transferred from Coronado National Forest, a unit of the National Forest Service, to the memorial. It comprised lots 2 and 7 of Section 18, Township 24 South, Range 21 East. This was where the visitor center, staff housing, and picnic area had already been located.

Some mining land in the Huachucas, as well as in Montezuma Canyon and its ravines, was excluded from the memorial by the 1960 legislation, including the Billy Boy, a claim within the State of Texas group, and the Z. T. Parker claim, later of the Victorio Company properties. The land reverted from the memorial to Coronado National Forest, National Forest Service. The mining claims remained with their owners. That property was described as the north half of the southwest quarter of the northwest corner of Section 13, and the north half of the southeast quarter of the northeast quarter of Section 14, Township 24 South, Range 20 East.

Each section contained twenty acres, for a total deletion of forty acres.[3] The State of Texas Mines in Montezuma Canyon were part of that land.

As the Coronado International Memorial formed its administration, the first order of business, then, called for the creation of its boundaries. The enabling legislation provided that the president of the United States would declare, by proclamation, any lands within the dedicated area for the memorial's use. Although the memorial was restricted from causing any recreational or other development within a sixty-foot strip north of the international boundary between the United States and Mexico, a basic description of the memorial's holdings was presented in the legislation. Based on the Gila and Salt River meridian, the original boundaries totaled 2,880 acres.[4] The basic grant of land that would establish Coronado International Memorial would be the start of a land acquisitions history filled with turns and twists.

The small strip of land along the border represented a small segment that was added by the 1960 legislation. The sixty-foot-wide strip straddled the border in the southeast corner of the memorial, lots 5 and 6 of Section 20, Township 24 South, Range 21 East, comprising 3.6 acres. In correspondence preparatory to the adjustment, it was depicted as an inadvertent exclusion from the original memorial boundaries.[5] Considerable confusion surrounded the status of this strip. For one thing, it did not appear to exist, according to most maps. Sections 19 through 24 of Township 24 South, Range 21 East, and the same sections to the east and west, began just north of the border. As they were abbreviated by their proximity to the border, they were shown on some maps as including only four lots, numbered 1 through 4, each comprising twenty-seven acres.

BLM plats depicted lots 1 through 4 that extended only from the north boundary of the section to the north side of a sixty-foot strip along the international border. The sixty-foot strip itself was split into four more, very small, lots. Lots 5 and 6 of Section 20 should have been within the boundaries of the memorial.[6] It was noted that the rest of the strip had been included within the original boundaries of the memorial.[7] Interestingly, later descriptions of the strip did not refer to any lot numbers above the number four.[8]

There was also doubt as to which agency administered the sixty-foot strip. The 1941 legislation that created the memorial specified that the NPS would be restricted in its activities within sixty feet of the border. Because that strip had been withdrawn in 1907 by presidential proclamation, the secretary of state had to be consulted prior to "any recreational or other development" within it.[9] The legislation that revised the memorial in 1960 was written to transfer the boundary strip from the National Forest Service. During consultation, the question was raised whether the Department of State actually controlled the land.[10]

The issue of the sixty-foot strip on the border would be revisited in just a few years. In the early 1960s the U.S. section of the international boundary and the Water Commission in El Paso, Texas, acted to divest itself of land within a sixty-foot-wide strip running along the border. The NPS moved to obtain those portions within the Coronado National Memorial and Organ Pipe Cactus National Monument, both in Arizona. Evidently, after a considerable amount of paper was shuffled, the land did change from one federal agency to another, though with little effect since it was already considered part of the memorial.

The sixty-foot border Arizona Strip within Coronado National Memorial included land already defined as within the memorial in 1941 as well that added in 1960.[11] The 1960 addition was within lots 3 and 4 of Section 20. In none of these sections is there a hint of lots 5 through 8. That, taken with the correspondence leading up to the 1960 addition, might suggest that "sections 5 and 6" did not actually exist, and were, in fact, added unnecessarily in 1960. The point was moot. No matter how the maps were marked, or when the land was acquired, it all belonged to the memorial.

As the NPS worked to rectify problems of development and control of the memorial through small boundary adjustments, private lands that would one day belong to the memorial were also in flux. The mining claims on the north side of Montezuma Canyon had just gained security from the 1960 adjustment. It had transferred forty acres from the memorial to Coronado National Forest in order to keep the mining claims and potential development out of the memorial and in the U.S. National Forest.

Part of that land belonged to the State of Texas mining properties belonging to Grace Sparkes. During the 1950s Sparkes had become interested in selling the State of Texas property. She improved the property and upped her asking price from $30,000 to $32,500, though it was said that she had not formally listed it. Supposedly, potential buyers had approached her about the property in 1957. Superintendent Philip Welles opined that Sparkes was asking more than the land was worth. However, he also recognized that the land had value to NPS over and above its monetary worth. It had a water source that was estimated as sufficient for the memorial's future development needs, and it contained structures that could be, and were at the time, used by the memorial. Its location, right on the main road through the memorial, probably increased its market value; it certainly made it more consequential to the memorial as well. Welles recognized a nuisance factor in the event that "persons unfriendly to the area or to the service" should buy the land.[12]

Sparkes preferred the idea of selling the land to the NPS for inclusion in Coronado Memorial. In 1958, she wrote that NPS had earlier expressed interest in some of the land, but she had then thought that she might return to mining. Her circumstances, as well as mineral prices, had changed, and Sparkes was determined to sell, preferably to NPS.[13] She mentioned its water resource and hoped that the buildings, still being remodeled, could become a ranger station. Sparkes hoped that in an upcoming expansion of the memorial, NPS could take over her land.[14] By then, the land and buildings that were added in 1960 had already been planned. During her lifetime, Grace Sparkes never did sell to NPS or anyone else. She died in 1963, leaving the State of Texas Mine property to her four nephews.[15]

In July 1970 Ruth M. Clark, a widow, and Charles A. and Paquita C. Smith, sold several mining properties, including the thirteen Doredor claims in the Hartford Mining District of the Huachuca Mountains that fell within the eventual boundaries of Coronado National Memorial. Evidently, the sellers were Bill Clark's widow and his partner's wife. The buyers were Coronado Investment Company, a partnership made up of Peter G. Wray and H. Wayne Pruett.[16] In 1973, the properties were transferred to Pruett-Wray Cattle Company, made up of the same partners.[17] By 1979, Pruett-Wray had changed its name to Victorio Land and Cattle Company and then to the Victorio Company.[18]

Back at the mouth of Montezuma Canyon, land was changing hands and developments were occurring, some of which would one day be problematical for the memorial. The remainder of Homestead Entry Survey 310, all of Homestead Entry Survey 311, and the Kudzmi Homestead were given by John A. and Inez Z. Jones to John Z. and Lawrence D. Jones "for and in consideration of the love and affection" of parents for their children in 1962.[19] The Jones brothers sold the total amount to Everett and Fred Baumkirchner and their respective wives, Margaret E. and Mary Ann, in 1965. The purchase price was not recorded, but John and Lawrence Jones carried a $45,000 mortgage on the property.[20]

The Baumkirchner brothers grew up in Miller and Hunter canyons of the Huachuca Mountains, the sons of a university-educated German immigrant who mined in the area. Over the years they owned several local businesses and built up a substantial ranching operation stretched along the east side of the Huachuca Mountains.[21] The Baumkirchners evidently obtained the Jones property for the purpose of speculation. They soon subdivided it and put portions on the market. The first tract was sold in September 1966. The Baumkirchners sold one acre that was later labeled Tract 101-15, to Calvin R. and Esther Teague.[22] The Teagues sold it to William L. Cashman and Ramona E. Cashman in April 1971.[23] In 2001 William and Jean Cashman continued to reside in this house and property, an inholding of Coronado National Memorial.

On July 21, 1967, the Baumkirchners sold two more small parcels of land within the Homestead Entry Survey 311. They also sold a one-acre portion to William and Louise Archie.[24] The Archies held the land until November 1972 and then sold it to Robert G. and Betty J. Chavez.[25] They, in turn, sold the property to Eileen Owens in April 1978.[26]

Also on July 21, 1967, the Baumkirchners sold two acres to Lawrence Edward Ray.[27] Ray borrowed $14,400 from the Farmers Home Administration of the U.S. Department of Agriculture for the purchase. The Farmers Home Administration held the deed to the property as collateral.[28] Next, Ray sold the property to James M. and Billie Jean Tyra in August 1971.[29] A month later, the Baumkirchners sold two acres to the Tyras.[30] Those two purchases placed the Tyras in possession of four acres. It appears that the Tyras borrowed money for both purchases from the Baumkirchners, money they repaid when they sold the land, known as Tract 101-11, to NPS in 1980.[31]

In 1971 the Baumkirchner brothers sold two more parcels of land. In August the brothers and their wives sold two one-acre lots to Dewitt and Doretta Ruth Green.[32] The Baumkirchners also sold a six-acre tract to a son of one of the brothers, Everett M. Baumkirchner Jr. In October 1971 the property was transferred pending payments totaling $6,000.[33] In 1980, when the younger Everett sold the land to the NPS, a warranty deed for that land was transferred from the elder Baumkirchners to him. It was probably given after the last money owed on the property was paid to the sellers and cleared the title for ownership by NPS and inclusion into Coronado National Memorial.[34]

In 1973 the Baumkirchners traded 541.43 acres to the National Forest Service "for and in consideration of. . . certain national forest land, which does not exceed in value the land herein conveyed." Included in the land exchange was most of their land in the area of the memorial. The National Forest Service now owned the entire Kudzmi Homestead, not yet within the memorial, and bought, from the Baumkirchners, an additional fifty acres in the memorial.[35] After the sale and exchange of land, the Baumkirchners subdivided the rest of their holdings except for one large parcel. That property was sometimes listed as two separate parcels although they were ultimately transferred together. A 1979 appraisal described a total of 94.23 acres that contained several building improvements, including rental units, residences, barns, and sheds. Access was by paved highway.[36]

The old Pyeatt Homestead also changed hands around the same time. In April 1973, according to a joint tenancy deed filed at the time, the Montezuma Ranch was sold to George F. and Elsie R. Weick of Illinois.[37] The Weicks would sell the property within a few years. After Richard Richards bought it in 1979, Elsie Weick would again become involved, as Richards's mother and creditor and, again, as a landowner. Weick's interest and involvement in the Montezuma Ranch would continue for the next few decades, at least.

All of the privately owned land discussed above was within the original homesteads at the mouth of Montezuma Canyon and on the north side of the canyon farther up into the Huachuca Mountains. The issue over its status came to a head at Coronado National Memorial in 1978. An anonymous and undated memo entitled "Boundary Adjustment: A Radical Proposal" discussed reasons for making significant adjustments to the boundaries of the memorial. It included additions to and withdrawals from the memorial. The portion of the memorial west of Montezuma Pass, according to the memo, was not really enjoyed by the visiting public except as a scenic backdrop. In addition, it represented 70 percent of the grazing land within the memorial. Both land and water resources had been damaged by overgrazing. Withdrawal of that land would relieve NPS personnel of the headache of patrolling and administering the overgrazing of the unused land.[38]

All of Montezuma Canyon was, said the memo, already thought of by the public to be part of the memorial.[39] It could be managed efficiently only if all of it was brought within the memorial. These concerns can be seen as addressing a changing vision of the memorial. First promoted as an overlook of the valley through which Coronado entered the United States, the pristine character of the view needed to be maintained if the memorial was to be worthwhile. Set aside to be enjoyed by the public for its natural beauty and resources, it would become a multiple-use area.

Notes

1. Frederick J. Brower, Acting Team Manager, Western Team, Denver Service Center to Regional Director, Western Region, February 19, 1974, WACC, Folder L 1417: Boundary Adjustments—Surveys & Reports F1.

2. Warrenty Deed, Cochise County Recorder's Office, Bisbee, Arizona, Deeds of Real Estate, Docket 217, pages 129-130. Southwestern Monuments Association to United States of America, Recorded May 14, 1962, Deed, John A. and Inez Z. Jones to Southwestern Monuments Association Signed and recorded May 22, 1959, Cochise County Recorder Deeds of Real Estate, Docket 217, pages 129-130. Also see A. M. Koehler, Acting regional Chief of Operations, NPS, to Earl Jackson, Santa Fe, NM, December 4, 1958.

3. An Act to Revise the Boundaries of the Coronado National Memorial and to Authorize the Repair and Maintenance of an Access Road Thereto, in the State of Arizona, and for Other Purposes, Approved September 2, 1960 (74 Stat 736) (Public Law 86-689), CORO Files.

4. Township 24 south, range 20 east, section 10, south half southwest quarter, south half southeast quarter; section 11, south half, southwest quarter; section 13, southwest quarter northwest quarter, south half; section 14, northwest quarter, south half, northwest quarter northeast quarter, south half northeast quarter; section 15, all; section 23, all; section 24, all; township 24 south, range 21 east, section 17, south half southwest quarter; section 18, southwest quarter, south half southeast quarter; section 19, all; section 20, lots 3 and 4; aggregating approximately 2,880.

5. Acting Director, NPS, to Regional Director, Region Three, NPS, Washington, DC, August 22, 1958, WACC, Folder L 1417: Boundary Adjustments—Proposed/Enacted Legislation F2.

6. Regional Chief, NPS Planning, Region Three, to Superintendent, Coronado National Memorial, Santa Fe, n.d. (possibly September 12, 1958), WACC, Folder L 1417

7. Acting Director, NPS, to Regional Director, Region Three, NPS, Washington, DC, August 22, 1958.

8. Request for Transfer of Excess Real Property and Related Personal Property, from Director, NPS, to Commissioner, United States Section, International Boundary and Water Commission, Washington, DC, February 1964, WACC, Folder L 1417: Boundary Adjustments—Proposed/Enacted Legislation F2.

9. An Act to Provide for the Establishment of the Coronado International Memorial, in the State of Arizona, Approved August 18, 1941 (55 Stat 630), CORO Files.

10. Acting Regional Director, Region Three, NPS, to Director, NPS, Santa Fe, n.d. (possibly October 8, 1958), WACC, Folder L 1417: Boundary Adjustments—Proposed/Enacted Legislation F2.

11. The Arizona Strip was created from the southerly sixty feet of the following subdivisions: Township 24 South, Range 20 East (Gila and Salt River Meridian), Section 22, Lots 1, 2, 3, and 4; Section 23, Lots 1, 2, 3, and 4; Section 24, Lots 1, 2, 3, and 4; Township 24 South, Range 21 East (Gila and Salt River Meridian), Section 19, Lots 1, 2,

3, and 4; Section 20, Lots 3 and 4; Totaling 32.504 acres more or less. See Request for Transfer of Excess Real Property and Related Personal Property, February 1964. See also, Donald E. Lee, Chief, Division of Land and Water Rights, NPS, to Bernard L. Boutin, Administrator, General Services Administration, March 5, 1964, and Boundary Status Map, October 1958, ILRPC Files, Land Ownership Record, WACC, Folder L 1417 and Folder L 1425, alphabetical listing by landowner's name, NPS Division of Land Acquisitions, July 10, 1979; Land Acquisition Plan, Coronado National Memorial, January 18, 1980 (and attached maps), ILRPC Files; Land Ownership Record, NPS, September 2, 1960, WACC, Folder L 1425: Land Holdings—Sparkes & Acquisition F17.

12. Welles to Regional Director, NPS, Hereford, September 15, 1957, WACC, Folder L 1425.

13. Sparkes to Senator Barry Goldwater, Hereford, September 11, 1958, WACC, Folder L 1425: Land Holdings—Sparkes & Acquisition F17.

14. Sparkes to Welles, Hereford, March 1950, WACC, Folder L 1425.

15. Gentry, McNulty & Tori, Attorneys at Law, to Acting Superintendent, Coronado National Memorial, Bisbee, October 14, 1965, WACC, Folder L 1425; also see other memos and letters in the same folder for improvements and sales prospects.

16. Warranty Deed, Ruth M. Clark, a widow, and Charles A. Smith and Paquita C. Smith, his wife, to Coronado Investment Company, a partnership comprised of Peter G. Wray and H. Wayne Pruett, co-partners, Recorded July 2, 1970, CCR, Deeds of Real Estate, Docket 645, 543–545.

17. Warranty Deed, Coronado Investment Company to Pruett-Wray Cattle Company, Signed May 1, 1973, CCR, Deeds of Real Estate, Docket 871, 481–483.

18. Deed (Joint Tenancy), The Victorio Company, an Arizona Corporation; formerly Victorio Land and Cattle Company, an Arizona Corporation; formerly Pruett-Wray Cattle Company, an Arizona Corporation, to James J. Wardle and Jacqueline S. Wardle, husband and wife, Signed December 18, 1979, CCR, Deeds of Real Estate, Docket 1388, 333–334.

19. Deed of Gift, John A. and Inez Z. Jones, of Santa Cruz County, Arizona, to John Z. and Lawrence D. Jones, Signed April 24, 1962, CCR, Deeds of Real Estate, Docket 300, 406–407.

20. Joint Tenancy Deed, John Z. Jones and Lawrence D. Jones to Everett Baumkirchner and Margaret E. Baumkirchner, husband and wife, an undivided half interest, Signed May 26, 1965, CCR, Deeds of Real Estate, Docket 389, page 21; Joint Tenancy Deed, John Z. Jones and Lawrence D. Jones to Fred and Mary Ann Baumkirchner, husband and wife, an undivided half interest, Signed May 26, 1965, CCR, Deeds of Real Estate, Docket 389, page 22; Realty Mortgage, Everett Baumkirchner and Margaret E. Baumkirchner, his wife, and Fred Baumkirchner and Mary Ann Baumkirchner, his wife, with John Z. Jones and Lawrence D. Jones, Signed June 1, 1965, CCR, Deeds of Real Estate, Docket 389, 23.

21. Jac Hein, *Sierra Vista: Its People and Neighbors: A Narrative History* (Sierra Vista, AZ: Banner Printing Center, 1983), unidentified photocopied pages, CORO Files.

22. Joint Tenancy Deed, Fred E. and Mary Ann Baumkirchner, and Everett M. and Margaret E. Baumkirchner, to Calvin R. and Esther Teague, Signed September 30, 1966, CCR, Deeds of Real Estate, Docket 456, 215.

23. Warranty Deed, Calvin R. Teague and Esther Teague, his wife, to William L. Cashman and Ramona E. Cashman, his wife, signed April 29, 1971, CCR, Deeds of Real Estate, Docket 767, 168.

24. Warranty Deed, Fred E. Baumkirchner and Mary Ann Baumkirchner, husband and wife, and Everett M. Baumkirchner and Margaret E. Baumkirchner, husband and wife, to William Arthur Archie and Eloise Archie, husband and wife, Signed July 21, 1967, CCR, Deeds of Real Estate, Docket 493, 280.

25. Warranty Deed, William A. Archie and Eloise Archie, his wife, to Robert G. Chavez and Betty J. Chavez, his wife, signed November 17, 1972, CCR, Deeds of Real Estate, Docket 831, page 427. Land was part of Homestead Entry Survey 311.

26. Warranty Deed, Robert G. Chavez and Betty J. Chavez, husband and wife, to Eileen G. Owens, an unmarried woman, signed April 28, 1978, CCR, Deeds of Real Estate, Docket 1250, 147.

27. Warranty Deed, Fred E. Baumkirchner and Mary Ann Baumkirchner, husband and wife, and Everett M. Baumkirchner and Margaret E. Baumkirchner, husband and wife, to Lawrence Edward Ray, an unmarried man, signed July 21, 1967, CCR, Deeds of Real Estate, Docket 491, 525.

28. Real Estate Mortgage for Arizona, Lawrence Edward Ray and Farmers Home Administration of the U.S. Department of Agriculture, September 27, 1967, CCR, Deeds of Real Estate, Docket 502, 478–479.

29. Joint Tenancy Deed, Lawrence Edward Ray, husband of Maria T. Ray, as his sole and separate property, to James M. Tyra and Billie Jean Tyra, his wife, signed August 13, 1971, CCR, Deeds of Real Estate, Docket 713, 392. After NPS acquired the surrounding property, this parcel became known as Tract 101–11, Parcel 1.

30. Joint Tenancy Deed, Fred E. Baumkirchner and Mary Ann Baumkirchner, his wife, an undivided half interest, and Everett M. Baumkirchner and Margaret E. Baumkirchner, his wife, an undivided half interest, to James M. Tyra and Billie Jean Tyra, his wife, Signed September 30, 1971, CCR, Deeds of Real Estate, Docket 1221, 457.

31. Warranty Deed, Fred E. and Mary Ann Baumkirchner, and Everett M. and Margaret E. Baumkirchner, to James M. and Billie Jean Tyra, March 25, 1980, CCR, Deeds of Real Estate, Docket 1413, 456–457.

32. Joint Tenancy Deed, Fred E. and Mary Ann Baumkirchner, and Everett M. and Margaret E. Baumkirchner, to Dewitt and Doretta Ruth Green, August 23, 1971, CCR, Deeds of Real Estate, Docket 862, 10–11. These lands were also part of the Homestead Entry Surveys. These two parcels became Tracts 101–12 and 101–14.

33. Warranty Deed, Fred E. Baumkirchner and Mary Ann Baumkirchner, husband and wife, and Everett M. Baumkirchner and Margaret E. Baumkirchner, husband and wife, to Everett M. Baumkirchner, Jr., Signed October 11, 1971, CCR, Deeds of Real Estate, Docket 940, page 71; Agreement, Fred E. Baumkirchner and Mary Ann Baumkirchner, his wife, as to an undivided half interest; and Everett M. Baumkirchner and Margaret E. Baumkirchner, his wife, as to an undivided half interest, and Everett M. Baumkirchner, Jr., a single man, Signed October 11, 1971, CCR, Deeds of Real Estate, Docket 732, 107.

34. Warranty Deed, Fred E. and Mary Ann Baumkirchner, and Everett M. and Margaret E. Baumkirchner, to Everett M. Baumkirchner, Jr., Signed March 19, 1980, CCR, Deeds of Real Estate, Docket 1410, page 2. Warranty Deed for Tract 101–16

35. The U.S. Forest Service purchased the Kudzmi Homestead, which was the remainder of Homestead Entry Survey 310, and a fifty-acre portion of the southwest corner of Homestead Entry Survey 311. Warranty Deed, Fred E. Baumkirchner and Mary Ann Baumkirchner, husband and wife, and Everett M. Baumkirchner and Margaret E. Baumkirchner, husband and wife, to Transamerica Title Insurance Company, as Trustee, Signed March 11, 1972, CCR, Deeds of Real Estate, Docket 841, 215–216; Warranty Deed, Transamerica Title Insurance Company to United States of America, Signed March 1, 1973, CCR, Deeds of Real Estate, Docket 841, 218.

36. Request for bids for appraisal of properties by A. W. Gray, Division of Land Acquisition, Western Region, NPS, May 4, 1979, ILRPC Files. When the Baumkirchners subdivided their holdings, they kept the biggest piece, later called tract 101–10. The property was generally located in Section 17, Township 24 South, Range 21 East, Gila and Salt River Meridian.

37. Joint Tenancy Deed, George H. Howe and Martha J. Howe, his wife, to George F. Weick and Elsie R. Weick, his wife, Wood Dale, Illinois, Recorded April 27, 1973, CCR, Deeds of Real Estate, Docket 853, 84.

38. "Boundary Adjustment—A Radical Proposal." WACC, Folder L 1417: Boundary Adjustments—Surveys & Reports F1.

39. Ibid.

Afterword

The effort to administer, preserve, and interpret the area of Montezuma Canyon will, no doubt, continue to evolve to meet the challenges and opportunities presented in the future.

—Joseph P. Sánchez, *Between Two Countries*.[1]

Innovative efforts and planning to manage, protect, and interpret the area of Montezuma Canyon and its environs will, no doubt, continue to evolve to meet the challenges and opportunities in the future. The historical themes, the cultural resources, and the development of the infrastructure of Coronado National Memorial have been intricately bound by the purpose for which the memorial was established. By the beginning of the twenty-first century, aside from its development, its long-standing history along that corner of the Arizona–Sonora border, and the struggle for identity within the NPS, Coronado National Memorial had come of age.

The original purpose for the establishment of Coronado National Memorial was articulated between 1940 and 1942 by the congressionally mandated Coronado Cuarto Centennial Commission, charged to commemorate the four hundredth anniversary of Coronado's exploration of the North. Thus, it was hoped that a joint international park would be established to demonstrate the harmonious relationships between the United States and Mexico, as well as to acknowledge the common history shared by the two countries.

Congress established Coronado National Memorial to commemorate a historical moment—the march of the Coronado Expedition that explored two thousand miles of North America between 1540 and 1542. The expedition moved northward through the Spanish claim represented by modern states in Mexico and the United States. Consequently, the Mexican states of Sinaloa and Sonora share a common history with Arizona, New Mexico, Texas, Oklahoma, and Kansas. At the time, the United States hoped to establish an international park based on that theme. The effort would require Mexico's cooperation.

Alas, Mexico proved to be an unwilling partner due to its anticolonial ideology following the Revolution of 1910. Thwarted by the lack of Mexican cooperation, the United States, in 1952, proceeded to create Coronado National Memorial instead of an international memorial. The ideas of harmonious relationships with Mexico and the sharing of a common history inspired by the legacy of the Coronado Expedition remained intact as the guiding themes that govern the purpose of the memorial. The task before the NPS in 1952 required that a plan be developed to accomplish such goals. The complementary physical development of the memorial began slowly in the late 1950s. Visionary management and development concept plans moved the dream of the memorial forward to become an actual place.

Montezuma Canyon turned out to be an excellent site for the memorial, because it was the scene of a slightly different and larger history than that originally conceived by the NPS. The many faces of Montezuma Canyon allowed for its histories to tie to the primary theme inspired by the moment of contact made by Francisco Vázquez de Coronado. Indeed, the Coronado Expedition represented the beginnings of a frontier movement that continued into the late nineteenth century as Spanish, and later Mexican, soldiers, ranchers, miners, and their families, as well as missionaries settled the area known today as southern Arizona. Missions and settlements were established along two river valleys. The first took place along the Santa Cruz River where settlements and missions known as Tumacacori, Tubac, San Xavier del Bac, and Tucson still stand. The second area was along the San Pedro River that attracted settlers to claim lands, north beyond Cananea between the Huachucas and the Mule Mountains, for ranching and mining. Some Mexican frontiersmen gravitated toward Montezuma Canyon and environs where early ranching and mining efforts took place. As the Hispanic frontier moved from south to north, another frontier movement pushed from east to west across the continent from the United States. Such was the legacy spawned by the Coronado Expedition that developed in time to form part of the cultural heritage of two nations.

The collision of the two frontiers occurred with the War of 1846 and the resulting Treaty of Guadalupe-Hidalgo in 1848. The area of southern Arizona, however, was acquired from Mexico through the Gadsden Purchase Treaty. Therefore, the later history of Anglo-Americans moving into lands formerly possessed by Mexican land grant owners as well as those traditionally claimed by Native Americans was merely another cycle of occupation seen time and again by tribes that once lived in those lands. Time marched forward to a point in 1942 when it became possible to preserve the common heritage of the area shared by two countries. The creation of Coronado National Memorial in 1952 ensured the accomplishment of that ideal.

Today, the biggest preservation enterprise in Montezuma Canyon and environs is Coronado National Memorial. Still, it is evident that prehistorical and historical protagonists made it all possible. Perhaps the most astonishing factor in the evolution of Coronado National Memorial was the will, the determination, and the drive of those who passed through and near Montezuma Canyon. Not only did the early Sonora–Arizona pioneers have these qualities, so too did the founders of the memorial and the first generations of NPS employees who implemented the first phases of its development. In the same way, their successors continue steadfastly to define Coronado National Memorial. All have made a difference in the creation, implementation, and operation of the memorial. The twenty-first century provides new challenges for the memorial, embedded in the politics, society, economies, and technologies of the new era before them. Although Coronado National Memorial had earlier struggled to define its identity, the passage of time and the efforts to develop the memorial's premises have pointed the way toward its future sustainability.

It is in the evolutionary development of Montezuma Canyon and its environs that the memorial has found a perspective and an indelible identity based on management traditions that have formed since its establishment. In the final analysis, Montezuma Canyon with its historical themes and cultural resources defines Coronado National Memorial. All that has happened there inclusive of prehistory, early Spanish contact with tribes in the area, Native American influences, Spanish colonial settlement, Mexican land grants, stock raising, and mining, the acquisition of Pimería Alta through the Gadsden Purchase Treaty by the United States, and the arrival of early Anglo-Americans and entrepreneurs is a part of that rich identity.

Coronado National Memorial is a part of the legacy that was forged by historic events associated with Montezuma Canyon. Above all, the long history of the federal presence in the region, whether it be that of the NPS sister agencies such as U.S. Forest Service, the BLM, the Immigration and Naturalization Service, or other such entities, is enhanced by the role of the NPS at Montezuma Canyon. Agencies of the State of Arizona have also contributed significantly to the development and care of the area. Although it took a collective effort to establish Coronado National Memorial, the historical process of what has occurred in and around Montezuma Canyon, once institutionalized by the NPS, has ensured its preservation for future generations. There was a moment when the memorial's existence was threatened, but it survived the test of time.

The issue of Coronado's route is still a matter of speculation. The exact trajectory of Coronado's route is still a topic of great interest. Recent studies regarding the Coronado Expedition point to the notion that there is still work to do in locating the route particularly through Sonora and Arizona. Perhaps interdisciplinary approaches between historians, archaeologists, geographers, and other disciplines could eventually solve the conundrum of Coronado's route, especially as innovative technologies open new doors to such an investigation.

In the nineteenth and twentieth centuries other issues concerning the border surfaced. By the middle of the first decade of the twenty-first century, it was evident that a new theme had emerged related to southeastern Arizona and Montezuma Canyon that cannot be ignored. The theme appears multifaceted. Its elements include illegal immigration, the *narcotráfico* (clandestine drug trade), as well as the smuggling of arms, people, and other issues. Associated with those topics are border surveillance; homeland security; associated law enforcement issues at Coronado National Memorial; relationships between NPS and other agencies in the area, particularly the U.S. Citizenship and Immigration Services; and, among other themes, present-day diplomatic relations with Mexico regarding border issues. On the other hand, perhaps a comprehensive history of national parks along the border needs to be written to provide a source that covers a broad perspective of the issues rather than a narrow or fragmented view dealing with individual parks, towns, and their environs. This is not to say that individual histories on this issue should not be done, but rather that they be put into perspective.

The history of humankind and land uses in Montezuma Canyon and environs is at the crux of the evolving Coronado National Memorial. Indeed, Coronado National Memorial plays an important role in the context of the rapidly developing southeastern Arizona. In many ways, the world came to Montezuma Canyon, as indicated by the history of Coronado National Memorial, which is intertwined with the history of others who have passed through or dwelt in Montezuma Canyon. In that regard, Montezuma Canyon holds the key to the many stories that can be told about the Arizona–Sonora borderlands.

Notes

1. Joseph P. Sánchez, Bruce A. Erickson, and Jerry Gurulé, *Between Two Countries: A History of Coronado National Memorial, 1939–1990* (Albuquerque, NM: Rio Grande Books, 2007), p. 215.

Bibliography

Libraries

Archivo General de la Nación, Mexico City
Archivo Histórico Diplomático, Secretaria de Relaciones Exteriores, Mexico, D.F.
Arizona Historical Society, Tucson
The Special Collections Library at Arizona State University, Tempe
The Arizona State Department of Mines and Minerals, Phoenix
The Arizona State Library, Archives and Public Library, Phoenix
Bisbee Mining and Historical Museum, Bisbee
Western Archeological and Conservation Center (WACC), Tucson
The Bancroft Library, University of California Berkeley

Documents

"Abandoned Mines a Danger to Humans, a Home to Bats." CNN.com nature. August 28, 2000.

Almada, Francisco R. *Diccionario de historia, geografia y biografia sonorense.* Hermosillo, Sonora, Mexico, Instituto Sonorense de Cultura, 1990.

Anonymous. "Eulalia Elias, 1786–1865." In *Arizona Women's Hall of Fame,* Arizona Historical Society, Museum Monograph, Central Arizona Division, Phoenix, AZ, 1987.

Baldwin, George P., ed. *The Black Hills Illustrated.* Philadelphia: Baldwin Syndicate: Black Hills Mining Men's Association, 1903.

Bancroft, Hubert Howe. *History of Arizona and New Mexico, 1530–1888.* San Francisco: History Company, 1890.

Bargalló, Modesto. *La Minería y la Metalurgía en la America Española durante la Epoca Colonial.* Mexico–Buenos Aires: Fondo de Cultura Economica, 1955.

Bohrer, Geoffrey T. "Siamese Triplets: Grace Sparkes, The State of Texas Mine, and the Coronado National Memorial." National Park Service, Coronado National Memorial, CORO Files, 1993.

Bolton, Herbert Eugene. *Coronado: Knight of Pueblos and Plains.* Albuquerque: University of New Mexico Press, 1949.

Bowden, J. J. "Private Land Claims in the Southwest." Master's thesis: Southern Methodist University, Dallas, Texas, 1969.

Calloway, Colin G. *First Peoples: A Documentary Survey of American Indian History.* Boston: Bedford/St. Martin's Press, 2005.

Coupal, J. S. *Synoptic Report of State of Texas Mine.* Phoenix, AZ: Arizona State Department of Mines and Minerals, 1940.

Day, Arthur Grove. *Coronado's Quest: The Discovery of the Southwestern States.* Berkeley: University of California Press, 1940.

Debo, Debo. *Geronimo: The Man, His Time and Place.* Norman: University of Oklahoma Press, 5th printing, 1989.

DiPeso, Charles C. *The Babocomari Village Site on the Babocomari River, Southeastern Arizona.* Dragoon, AZ: Amerind Foundation, 1951.

——. *The Sobaipuri Indians of the Upper San Pedro River Valley, Southeastern Arizona.* Dragoon, AZ: Amerind Foundation, 1953.

Dobkins, Betty Eakle. *The Spanish Element in Texas Water Law.* Austin: University of Texas Press, 1959.

Elías Gonzales, José María. *Diario de las operaciones practicadas por el Señor Comandante General del Estado José María Elías Gonzales.* Archivo Historico de Hermosillo, Sonora, folio 1, Reel 15, December 30, 1849, Arizona Historical Society, Tucson.

Fergusson, Erna. *Our Southwest.* New York: Alfred A. Knopf, 1940.

Fischer, Howard. "Heir Prefers a Fight to Leaving Park Home." *Arizona Daily Star,* September 13, 1979.

Flint, Richard, and Shirley Flint, eds. *The Coronado Expedition to Tierra Nueva: The 1540–1542 Route Across the Southwest.* Niwot: Colorado University Press, 1997.

Gladwin, Harold Sterling. *Excavations at Snaketown,* vol. 4, *Reviews and Conclusions.* Medallion Papers, No. 38. Globe, AZ: Gila Pueblo, 1948.

——. *A History of the Ancient Southwest.* Portland, ME: Bond Wheelwright, 1957.

Gómez Robledo, Antonio. *México y el Arbitraje Internacional.* Mexico, D.F.: Editorial Porrúa, 1965.

Granger, Byrd Howell. *Arizona's Names (X Marks the Place).* Tucson: Falconer, 1983.

Hadley, Diane. "Inter-Ethnic Contacts in the Borderlands: The Apache Campaign of José María Elías Gonzales." Unpublished manuscript, Arizona Historical Society, Tucson, AZ.

Hammond, George P., and Agapito Rey, trans. and eds. *Narratives of the Coronado Expedition 1540–1542.* Albuquerque: University of New Mexico Press, 1940.

Herring, Patricia Roche. "The Silver of Real de Arizonac." *Arizona and the West* 20, no. 3 (1978): 245–58.

Hodge, Frederick, and Theodore H. Lewis, eds. *Spanish Explorers in the Southern United States, 1528–1543.* Austin: Texas State Historical Association, 1984. Originally printed 1907.

Humphrey, Robert R. *90 Years and 535 Miles: Vegetation Changes along the Mexican Border.* Albuquerque: University of New Mexico Press, 1987.

Hunt, Aurora. *The Army of the Pacific: Its Operations in California, Texas, Arizona, New Mexico, Utah, Nevada, Oregon, Washington, Plains Region, Mexico, etc. 1860–1866.* Glendale, CA: Arthur Clark and Company, 1951.

Jiménez Núñez, Alfredo. *El Gran Norte de México: Una frontera imperial en la Nueva España 1540–1820*. Madrid: Editorial Tébar, 2006.

Jones, Oakah L. *Pueblo Warriors and the Spanish Conquest*. Norman: University of Oklahoma Press, 1966.

Kinnaird, Lawrence, trans. and ed. *The Frontiers of New Spain: Nicolas de Lafora's Description, 1766–1768*. Berkeley, CA: Quivira Society, 1958.

Klinck, Rickard E. "In the Land of Coronado." *Arizona Highways* (September 1957).

McCroskey, Mona Lange. *Grace Marion Sparkes: Matriarch of the Early Arizona Tourist Industry*. Master's thesis, Arizona State University, Tempe, AZ, 1987.

Memorial and Affidavits Showing Outrages Perpetuated by the Apache Indians in the Territory of Arizona for the Years 1869–1870. Published by Authority of the Legislature of the Territory of Arizona. San Francisco: Francis & Valentine, printers copy available at Arizona Historical Society, Tucson, AZ.

"The Mule Pass Mines." *Arizona Star*. November 14, 1878. Copy available at Arizona Historical Society, Tucson, AZ.

Nentwig, S. J., Juan. *Descripción Geográfica, Natural y Curiosa de la Provincia de Sonora*, edited by Germán Viveros. Mexico City, Mexico: Archivo General de la Nación, 1971. Originally published 1764.

Officer, James E. *Hispanic Arizona, 1536–1856*. Tucson: University of Arizona Press, 1987.

Orton, Richard H. *Records of California Men in the War of the Rebellion*. Sacramento, CA: State of California, 1890.

Prezelski, Tom. "Lives of Californio Lancers: The First Battalion of Native California Cavalry, 1863–1866." *Journal of Arizona History* 40 (Spring 1999).

Raat, W. Dirk, and Michael M. Brescia. *Mexico and the United States: Ambivalent Vistas*, 4th ed. Athena: University of Georgia Press, 2010.

Rea, D. B. "The Mines of the Cananea." *Arizona Star*, November 21, 1878. Copy available at Arizona Historical Society, Tucson, AZ.

"Reminiscences of Rafael Elias, 81-Year-Old Pioneer." *Bisbee Daily Review*, July 29, 1934. Copy available at Arizona Historical Society, Tucson, AZ.

Reynolds, Mathew G. *Spanish and Mexican Land Laws*. St. Louis, MO: Buxton and Skinner Stationery Company, 1895.

Sánchez, Joseph P. "A Historiography of the Route of the Expedition of Francisco Vázquez de Coronado: General Comments." In Flint and Flint, *The Coronado Expedition*, 31–35.

——. "Cíbola to Río de Cicúye." In Flint and Flint, *The Coronado Expedition*, 215–25.

——. *Comparative Colonialism, the Spanish Black Legend, and Spain's Legacy in the United States: Perspectives on American Latino Heritage and Our National Story*. Denver, CO: National Park Service, U.S. Department of the Interior, 2013.

——. "Compostela to Cíbola." In Flint and Flint, *The Coronado Expedition*, 138–48.

——. *Early Hispanic Colorado, 1678–1900*. Albuquerque, NM: Rio Grande Press, 2015.

——. "Pedro Fages in Sonora, 1767–1768 & 1777–1782." *New Mexico Historical Review* 51: (1976): 281–94.

——. "Río Cicúye to Quivira." In Flint and Flint, *The Coronado Expedition*, 281–301.

Sánchez, Joseph P., Bruce A. Erickson, and Jerry Gurulé. *Between Two Countries: A History of Coronado National Memorial, 1939–1990.* Albuquerque, NM: Rio Grande Books, 2007.

Sánchez, Joseph P., Carol Shively, Ted Alexander, and Robert Spude. *Hispanics and the Civil War: From Battlefield to Homefront.* National Park Service, U.S. Department of the Interior, 2011.

"The San Rafael Mines." *Arizona Star,* December 5, 1878. Copy available at Arizona Historical Society, Tucson.

Sanderson, Steven E. *Agrarian Populism and the Mexican State: The Struggle for Land in Sonora.* Berkeley: University of California Press, 1981.

Saugey, David A. "U.S. National Forests: Unsung Home to America's Bats." *Bats* 9, no. 3 (Fall 1991): 3–6.

Sayles, E. B. *The San Simon Branch: Excavations at Cave Creek in the San Simon Valley. I. Material Culture.* Medallion Papers, no. 34. Globe, AZ: Gila Pueblo, 1945.

Schroeder, Albert H. Fray "Marcos de Niza, Coronado and the Yavapai." *New Mexico Historical Review* 30, no. 4 (1955): 265–96.

——. "Coronado and the Yavapai." *New Mexico Historical Review* 31, no. 1 (1956): 24–27.

Seymour, Deni J. *Where the Earth and Sky Are Sewn Together: Sobaipuri-O'odham Context of Contact and Colonialism.* Salt Lake City: University of Utah Press, 2011.

Sierra, Carlos J., compiler and editor. *El Chamizal, monumento a la justicia internacional.* Mexico, D.F.: Secretaría de Hacienda y Crédito Público, 1964.

Smith, Cornelius C. Jr. *Fort Huachuca: The Story of a Frontier Post.* Washington, DC: Department of the Army, United States Government Printing Office, 1981.

Sonnichsen, Charles Leland. *Colonel Greene and the Copper Skyrocket; The Spectacular Rise and Fall of William Cornell Greene: Copper King, Cattle Baron, and Promoter Extra-ordinary in Mexico, the American Southwest, and the New York Financial District.* Tucson: University of Arizona Press, 1974.

Stewart, Yvonne G. "Montane Cochise Culture Sites in Coronado National Memorial," *Proceedings of the First Conference on Scientific Research in the National Parks, vol. 2.* New Orleans, LA, November 9–12, 1976, edited by Robert M. Linn. Sponsored by National Park Service and American Institute of Biological Sciences. Washington, DC: United States Department of the Interior, National Park Service Transactions and Proceedings Series, 1979.

Sweeney, Edwin R. *Mangas Coloradas: Chief of the Chiricahua Apaches.* Norman: University of Oklahoma Press, 1998.

Toops, Connie. "Going to Bat for Bats." *National Parks: The Magazine of the National Parks and Conservation Association* 75, no. 1–2 (2001): 28–31.

Tuthill, Carr. *The Tres Alamos Site on the San Pedro River, Southeastern Arizona.* Dragoon, AZ: Amerind Foundation, 1947.

Van Cleve, Peter M. "History of Mining in the Coronado National Memorial." National Park Service, Coronado National Memorial, CORO Files, 1997.

Wagoner, Jay J. *Early Arizona: Prehistory to Civil War.* Tucson: University of Arizona Press, 1975.

Wagstaff, Robert M. "Coronado's Route to Quivira: The Greater Weight of the Credible Evidence." In *West Texas Historical Association Yearbook,* Vol. 42, 137–66. Abilene, TX, 1966.

Weber, David J. *Bárbaros: Spaniards and their Savages in the Age of Enlightenment.* New Haven, CT: University of Yale Press, 2005.

"What Is Your Favorite Park Doing for Bats." *Bats* 13, no. 1 (Spring 1995): 10.

Wilson, John P. *Islands in the Desert: A History of the Uplands of Southeastern Arizona.* Albuquerque: University of New Mexico Press, in cooperation with the Historical Society of New Mexico, 1995.

About the Author

Dr. Joseph P. Sánchez, PhD, retired from the National Park Service in 2014 after thirty-five years of service. During his time with the NPS, he served as superintendent of Petroglyph National Monument (2003–14). He is the founder and director of the Spanish Colonial Research Center at the University of New Mexico (1985 to present). Sánchez is also founder and editor of the *Colonial Latin American Historical Review (CLAHR)*. Before his career with the NPS, Sánchez was a professor of colonial Mexican history and director of the Mexican American Studies and Research Center, both at the University of Arizona, Tucson. He has taught at Santa Ana College in California; the University of New Mexico; and the Universidad Autónoma de Guadalajara. He has published several studies on the Spanish frontiers in California, Arizona, New Mexico, Texas, and Alaska. His numerous scholarly articles and book-length publications include *New Mexico: A History*, coauthored with Robert Spude and Art Gómez (2013); *Early Hispanic Colorado, 1678–1900* (2015); and *From Saltillo, Mexico, to San Antonio and East Texas: An Historical Guide to El Camino Real de Tierra Afuera and Camino Real de los Tejas during the Spanish Colonial Period* (2016), compiled and edited by Joseph P. Sánchez and Bruce Erickson.

Index

The letter "t" after a page number indicates table data.